나만의 비밀 영어사전

나만의 비밀 영어사전

발행일	2017년 1월 16일		
지은이	Nicholas Won		
펴낸이	손 형 국		
펴낸곳	(주)북랩		
편집인	선일영	편집	이종무, 권유선
디자인	이현수, 이정아, 김민하, 한수희	제작	박기성, 황동현, 구성우
마케팅	김회란, 박진관		
출판등록	2004. 12. 1(제2012-000051호)		
주소	서울시 금천구 가산디지털 1로 168, 우림라이온스밸리 B동 B113, 114호		
홈페이지	www.book.co.kr		
전화번호	(02)2026-5777	팩스	(02)2026-5747

ISBN   979-11-5987-379-9 03740(종이책)   979-11-5987-380-5 05740(전자책)

이 도서의 국립중앙도서관 출판예정도서목록(CIP)은 서지정보유통지원시스템 홈페이지(http://seoji. nl.go.kr)와 국가자료공동목록시스템(http://www.nl.go.kr/kolisnet)에서 이용하실 수 있습니다. (CIP제어번호 : CIP2017000859)

(주)북랩 성공출판의 파트너

북랩 홈페이지와 패밀리 사이트에서 다양한 출판 솔루션을 만나 보세요!

홈페이지 book.co.kr   1인출판 플랫폼 해피소드 happisode.com
블로그 blog.naver.com/essaybook   원고모집 book@book.co.kr

미드가 들리지 않는
당신을 위한 실생활 밀착 표현과
고급 슬랭 집대성

나만의
비밀
영어사전

Nicholas Won 지음

북랩 book Lab

┃ Prologue ┃

외국어는 욕부터 배운다는 말이 있습니다. 남의 나라 말을 배울 땐 비속어부터 배우는 것이 우선이고, 비속어는 많은 노력을 하지 않아도 쉽게 배울 수 있다는 의미입니다. 충분한 타당성이 있는 말입니다.

영어에서의 비속어, 즉 슬랭(Slang)이란 쉽게 설명하면, 원어민들의 실생활 밀착 영어입니다. 슬랭은 언어 표현을 다양화해주기도 하지만, 그 의미를 모르면 심각한 오해를 일으킬 수 있으므로 반드시 익혀야 합니다. 예를 들어 'Have a blast'라는 슬랭은 '좋은 시간을 보내라'라는 뜻을 가지고 있는데, 'Blast'가 단지 폭발이라는 뜻만 가지고 있는 것으로 알고 있다면, 하나의 단어, 하나의 문장의 의미만이 아니라 이 이후에 이어지는 대화 전체를 이해할 수 없게 됩니다.

영어에서는 Literal Meaning(글자 그대로의 의미)보다는 Figurative Meaning(비유적 의미), 즉 어떤 단어나 구절이 어떻게 사용되는가에 따라 해석이 달라집니다. 이걸 학습하는 것이 중요합니다. 예를 들면, 우리는 "Mind your own business!"라고 말하는 대신 "Fuck off!"라고 말하는 것을 자주 들을 수가 있습니다. 앞의 표현은 너무나 점잖은 표현이라 말하는 사람의 기분 상태를 상대방에게 제대로 전달해 주지 못한다고 느꼈는지 비속어를 사용한 것입니다. 여기에서 'fuck'의 뜻은 문자적 의미(Literal Meaning)와 상관없습니다. 우리가 '개새끼야!'라고 해도 '개의 자식'이란 뜻이 아닌 것과 마찬가지입니다. 'Fuck'의 의미가 문자대로(Literally) 사용되면 영화 등급이 PG13(13세 미만은 보호자 동반이 요망되는 영화 등급)에서 R(Restricted - 17세 미만 보호자 동반 요망)로 바뀝니다. 다시 말하면 원어민이라면 만 13세만 되어도 'fuck'이란 말을 제대로 쓸 줄 안다는 것입니다. 'Fuck'이란 말을 적절히 쓰고, 그 함의(Implication)를 해석할 줄 안다는 뜻입니다.

어떤 면에서는 이러한 언어들의 선행적인 이해가 평범한 표준 영어를 이해하는데 많은 도움을 주고 있습니다. 실제 외국인들의 대화를 듣고 이야기하다 보면 무수한 슬랭(우리나라의 사투리와 마찬가지로)들이 보편적으로 사용되고 있고, 젊은이들을 중심으로 다시금 새로운 언어로 변화하고 발전하는 것을 볼 수 있습니다. 그러므로 이러한 언어들을 이해하는 것은 분명 영어 공부를 하는 사람들에게 쉽게 다가설 수 없는 외국어를 자신의 것으로 받아들이는 지름길일 수도 있습니다.

하지만 슬랭은 영어를 이해하는데 쉽게 접근할 수 있는 수단임과 동시에 다소 넘기 어려운 벽이기도 합니다. 이런 슬랭들을 학교에서 가르쳐 주나요? 그렇지 않습니다. 정규 교과 과목에 슬랭은 없습니다. 슬랭은 교과서에는 나오지 않습니다. 그렇지만 원어민들은 다들 씁니다. 입 밖으로 내지는 않더라도 그 의미는 다 알고 있습니다. 안 가르쳐도 아는 게 슬랭입니다. 또한 안 가르쳐도 어떤 상황에서 슬랭을 써야 적절한지도 잘 알고 있습니다.

또 짧은 시간 안에 그 많은 슬랭을 배우는 데는 한계가 있습니다. 모르는 슬랭이 나타날 때마다 누가 바로 옆에서 한국말로 바로바로 가르쳐 주지 않는 이상은 눈치나 경험으로 몸으로 체득하기에는 너무나 많은 시간이 필요하게 됩니다.

그리고 자주 사용되고 있는 슬랭이라 하더라도 그 특성상 일반 사전에는 등재되어 있지 않은 경우가 많고, 등재되어 있다고 해도 예문이 없는 경우가 많아서 처음 접하면 그 의미를 도저히 이해하지 못해 당황할 때가 많습니다. 또 미국 영화나 드라마의 한국어 자막에서는 아예 그 뜻을 생략해 버리거나 암시하는 정도로 처리해 버리는 경우도 다반사입니다.

우리가 성인 대상의 미국 영화, TV 드라마, 코미디 프로그램을 볼 때나, 현지에서 원어민들 사이의 대화를 들을 때 듣기가 잘 안 되는 이유는 현지 원어민 성인들이 사용하는 슬랭들을 모르고 있기 때문인 경우가 많습니다. 그래서 그런지 중산층의 표준 영어보다는 다양한 계층의 말을 쉽게 접할 수 있는 미국 드라마 시청이 최근 영어 학습의 한 방법으로 유행하고 있고, 미국 드라마에서 들을 수 있는 표현들을 소개해 주는 학습서들도 많이 출간되고 있습니다.

사실 영어 학습은 영어사전과 친해지는 일부터 시작되고, 영어 학습의 성패는 학습 단계에 맞는 사전을 잘 선택하고 잘 활용하는데 있다고 해도 과언이 아닙니다. 여느 외국어 학습과 마찬가지로, 영어도 어느 정도 단계에 오르면 자기 주도 학습이 중요한데, 다양한 미디어를 활용하여 학습하게 되는 고급 단계에 들어가면 일반 사전에 우선 등재되어 있지 않은 단어들, 특히 속어의 의미를 빨리 알려줄 수 있는 사전이 필요하지만, 그런 사전을 찾기가 쉽지 않았습니다.

이제 『나만의 비밀 영어사전』이 이런 문제를 어느 정도 해결해 줄 것입니다.

『나만의 비밀 영어사전』은 실생활에서 많이 사용되는 슬랭, 슬랭에 가까운 단어와 표현들, 그리고 성인들이 자주 사용하는 비유적 표현, 온라인 채팅에서 볼 수 있는 약어들을 그 예와 함께 사전 형식으로 구성한 것으로, 성인을 주 독자층으로 하는 영문 소설들, 또한 17세 이상의 시청자들을 위한 드라마, 성인 대상의 영화 등에서 자주 접하는 속어들을 총망라하여, 한 영으로 그 의미를 풀어 놓았고, 그 용례도 실어 놓았습니다. 따라서 일반 영한사전이나 영영사전에서는 그 의미를 바로 찾기가 어려워 해석이 잘 안 되는 부분이 나올 때 이 사전이 큰 도움이 될 것입니다. 영문 소설 독해 또는 미국 드라마를 자막 없이 시청하는 수준의 영어 학습자분들에게는 반드시 필요한 사전이라고 할 수 있습니다.

사전을 첫 페이지부터 읽는 것처럼 비효율적인 영어 학습 방법은 없을 것입니다. 하지만 『나만의 비밀 영어사전』은 첫 페이지부터 가볍게 읽어 보기를 권해 드립니다. 그 이유는 본 사전에 포함된 단어와 표현들은 실제 생활에서 원어민 성인들이 아주 많이 사용하고 있는 표현들이고, 어떤 상황에서 어떤 표현들이 사용될지 모르기 때문에, 가능한 빠른 시간 내에 많은 속어를 접해보는 것이 필요하기 때문입니다. 처음부터 전체를 다 읽어 볼 시간이 없으시다면 우선 '**Bold**체'로 되어 있는 중요 속어들만이라도 먼저 꼭 기억해 놓아야 합니다. 또한 슬랭 표현들은 '*italic*체(기울어진 글자체)'로 구분했으니 참고하시기 바랍니다.

소통이란 상대방에게 나를 맞추는 것입니다. 나와 대화하는 상대방이 슬랭을 많이 쓰는 것 같다면 부끄러워 마시고 슬랭을 사용해 보기를 권해드립니다. 그렇게 하기 위해서는 먼저 어떤 상황에서 어떤 슬랭들을 사용하는지 알아야 합니다. 그 모든 것이 『나만의 비밀 영어사전』에 다 들어 있습니다.

감사합니다.

Nicholas Won

❙ Contents ❙

step. 00

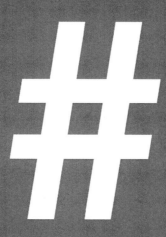

- **10** 아주 매력적인 여성이나 남성 (10점 만점에 10점); Very attractive person; a person who, on a scale of 0 to 10, is the best. From the movie '10', featuring Dudley Moore and Bo Derek.

- **1st base** (데이트에서) 키스(에 성공)하다; To kiss, make out.

  • He got to the 1st base with her.

- **2nd base** (데이트에서) 가슴을 만지(는데 성공하)다; To put one's hands up a person's shirt, with hand-on-skin contact, e.g. the fondling of breasts.

  • He got to 2nd base on the 1st date.

- **3rd base** (데이트에서) 성기를 만지(는데 성공하)다; To stimulate the genitals with one's hand.

  • He got to 3rd base.

- **3rd degree** (경찰 등의) 고문, 엄한 심문. (또는 third); Interrogation

  • She really gave me the third degree.

- **5-0** 경찰; The police. Pronounced as "five oh."

  • 5-0 at the party!
  • The 5-0 are coming to break up the fight.

- **69** 남녀 동시 구강성교 행위; To receive and perform oral sex at the same time. Pronounced as "sixty-nine."

  • The two girls were in a 69, licking each other's pussies.

- **86** 제거하다. 내쫓다. 서비스를 거부하다; To stop selling an item in a restaurant, because there is no more; to eject from a venue.

  • I was 86ed from the bar last night.

10

A

□ *a dog with two dicks*　　　　아주 행복한, 아주 운이 좋은; A mythical creature who is extremely happy or fortunate.

　• I'm happier than a dog with two dicks.

□ *a.c./d.c.*　　　　양성애(兩性愛)의; Bisexual

　• Hey, did you hear about Brittney. I think she's AC DC!

□ ABC party　　　　옷만 빼고는 다 입을 수 있는 파티; Anything But Clothes party, where you wear anything but clothes. ex: trash bags, saran wrap, lampshades, trashcans, tape, cardboard boxes, etc.

　• Dude that ABC party last night was raging. There's nothing better than seeing girls with just a piece of tape on.

□ *abso-fucking-lutely*　　　　Absolutely의 속어적 강조; Absolutely; without a doubt. The insertion of "fucking" places emphasis on the use of "absolutely."

　• I have abso-fucking-lutely too much homework.

□ acid　　　　환각제. LSD; The hallucinogenic LSD(Lysergic acid diethylamide).

　• Do you think he could sell me some acid?

□ acid freak　　　　LSD 상용자; LSD user

　• It's more common that hackers are like hippies or acid freaks or mad scientists or car mechanics.

□ acid head　　　　LSD 상용자; LSD user

　• Paul was an acid head and enjoyed tripping on LSD.

□ action　　　　성교; Act of having sex.

　• Hey, you get any action last night?

□ *Adios, MOFO!*　　　　"Goodbye"를 의미하는 Standard Spanish인 adios 에 mother fucker를 의미하는 MOFO를 추가한 것; Goodbye, mother fucker.

12

□ **AFU**　　　　　엉망진창; Acronym of "all fucked up." A shortened version of SNAFU.

　• That is totally afu, dude!

□ **ain't nothing but a chicken wing**　　문제없다. 대수롭지 않다; To be okay; not a big concern. "Thing" and "wing" are typically pronounced "thang" and "wang" respectively.

　• To me it ain't nothing but a chicken wing.

□ **airbrain**　　　　바보, 얼간이; An unintelligent person.

□ **airhead**　　　　바보, 얼간이; An unintelligent person; "dimwit" . Contains strong connotations of obliviousness or forgetfulness. Origin: term implies the person's head contains nothing but air.

　• He's confused again. What an airhead!

□ **AKA**　　　　　별칭; Alias, acronym of "Also Known As."

　• That man by the bar is Frank, A.K.A. "the lady killer."

□ **a-list**　　　　최고 부류[대열](에 속하는 인사들); A metaphorical list of the post popular people.

　• Bridal couples arriving by helicopter? Old news on the Indian wedding circuit. So is hiring a Bollywood actor to perform or just rub shoulders with guests. The practice of hiring celebrities is so common that there's even an industry price list for A-listers. Shahukh Khan, India's biggest star, is quoted at $750,000, while movie heartthrob Salman Khan lists at about half that price.

□ **All foam, no beer**　　멍청한, 지능이 낮은; Stupid; retarded

□ **all that (and a bag of chips)**　　끝내주는[굉장히 매력적인]; Of the highest quality.

　• He thinks he's all that.

□ **all the way**　　　(이성과) 갈 데까지 가다, 성교하다; Copulation, especially in "go all the way."

• I did not go all the way with him, however.

□ **all-nighter** 철야 시합[집회, 공연 따위]; 철야 영업소[상점]; An all-night period of awakedness to finish a task.

• I had to pull an all-nighter before the final.

□ **• ambulance-chaser** (교통사고를 쫓아다니는) 3류[악덕] 변호사; An unethical attorney who solicits business at the scenes of accidents or in hospitals, in exchange for a percentage of the damages that will be recovered in the case.

• Your friend should get one of those ambulance chasers and file a lawsuit.

□ *AMF* 안녕 친구, 꺼져라 이놈아; Acronym of "adios mother fucker." One typically says this when one has caused an object to go a long distance, or to the wrong location, e.g. in the game of golf.

• There goes that ball… AMF!

□ **amp up** (출력을) 높이다. 증가시키다. 흥분하게 만들다; To increase.

• Meanwhile, in the ice rink, Rhona Martin, our one real contender, was amping up Britain's curling team.

□ **amped** 멋진, 굉장한, 몹시 흥분한 (about); (마약으로) 흥분한; Angry, annoyed, offended; Excited, energetic, cool, awesome

• Dude, his new skateboard is so amped!
• It's been a rough week but we're going skiing Saturday, I am so amped!

□ **amped up** 몹시 흥분한 (about); (마약으로) 흥분한; Excited, or hopped up on AMPhetamines.

• That dude is all amped up because he just snorted 60 dollars of ice in one line!

□ *anal* 항문 성교; Anal sex.

• Are you into anal?

□ **anal** (사람이) 지나치게 깔끔한, 신경질적인; Shortened form of anal retentive.

14

- Quit being so anal!
- You're very anal today.

□ *anal retentive*   (사람이) 지나치게 깔끔한, 신경질적인; Uptight, stingy, conservative; by the book. Usually shortened as anal.

- My boyfriend is really anal retentive about his car.

□ and a half   (보통 것보다 더) 놀라운[굉장한/중요한]; Used to indicate an extreme condition or an excessive amount.

- That was a soccer game and a half.

□ and stuff   ~같은 (시시한) 것; Et cetera. Usually implies that the speaker has more to say, but is just too lazy to say it or does not want to divulge the information.

- Do you find yourself watching TV and stuff?

□ *anilingus*   (성적 흥분을 위한) 항문을 입으로 자극하기; The use of the mouth or tongue to stimulate the anus of another person; Anilingus (from anus+lingus (Latin Lingere: to lick), also spelled analingus, also referred to or described as anal/oral contact or anal/oral sex, is a form of oral sex involving contact.

□ antsy   안달하는; Jumpy

- He was antsy, waiting for the test results.

□ apple polisher   아첨꾼; A sycophant; toady

- That apple-polisher gave me quite a laugh, but I can't stand him.

□ *Are you fucking kidding me?*   지금 날 놀리는 거냐?; I can hardly believe what you are saying.

□ *arse*   엉덩이, 둔부(ass, buttocks); Australian, British and Irish word for a person's rear end.

- I'm sitting on my arse.

□ **arsehole**　　　　　똥구멍(asshole); 바보, 어리석은 놈; Asshole

• Quit being an Arsehole!

□ **as 형 as a bastard**　매우[더없이] ~한; Intensifies the named adjective to an extreme degree.

□ **as 형 as a bitch**　　Intensifies the named adjective to an extreme degree.

□ **as 형 as fuck**　　　Intensifies the named adjective to an extreme degree.

□ **as 형 as hell**　　　Intensifies the named adjective to an extreme degree.

□ **as 형 as shit**　　　Intensifies the named adjective to an extreme degree.

□ **as fuck**　　　　　　매우[더없이] ~한; An intensifier. To a great extent
or degree; very.

• That car is nice as fuck.

□ **as heck**　　　　　　매우[더없이] ~한; An Intensifier. To a great extent
or degree; very.

• People from my town rarely go to college. They sure as hell – sorry, miss
– they sure as heck don't go to L.A. to college.

□ **as hell**　　　　　　매우[더없이] ~한; An Intensifier. To a great extent
or degree; very.

• Something about the girl was sexy as hell. She had such an innocent face.

□ **as shit**　　　　　　매우[더없이] ~한; An intensifier. to a great extent
or degree; very.

• It is hot as shit in here.

□ **ASL**　　　　　　　나이, 성별, 거주지; Online chatting acronym of
"age, sex, location?" An inquiry of one's age, gender, and location.

16

- ASL?

□ **ass** 바보, 멍청이; Idiot, Fool

- You ass! They don't speak German in Mexico.

□ **ass** 궁둥이, 엉덩이. 항문; Buttocks

- Adam marveled at her ass.

□ ass 고집불통; One who exhibits complete ignorance and disregard for social norms, customs, and practices.

- Don't be such an ass.

□ **ass** 기분 나쁜 것, 기분이 몹시 안 좋음; Anything displeasing.

- I feel like ass today.

□ **ass backwards** 거꾸로, 뒤죽박죽으로; Chaotic, in a mess.

- He did the work ass backwards, so I had to do it again.

□ **ass cheeks** 궁둥이, 엉덩이; Buttocks

- That shit was so big that it hurt my ass cheeks on the way out.

□ **ass clown** '사회성이 없고 둔감한 사람'을 비하하여 일컫는 말; A general term describing intellectually challenged people or a fool of great magnitude.

- Those people in the personnel office are such ass-clowns.

□ **ass crack** 항문; The cleft between the buttocks.

- Your ass crack is showing.

- **ass out**   모임에 빠지다. 접근을 못하게 되다; To not attend a social gathering after already agreeing; to be prevented access to a location because others are engaging in sexual congress within.

> • Everyone knows she's gonna ass out tonight.
> • I had to sleep in the lounge because I got assed out of my dorm room.

- **ass out**   돈이 하나도 없는; Without money; BROKE.

> • I can't go to the show tonight, I'm ass out.

- **ass up**   지저분하게 하다. 더럽히다; To make something like ass. For example, making something "smell like ass."

> • He assed up the room.

- **ass up**   실수하다. 못 쓰게 만들다; To mess up.

> • I think we assed up the acquisition.

- **ass-backwards**   거꾸로, 뒤죽박죽으로; In reverse or totally incorrect.

> • That computer must have been set up ass-backwards; most of the buttons don't work.

- **ass-dough**   쉽게 벌리는 돈, 앉아만 있어도 벌리는 돈; Easy money you make while you are sitting on your ass.

> • Bill: I have a great job! All I do is sit on my ass and make money!
>   Fred: Yep good ol' ass dough. You're living the dream, buddy.
> • Dosen't get any better than ass dough.

- **assful**   불쾌한, 화나는, 싫은; Displeasing

> • Her new hair style is pretty assful.

- **asshoe**   멍청한 창녀; 항문 성교를 좋아하는 창녀; A person considered sexually promiscuous who likes anal sexual intercourse; a dumb prostitute.

> • Don't be an asshoe!
> • She's an asshoe!

□ **asshole**   항문; Anus

• My asshole itches.

□ **asshole**   멍청이, 똥 쌀 놈; 지긋지긋한 것[곳]; A person who is offensive, pompous, rude, unkind, impolite, etc.; "jerk"

• Look, I've got four assholes from your hometown here to collect your belongings. What do you want me to tell them?

□ *asshole buddy*   친구, 짝패; 호모들; A friend with whom a scumbag can be himself. more commonly used in the American South than in other regions, to denote two very close male friends who have come to know each other intimately, though not necessarily sexually. Even if they are having sex, they may nonetheless identify as straight.

• Lonnie and Joe Bob? You hardly ever see one without the other. They've been asshole buddies for years.

□ *ass-kicking*   멋진, 훌륭한; Excellent

• They headhunted me because of my ass-kicking performance stats.

□ *ass-kiss*   아첨하다; To seek favor through flattery; to be a sycophant or toady.

• They just want their asses kissed.

□ *ass-kisser*   아첨꾼; An obsequious person.

• That ass-kisser, Peter, is always telling the boss how great he is.

□ ass-load   대량, 많은 양; A great quantity. More than a butt-load but less than a shit-load.

• I would have bought that comic book collection, but they wanted an ass-load of money for it.

□ *ass-sucker*   아첨꾼, 알랑쇠; Someone who succumbs to authority, doing whatever authority figures ask and attempting to please them in every possible way.

- He was a real ass-sucker.

□ *asswipe*   1. 화장지(의 대용품). 2. 빌어먹을 놈; 얼간이; 알랑쇠; One who behaves in an offensive, pompous manner.

- It didn't help much that Karl Wellingham was a Major League, Grade-A asswipe.

□ astronaut lady   우주 최고의 미모를 갖춘 여자; A lady with "astronomical" beauty. One special girl that you would only find in this universe.

- You're an astronaut lady, that's how beautiful you are.

□ ate up   엉망진창인; Not "squared away" (i.e. not organized or prepared: a mess.)

- Damn, your room is ate up.

□ *ATM*   항문 대 구강성교; Ass to Mouth Sex.

- He ATMed her.

□ *Aunt Flo*   월경; Menstrual period. Sometimes abbreviated AF. Also Aunt Flo and cousin Red.

- I had unexpected company last night⋯ Aunt Flo and cousin Red came to visit.

□ awesome possum   awesome의 변형; Variant of "awesome"

- That party was awesome possum.

□ *axe wound*   도끼 자국 (여성의 성기); Vulva ("vagina")

- She's got a nice axe wound.

□ **A-yo**   (아주 친한 사이의) 인사말 "Hey!"와 동의어; A greeting. Synonymous with "Hey!", "What's up?" etc.

- A-yo, Jessie, what's going on?

20

B

□ **B. and D.**   학대. 변태 성행위; Bondage & Discipline.

• Though it's still a fairly taboo subject, B and D is rather common.

□ **B.J.**   구강성교; Blow job.

• Tom: Dude, I just got the sweetest B.J., she did it like a pro.
 Jack: Oh really? Who was she? I want some of that B.J. action.

□ **b.s.**   Bullshit의 두음 문자. 허튼소리. 거짓말; Lies; words or actions meant to be deceptive.

• That's a bunch of b.s.!

□ **B4**   Before의 on-line chatting상의 줄임말; Before. On-line chat acronym.

• I knew you B4 we went to the same school together.

□ **babe**   계집아이; 성적 매력이 있는 여성; Affectionate term for one's significant other; a particularly attractive woman.

• Hey babe, could you grab me a beer?

□ **babe magnet**   사람을 유혹하는 것; 매력적인 남자; Attractive male.

• Guy A: That guys a babe magnet.
 Guy B: Let's beat him up.
 Guy A: Yeah.

□ **babelicious**   성적 매력이 있는 여성; Babe+Delicious. Describes the sexiness of a female.

• Man, check out that babelicious chick over there.

□ **baby**   (예쁜) 젊은 여자, 계집애; 연인; Affectionate term for one's significant other.

• Hey baby, could you grab me a beer?

□ **baby daddy** (여성의 입장에서) 아기 아빠; The father of a woman's child.

- That man isn't my boyfriend, he's my baby daddy.

□ **babygirl** 여자친구; Girlfriend

- When my girlfriend started calling my best friend "babygirl", I knew it was over.

□ **BAC** 혈중 알코올 농도; Blood-alcohol concentration.

□ *back asswards* 잘못한, 이상한 방향으로 일이 처리된; Done or performed incorrectly, strangely, opposite from the correct way, or clumsily.

- Sorry, I'm back asswards today.
- Why do you have to do everything back asswards?

□ *back door* 항문; Anus

- I went in through the back door.

□ *back end* 항문; Anus

□ **back like bull, brain like bird** 멍청한, 지능이 낮은; Stupid/Retarded

□ **backhanded compliment** 빈정대는 투의 칭찬; What might at first sound like a compliment but could/should really be taken as an insult when considered in its entirety.

□ *bad ass* 끝내주는; Very good, excellent; cool; awesome

- He's a bad-ass guitar player.
- That was a bad-ass concert.

□ **bad rap** (오심으로 인한) 억울한 죄, 부당한 형벌, 부당한 비난; False accusation.

- He gets a bad rap, but he's a cool dude.

□ *bad shit* 어려운 문제; Difficult problem.

□ *balcony*   (아주 큰) 유방; Big breast.

• She's got a balcony you could do Shakespeare from!

□ *bald man in a boat* 클리토리스; Clitoris

• Licking the bald man in the boat will make your woman CUM!

□ *ball*   성교하다; To have intercourse.

• If I put a sock on the doorknob, don't come in: it means I'm going to ball my girlfriend.

□ **ball**   아주 즐거운 한때; A great time.

• Man, why did we have to leave so early? I was having a ball!.

□ **ball**   고환(睾丸); Testicle

• Adam felt warm fingers caressing his balls? Allie keeping him erect, he thought.

□ **ball**   성공하다; To be successful. Typically used to refer to men, and often implies an abundance of money, women, nice clothes, expensive cars, etc. Also big balling.

• He is a baller; he keeps three or four females at all times.

□ **ball up**   혼란하게 시키다[하다]; [계획 따위]를 망치다; To mess something up.

□ **ball-buster**   매우 힘든 일. 남을 혹사시키는 사람; Ball-breaker. A person or task which is excessively demanding or punishing.

• My slave-driving boss expects me to work over the weekend. What a ball-buster!

□ **balled-up**   못쓰게 된, 대혼란의; Confused, in a mess.

□ **balls**   용기, 근성, 배짱; Bravado, courage; GUTS

• Randy and Andy Smith knew their dad had no balls. He had always been a pussy.

□ **balls**　　　　　　고환(睾丸); Testicles

• Adam closed his eyes for a moment and then felt two tongues working on his balls.

□ **balls of steel**　　　용기, 근성, 배짱; Metaphorical testicles that people with courage or gall have.

• You must have balls of steel showing your face in here.

□ **balls out**　　　　무모하게; With reckless abandon and extreme courage.

• Those motorcyclists took that steep hill balls out!
• You just have to go balls out to win this game.

□ **balls to the wall**　　끝까지, 극단적으로, 최후까지; Extreme, all out.

• That guy went balls to the wall to win that race.
• This is the last game of the season, boys! So, it's balls to the wall!

□ ***Balls!***　　　　헛소리 마!; I don't believe it(you); Exclamation of disappointment.

□ **balls-up**　　　　엉망으로 한[망친] 것; Errors

□ **ballsy**　　　　　대담한, 위세 좋은; 의욕적인, 정력이 왕성한; Brave; courageous

• That was one ballsy move.

□ **baloney**　　　　무의미, 잠꼬대 같은 소리, 허황된 말; Nonsense

• Baloney!

□ **bam**　　　　　"쾅"(하고 치다, 터지다, 소리를 내다 등); A sound, mostly that of an impact or collision; "There you go; and then suddenly, ~" ; etc. Usually spoken with increased volume.

25

• I had the interview, and then – bam – I was in upper management!

□ **bamboozle**
dupe; hoodwink

속이다; To deceive using underhanded methods;

• The card cheat bamboozled me out of my money!

□ *bananas*
able; ridiculous

바보 같은, 멍청한. 바보같이!, 멍청아!; Unbeliev-

□ *bananas*

열광한, 흥분한; Excellent

• Penny: Dave, this sandwich is bananas.
Dave: Thanks, Pen.
• That Chris Tucker movie was bananas.

□ **bang**
punch, slap

~을 쾅[탕]하고 닫다, ~을 찰싹 때리다; To hit,

• If he keeps saying that, watch me walk over and bang him.

□ *bang*
with.

(여성과) 성교하다; To have sexual intercourse

• I banged that girl I took home from the bar last night!

□ *bang*

마약 주사를 놓다; To inject drugs intravenously.

• Mark had to go into the bathroom. He's bangin' something.

□ **bang out**

때려눕히다; To hit or cause bodily injury.

• If you don't shut up, I'm going to bang you out.

□ **bang up job**

기대에 넘는 성과를 내다; An accomplishment that
goes above and beyond what is expected; a good job.

• She did a bang up job on the proposal.

26

- *bangable* 성적으로 매력 있는; A person that you would have sex with; not a gorgeous person but an average person.

  • John isn't gorgeous, but he's bangable.

- banging 끝내주는; The bomb, extremely good.

  • That new cd is bangin!

- *banging* 아주 매력적인; To be very attractive; To be stylish.

  • She was banging at that party!
  • Her outfit is bangin!

- bar hop 여러 술집을 돌아다니며 술을 마시다; To visit several bars during a single outing.

  • We're going bar hopping later. Want to come with?

- *bareback* 콘돔을 쓰지 않는 성교; Of unprotected sex.

  • She likes it bareback.

- barf 토하다, 게우다; 토한 것; To vomit.

  • You got barf on your shoes.

- barkeep 술집 주인[판매원]; 바텐더(bartender); Bartender

  • Hey, barkeep, could I get another one?

- barn door 바지 앞의 지퍼; The fly (zipper) on one's pants.

  • Your barn door is open.

- barrel (along) [차를] 고속으로 몰다; To speed.

  • A rusted, yellow MODEL-T barrels along the rickety dock.

- **bash** 세게 때리다, 때려 부수다; To hit somebody a solid blow.

• Why do you have to bash my beliefs?

□ bash *somebody* up   ~를 강타하다; Defeat physically, hit strongly.

• I was threatened with a knife, bashed up and robbed.

□ **bastard**   놈, 녀석; 싫은 사람[것]; A mean or nasty person.

• Holden thinks about how much of a moron and a bastard he is.

□ bastard   아주 어려운 문제; Very difficult problem.

• This problem is a bastard!

□ **Batman and Robin**   항상 같이 다니는 친구 사이; Batman and Robin refers to the partnership between Batman and Robin, two superhero characters; inseparable friends.

• Those two are so Batman and Robin.

□ **bats (in the belfry)**   정신 이상의, 미친; Crazy

• Maybe she has bats in her belfry.

□ *batshit crazy*   미친, 제정신이 아닌; Extremely crazy.

□ **battered**   심하게 취한; Extremely intoxicated.

• I got totally battered last night.

□ **batty**   머리가 돈, 미친; 어리석은; Crazy, usually in reference to a person.

• That music is driving me batty.

□ bawl *somebody* out ~에게 호통치다; To cry loudly.

• Someone in the audience bawled out `Not him again!'

□ **bazillion**   엄청 큰 금액이나 양; A very large number.

□ *bazonga*   젖퉁이, 큰 젖퉁이; A breast. Usually used in the plural.

• She's got some nice bazongas.

□ *BDSM*   속박과 훈육, 사디즘과 마조히즘; Acronym for "bondage, dominance, sadism(submission), masochism"

□ **be a sucker for**   ~라면 사족을 못 쓰다; Very difficult to resist.

□ **be all about**   ~이 최고[전부]다. ~에 미쳐있다; To be extremely enthusiastic for.

• I'm all about sports right now.

□ **be easy**   조심하시오! 조심해라; Take care, have a good one.

• I'm out… be easy.

□ **be mellow**   (특히 술을 마셔서) 느긋해진; Kind or less extreme in behavior as a result of drinking.

□ **be on the up-and-up**   정직한, 신뢰할 수 있는; To be honest.

□ ***be pissed (off)***   화가 나다; To feel angry.

□ *be scared shitless*   몹시 겁먹어; To be scared very much.

□ **be scared to death**   몹시 겁먹어; To be scared very much.

□ **be turned on by**   ~에 끌리어; To be attracted by.

□ **beak**   (사람의) 코; Large, abnormally sharp nose.

• Todd Eckel has a massive beak!

□ **Beamer**   BMW 자동차; A BMW automobile.

• Suspect tried to boost Witman's Beamer.

29

□ *bean*   클리토리스; A slang term for the clitoris.

• She was flicking her bean all night.

□ *bean count*   (여성들의) 가슴을 쳐다보다; To stare at breasts, usually in cold weather.

• We just sat on the porch bean counting.

□ bean counter   [경멸적] 통계 전문가; (관청/기업의) 경리 담당자, 경리 사원; 숫자[머릿수]만 따지는 사람; Derogatory term used in referring to ac-countants.

• I would hate to be a bean counter for a living. I would rather be poor and have a personality.

□ beans   적은 양; A small amount.

□ *bearded clam*   여성의 성기; Female genitalia.

• He touched my bearded clam!

□ beast   짐승 (같은 사람); A person or thing that looks tough, ripped, cut, or has an intimidating presence.

• Nate is a huge beast.

□ beat   돈을 떼이다; To cheat by not paying.

• You got beat for 20 bucks.

□ **beat**   지쳐 빠진; Tired, spent

• After two games of football, man, I am beat.

□ *beat one's meat*   자위하다; To masturbate. Note: applies only to males.

• I beat my meat instead of having intercourse.

- **beat down** 을 때려눕히다, 타도하다; To verbally berate into submission (publicly); to physically rough up or convincingly administer authority over another person or thing.

  • Mr. Smith beat down that dude who came up on his porch asking for money.

- *beat it* 자위하다; To masturbate

  • I like to beat it while watching lesbian porn.

- **Beat it!** 나가!, 썩 꺼져!; To go away; to leave; to send away without ceremony. If you don't like somebody just tell them beat it.

  • A: Excuse me miss/sir, can you please spare some change?
    B: Beat it!

- *beat off* 자위하다; To masturbate.

  • I've heard he beats off twice a day.

- *beat one's ass* 혼을 내다, 때리다, 이기다; To beat somebody up.

- *beat one's meat* 자위하다; To masturbate.

  • Give me some lotion, I need to beat my meat.
  • Hand me that Gatorade, I need to beat my meat.

- beat *somebody* to a pulp 혼을 내다, 때리다, 이기다; To beat somebody up.

- *beat somebody's ass* 혼을 내다, 때리다, 이기다; To beat somebody up.

- *beat somebody's ball* 혼을 내다, 때리다, 이기다; To beat somebody up.

- *beat somebody's bun* 혼을 내다, 때리다, 이기다; To beat somebody up.

31

□ **_beat somebody's butt_** 혼을 내다, 때리다, 이기다; To beat somebody up.

□ beat the (living) daylights out of 혼을 내다, 때리다, 이기다; To beat somebody up.

□ **_beat the crap out of somebody_** 혼을 내다, 때리다, 이기다; To beat somebody up.

□ beat the hell out of 심하게 때리다; To beat violently.

• "It's not surprising that they would say there's no right to beat the hell out
of the officer," Bodensteiner said.

□ **Beat the hell out of me!** 도무지 무슨 말인지 모르겠다; I don't know.

□ **_beat the shit out of_** 심하게 때리다; To beat severely.

• Some sick twist beat the shit out of her.

□ **beater** 매력 없는, 탐탁지 않은 사람; Unattractive or undesirable. Applied to a person.

• I got together with her at a party once, but she was kind of beater.

□ **Beats me!** 몰라, 두 손 들었어; I don't know.

• Person 1: "Wow, how did you get that bruise?"
Person 2: "Beats me!"

□ **_beautimus_** 매력적인 여성; Attractive female.

□ **_beaver_** 여성의 성기, 여성의 비하; Vagina; a derogatory term
for a woman.

• Let's go scope out some beaver.

□ **_beaver shot_** 두 다리를 벌려 성기를 드러낸 여자 사진; A porno-
graphic photograph graphically displaying the "beaver" (i.e. external female genitalia.)

- I might give you her beaver shot.

B

□ **beef** 불평, 불만; 말다툼, 싸움; A complaint or disagreement.

- He has a beef with anyone who tells him otherwise.

□ ***beef curtain*** 커져서 늘어진 여성의 음순; Big, saggy pussy lips.

- Being stuck in a blizzard, I was very thankful my girlfriend had her warm beef curtains to keep my dick from getting frost-bitten and fall off.

□ ***beefcake*** (남성의) 육체미[누드] 사진; 핸섬하고 늠름한 남성; A muscly man.

- Massive-breasted heiress, 38, seeks witty Nobel-awarded intellectual beef-cake gardener-chef-poet with stonking pecs.

□ **beefy** 우람한; Muscular guys having notable sexual attraction, such as six-pack abs or big arms.

- Look at him! He is so beefy!

□ **behind** 엉덩이; Buttocks

- He slapped her on the behind.
- Shelly plopped her wet behind on his lap and kissed him before cuddling up to him.

□ **belly up** 죽다, 도산하다; Bankrupt, failed, dead

- One of my goldfish went belly up last night, now I have to flush it.

□ **bellyacher** 불평을 늘어놓는 사람, 불평가; A person who complains or moans as if s/he had a stomachache.

- Grace can be cute but she is always bellyaching.

□ **belt** (혁대 따위로) ~을 후려치다; To strike a strong blow with a belt or one's fist.

- I will belt you upside your head if you look at my lady's teats one more time!

33

- belt (along) 질주하다; To move with great speed or to hurry.

- *Belushi* 코카인에 헤로인 모르핀 또는 암페타민을 섞은 마약 (주사); Combined intravenous injection of cocaine and heroin, more commonly referred to as a speedball.

  - Some friends asked if I wanted to try a belushi, but it's a bit too hardcore for my tastes.

- Benjamin 미 100달러 지폐; Short or slang expression for a 100(hundred)-dollar-bill because Benjamin Franklin's face is on the front side of it.

  - What is in this bag? It's full of Benjamins!

- *bet (one's) ass* (~을) 확신하다, 절대 ~이다; Statement that something is true.

  - And you can bet your ass that belongs to him.

- bet the farm 전 재산을 걸다, 큰 도박을 하다, 절대 확신하다; To risk everything.

  - Mike bluffed with his ace high and bet the farm.

- BF 남자친구; Boyfriend

  - Is he your new BF?

- BFF 영원한 절친; Acronym for "best friend(s) forever"

  - My BFF Becky texted and said she's kissed Johnny.

- bi 동성애자; Bisexual

  - I wondered if she was bi.

- **Big deal!** [감탄사적; 야유/조소를 나타내어] 그게 무슨 대수라고!; I don't care. This is not important or interesting; sarcastic interjection to espouse one's belief that the subject isn't a big deal.

• So you gained a few pounds. Big deal!

□ *big O*   오르가슴; An orgasm.

• Did you give her the big O?

□ big 'uns   뚱보; Obese people.

□ bilge   부질없는 이야기(생각). 허튼소리; Lies

□ bill   100달러; One hundred dollars.

• That'll cost you six bills.

□ *bimbo*   섹시하지만 멍청한 여자, 난잡한 여자; A female who's attractive but unintelligent, or a promiscuous female.

• She looks like a bimbo.

□ bio break   (채팅이나 회의 도중) 화장실에 가기 위한 짧은 휴식; A bathroom break. Term is generally used during meetings, presentations, etc.

• Do you guys need a bio break? Let's break for ten, and then I'll continue the presentation.

□ *bird*   매력적인 소녀, 여자; 여자친구; A female, usually attractive. Origin: British.

• That bird is fine!

□ birdbrain   새대가리, 멍청이; An unintelligent person.

• That birdbrain delivered the wrong box again.

□ birdbrained   멍청한, 새대가리의; Stupid, unintelligent

• Making fun of your birdbrained theories is a far cry from hostility, but it is a lot of fun.

□ **birth control glasses** (군에서 지급해 주는) 못생긴 안경; The brown —framed prescription eyeglasses issued to new recruits in the U.S. Military, and perceived as notoriously unattractive.

• Adam noticed he also had braces to go with his birth-control glasses. This kid had better hope to make a lot of money if he ever wanted to get laid.

□ **birthday suit**   맨살, 알몸; Nudity

• The guests at the pool party were dressed in their birthday suits.

□ **bitch**   ~에게 불평[우는 소리]을 하다; To complain; whine

• She called me back to bitch me out for turning down the honor of working with her.
• She's always bitching about people she hates.

□ **bitch**   불쾌한 것, 까다로운 것; An extremely difficult or unpleasant problem.

• Doing my homework is such a bitch.

□ *bitch*   (일반적으로) 여자(를 낮춘 말); A general (if de-rogatory) term to refer to females.

• "I just want to roll down the windows and scream to all the girls we pass," she continued. "I've a huge cock in my pussy, bitches. I'm getting fucked by two people I love and you're just driving around looking."

□ **bitch and moan**   언제나 불평만 해대다; Complain all the time.

• The guy bitches and moans, or doesn't participate because he does not want to be part of the group.

□ **bitch out**   겁이 나서 (어떤 일에서) 빠지다; To not do something out of fear; CHICKEN OUT.

• He promised to go with me to the party but at the last minute he bitched out.
• I knew Tony would bitch out.

□ **bitch session**   사람들이 모여서 불평불만을 해대는 비공식적인 모임; An informal gathering where people gripe and air their grievances.

36

• Where's Jim? Is he holding a bitch session again with other workers?

□ bitching　　　　　　기막히게 좋은, 끝내주는; Excellent, wonderful

• That's a bitchin' bike!

□ bitchy　　　　　　　욕하는, 흉보는; Saying unkind things about someone.

• I'm sorry. I know I was bitchy on the phone.

□ bite it　　　　　　　(수수께끼 질문 따위에서) 패배를 자인하다; To be
defeated.

□ *Bite me!*　　　　　　꺼져! 저리 가!; A contemptuous dismissal; a command, similar to "Go to hell!" (i.e. "Leave me alone!", "Go away!" etc.)

□ *Bite me on the ass!* 꺼져! 저리 가!; A contemptuous dismissal.

□ *Bite my ass!*　　　　꺼져! 저리 가!; A contemptuous dismissal.

□ bite *somebody's* head off　　　심하게 꾸짖다; Attack verbally, used
especially in cases the attack is out of proportion to the situation; to
reprimand.

□ bite the big one　　죽다; To die or to get killed.

• Do you think Joe will bite the big one?

□ **bite the dust**　　　1. 헛물을 켜다[실패/패배하다] 2. 죽다; To die, to
utterly defeated.

• And it's not just the small foreign companies that are biting the dust.

□ *bite the pillow*　　　항문 성교의 상대가 되다; To be on the receiving
end of anal sex.

□ bitty　　　　　　　　[어린이 말] (아주) 조그만; Little, small, insignificant

- It's a bitty little thing, isn't it?

□ *BJ* Blow job(구강성교)의 두문자; Acronym for "blow job", i.e. fellatio.

- She gave him a BJ.

□ blabbermouth 입이 싼 사람; A person who talks too much. Usually implies they reveal secrets.

□ black tar (농축한) 검은 헤로인; A type of heroin.

□ blah 기분이 좀 안 좋은; Unwell

- I'm feeling kinda blah today.

□ blam 빵, 탕(총 따위의 소리), 탁(문을 세게 닫는 소리 따위), 세게 치다; To punch hard.

□ *blast* 사정하다; To ejaculate.

- I just blasted her in the ass.

□ blast 뭔가 특히 좋은 것(재미있는 것); Something very fun.

- I've done more at twenty-two than most people do their whole lives. I partied my ass off. There were so many women. I smoked so much weed… I had a blast.
- That party was a blast!

□ blaze 마리화나를 피우다; To smoke marijuana.

- You got some pot? Then let's blaze.

□ blaze 아주 매력적인 사람; An extremely attractive person.

- That guy is a blaze!

□ blazing 아주 매력적인; Extremely attractive.

- That girl is blazing.

- **bleeding** 몹시, 형편없는 (강조의 용법); A somewhat less offensive replacement for "fucking"

  • What the bleeding hell do you think you're doing?

- **bling** 반짝이는 (보석 종류의); Shiny, used to describe jewelry.

  • My ring is bling.

- **bling bling** 반짝이는 (보석 종류의) 장신구. 값비싼 장신구; Any expensive, flashy, or shiny jewelry, usually gold or silver, esp. bracelets, chains, earrings. Used to relate something that's fancy.

  • ⟨after a Mercedes Benz passes by⟩ Bling Bling!
  • She was looking hot in her bling-blings.

- **blithering idiot** 순진한 멍청이; A stupid person who insists on spouting his or her ill-conceived ideas.

- **blitzed** 술 취한; 녹초가 된; Extremely drunk.

  • Last night, my friends and I got totally blitzed.

- **blockhead** 바보, 멍청이; A silly, unintelligent, or foolish person.

- **blonde** 멍청한 금발 미녀; Dumb or stupid. Used on anyone who acts stupid or to describe yourself when you do something stupid.

  • Geeze, how could I forget that? I'm such a blonde!

- **blood in, blood out** 갱단에 들어갈 때 피로 서약하고, 탈퇴할 때도 피를 보고 나옴; Just like a gang makes you take a beating to get in and take a beating to get out.

- **blooper** (사람들 앞에서 범하는 당황스러운) 실수; An embarrassing verbal faux pas or public mistake.

- **blow** (비밀을) 불다[들통나게 하다]; To expose, to betray a secret.

- **blow**   (지체 없이) 떠나가다; 줄행랑치다; To leave, to depart speedily.

> • Gotta blow, catch you later.

- **blow**   마리화나를 피우다; To smoke marijuana. To snort cocaine.

> • Let's blow some coke.

- ***blow***   펠라티오[구강성교]를 하다; To perform fellatio.

> • Will you stop acting like I'm blowing bums for rock, for Christ's sake?

- **blow it**   실수하다, 얼빠진 짓을 하다; To botch, destroy; to completely fail a task.

> • I really blew it during the presentation.

- ***Blow it out your ass!***   엿 먹어라!; A contemptuous dismissal.

- **Blow it out your ear!**   엿 먹어라!;A contemptuous dismissal.

- ***blow job***   구강성교[성애], 펠라티오; Fellatio.

> • For the next few minutes, she fought off every attempt Shelly made to dislodge her from the cock and the only sounds from the back were Adam's grunts and the sounds Allie's mouth made as she gave him a sloppy, wet blowjob.

- **blow me**   제기랄. 저리 꺼져 등의 의미; Taunt similar to fuck you. a sign of disrespect. an angry retort; "bite me". Literally: "Suck my penis."

> • Hey buddy, if you don't like my attitude, you can blow me.

- ***blow me***   구강성교를 하라는 명령어; A command to perform oral sex. Literally: "Suck my penis."

- **blow off**   무시하다. 퇴짜 놓다; To purposely miss an engagement; to skip out on something after committing; to ignore.

40

- She has better thing to do that night so she will blow off the boring plans.

□ **blow** *one's* **cool**   감정적이 되다, 흥분하다; To become angry; to lose control.

- Her mean words made him blow his cool.

□ blow *one's* fuse   화를 내다; To become angry or lose control.

□ *blow one's load*   사정하다; To ejaculate.

- I accidentally blew my load on her pillow.

□ **blow** *one's* **mind**   미치다; To become insane; to amaze.

- That concert blew my mind.

□ blow *one's* stack   미치다!; To become angry or lose control.

□ blow *one's* stopper   미치다!; To explode with anger.

□ blow *one's* top   미치다!; To explode with anger; to become angry.

□ *blow one's wad*   사정하다; To ejaculate.

□ blow smoke   허풍을 떨다, 쓸데없는 이야기를 하다; To promote an illusion or fantasy about oneself; to make unfounded or exaggerated remarks or claims.

- He was talking big about how he knew math, but when I talked to his math teacher it turned out that he was just blowing smoke.

□ blow *someone* away   사살하다; 압도하다, ~에 완승하다; To kill, usually with a firearm.

- She is going to blow him away!

□ blow *someone* out of the water   기습 공격하다; To launch a surprise attack of devastating proportions.

- blow *something* sky-high   파괴하다; To destroy or ruin.

- blow *something* wide open   비밀을 폭로하다; To make something public that had been secret.

- blow the coop   탈출하다, 갑자기 떠나다; To leave suddenly; to escape from prison.

- blow the lid off   비밀을 폭로하다; To make something public that had been secret.

- **blow the whistle on**   밀고하다; To bring something to an end; to inform authorities about wrongdoing in order to stop it.

- **blow up**   ~에게 화를 내다[분통을 터뜨리다]; To lose control; to become extremely angry.

  • He totally blew up at me after I wrecked his car.

- blow up   과장하다; To make exaggerated claims.

- *blowjob*   펠라티오[구강성교]; Fellatio

  • Kyle: And what award did you win tonight?
  Porn star: Best blowjob.
  Kyle: Best blowjob? That must be an amazing blowjob.

- blowout   파티; A big party.

- blue   (미국 정치) 민주당 지지 지역; In the United States, supportive of, run by, or dominated by the Democratic Party.

- *blue balls*   (몹시 흥분하고 있으면서 사정하지 못할 때의) 하복부의 아픔, 고환의 통증; A painful sensation in the balls (testicles) caused by prolonged sexual arousal that does not end in ejaculation.

  • Hank: Let me ask you a question: in your experience, what's the best way to get rid of blue balls? Britt: Don't get married.

◻ **blurb** (책 표지 따위의) 짧고 과장된 광고, 선전문, 추천문, 호의적 단평(短評); A short description of a book, film, musical work, or other product written and used for promotional purposes.

• Anyway, there was a big blurb about Ashley Malibu and Daystar. I was going to call her tonight to congratulate her.

◻ *bob head* 펠라티오[구강성교]를 하다; To practice fellatio, oral sex.

• Marcia doesn't like to bob head.

◻ *boff* 성교하다; To have sex.

• Did you finally boff her?

◻ *Bogart* 돌아가며 피우는 마리화나를 독점하다; To steal, monopolize, or hog.

• Don't Bogart my cookies!

◻ **boilermaker** 물 대신 맥주를 입가심으로 마시면서 드는 위스키, 폭탄주; A whiskey with a beer chaser.

• The waitress brought them two boilermakers.

◻ *boink* 성교하다; To have sex with someone.

• He boinked her last week.

◻ **bomb** 대성공; The best, outstanding

• That movie is really bomb!

◻ **bombed** (술/마약에) 취한; Extremely drunk.

• Adam got totally bombed at the party last night.

◻ *bone* (발기한) 남성의 성기; 발기; The penis, especially when erect.

• He gave her his bone.

□ **bonehead** 멍청이, 얼간이; An idiotic or foolish person.

• You bonehead!

□ *boner* 발기한 남성의 성기; 발기; An erection.

• My boner is showing through my pants.

□ **boner** 어처구니없는 실수, 큰 실수; A clumsy error.

• I studied for that test for weeks, but I still managed to boner it. I got a D!

□ **bong** 마리화나용 물 파이프; Pipe with a water filtration system used for smoking marijuana.

• He likes to smoke a bong-load about twice a week.

□ **bonkers** 술 취한; 정신이 돈, 미친(mad); 제정신이 아닌; Some-one who loses their temper uncontrollably or suddenly acts insane.

• He just went bonkers.

□ **boo** 여자친구나 남자친구; Boyfriend or girlfriend.

• Me and my boo are going out to watch a movie.

□ *boob* 유방; Breast

• She just wanted to walk from group to group, rubbing their shoulders or playing with their boobs.
• Serious question for you: are you a boob man, ass man, leg man? What's your preference?
• She got hit in the boob.

□ *boob job* 유방 확대 수술; Breast enhancement surgery.

• "I was going to be a dancer," Rebecca confided to Adam. "I have the legs for it, I think, but I didn't have enough up top and I wasn't willing to get a boob job."

□ *booby* 유방; Breast

• She just wanted him to notice her butt and boobies.

□ boodle 많은 양의 돈; A large but unspecified amount of money.

□ boogie 춤추다, 빨리 움직이다; To dance or move quickly.

□ boondocks [단수 취급] 오지, 벽지; 황야; (미개척의) 삼림 지대; A place that is far from the current location.

• You know you live in the boondocks when you can't see your house from the road.

□ boonies [단수 취급] 오지, 벽지; 황야; (미개척의) 삼림 지대; A remote, usually brushy rural area.

• My Mom got pissed at me for doing some of the things I used to do. She shipped me off to my aunt in the boonies. I thought I was a bad-ass, you know. Turns out farm kids can deliver a pretty good ass-kicking when the time comes.

□ boot ~을 해고하다. 쫓아내다; To fire; get rid of; throw out, to expel.

• He got booted from the club.

□ *booth babe* 전시장 부스에 있는 매력적인 여자; An attractive female member of staff sent to hand out pamphlets and attract attention for the company.

• God, I'm stuck playing booth babe again… I swear, this is a discrimination suit waiting to happen.

□ bootleg 불법으로 제작[판매]하는 것; 밀조품, 불법 복사품, 해적판; A pirated copy of something; Anything cheap, second-rate, or cheesy, regardless of whether its stolen or copied, especially by teenagers.

• Person A: He got those shoes at Payless. Person B: Yeah, that's bootleg.
• Ahhh, I remember those great nights where I used to get BOOTLEG copies of music on Napster.

□ **bootlicker**   아첨꾼, 알랑거리는 사람; A servile flatterer; a toady or sycophant.

• BDK is always kissing Capt. Connoly's ass, what a bootlicker!

□ *booty*   엉덩이; Buttocks

• That girl over there has some large-ass booty!

□ *booty call*   성관계를 갖기 위해서 갖는 만남. 또는 그것을 위한 전화; A last-minute or previously unplanned request to meet up with someone with the intention of having sex.

• He called me at 3 a.m. last night for a booty call.

□ *bootylicious*   섹시한; Attractive; possessing shapely rear end.

• The bootylicious queen has declared that working on Broadway would be her ideal job.

□ **booze**   알코올. 술; Alcohol

• I heard you don't handle your booze so well any more.
• I've never seen her pass up free booze in my life.

□ **bop**   (주먹/막대기 따위로) ~을 때리다, 치다; To hit, strike

• Son, you know you shouldn't bop your brother. A bop in the head is not nice!

□ **bork**   망가트리다, 부수다; To break, ruin, destroy

• I think I borked your computer.

□ **borked**   망가진, 부러진, 고장 난, 깨진; Broken, not functioning.

• I think your computer is borked.

□ **boss**   아주 좋은; Excellent, wonderful

• He has such a boss car.

□ *bottom*   엉덩이, 둔부; Buttocks

- One of Adam's hands stroked Allie's sides and her bottom; the other tweaked and rubbed her nipple softly.
- Adam gave her bottom a gentle squeeze.

□ bottom-feeder   밑바닥 인생(다른 사람의 불행이나 다른 사람들이 버린 물건을 이용하여 돈을 버는 사람); A despicable person; a useless or low-class person.

- You are either incompetent – or a dedicated bottom feeder of the bankers.

□ bounce   떠나가다; To depart.

- I am getting a bit tired of this party, so let's bounce.

□ bouncer   (극장/댄스 홀 따위의) 경비원(guard); 경호원(body-guard); Security, generally at a club, bar, or party.

- I pushed the girl that slapped me and then the bouncers threw me out.

□ *box*   여성[남성]의 성기; Vulva

- Derrick dipped his head down to capture a nipple in his mouth as Jenny felt the first inch of the invader in her box. Shelly said. "I'll keep my box wrapped around this pole until you can have your taste."
- I was going to finger her tight box good while she pulled on your cock.

□ *box*   매력적인 여성; An attractive female.

□ *box lunch*   쿤닐링구스(입술이나 혀로 여성의 성기를 애무하는 행위); Cunnilingus

- Damn, my girl was just begging for a box lunch… I didn't mind giving her one.

□ bozo   녀석, 멍청이; 거친 사람, 골치 아픈 사람; Fool

- You are such a bozo.

□ bra   형제; Synonymous with "bro"

□ **brainiac**   아주 똑똑한 사람; A very intelligent person; brain+Steve Wozniak(Apple의 공동창업자)

□ **brat**   애새끼, 꼬마 녀석; A poorly-behaved child.

• The kid I babysit is such a brat.

□ ***break one's ass***   뼈 빠지게 일하다; To work very hard.

□ ***break one's balls***   뼈 빠지게 일하다; To work very hard.

□ ***break one's buns***   뼈 빠지게 일하다; To work very hard.

□ ***break one's butt***   뼈 빠지게 일하다; To work very hard.

□ **break out**   탈출하다, 떠나다; To escape, leave

□ break *somebody's* chops   뼈 빠지게 일하다; To work very hard.

□ ***break somebody's ass***   물리치다, 혼내다; To beat up; to harass or annoy.

□ ***break somebody's balls***   물리치다, 혼내다; To beat up; to harass or annoy.

□ ***break somebody's buns***   물리치다, 혼내다; To beat up; to harass or annoy.

□ ***break somebody's butt***   물리치다, 혼내다; To beat up; to harass or annoy.

□ **break up**   크게 웃다[웃기다]; To cause laughter.

□ **break wind**   방귀 뀌다; A replacement for "Fart". Mostly used by people(s) over the age of 55.

48

- What the heck is that smell? Did you just break wind?

□ **breeze**   갑자기 떠나다; To leave.

- Yo, this party is wack. I'm about to breeze.

□ **brew**   맥주; A beer.

- Would you like to come in for a brew?

□ **bring off**   성공하다; To succeed.

□ **bring *someone* down a peg**   ~의 자만심[콧대]을 꺾다[~에게 자기 수준을 깨닫게 하다]; To lower someone's high self-opinion.

- He needed to be taken down a peg or two.

□ **bro**   (남자를 다정하게 부를 때) 친구; Friend; commonly used in greetings.

- What's up, bro?

□ **broad**   여자(woman); 품행이 나쁜 여자, 매춘부; A female.

- Come on, you're old enough to figure this out. I'm nailing this broad.

□ **bronze**   경찰; The police.

- The bronze are up ahead, slow down.

□ ***brown eye***   항문; Anus

- You've got to be gentle with the brown eye.

□ **brown nose**   (남에게) 알랑거리다, 아첨 떨다; To fawn over a superior.

- She is the biggest Brown Nose in the company!
- John is a total brownnoser because he is always sucking up to the teacher.

- *__brown star__*   항문; Referred to as the anus, often characterized by 'striations' that are in a star pattern.

> • Wow, that girl has some nice striations on her brown star.

- **brush off**   ~을 무시하다. 외면하다; To ignore someone, sometimes completely and regard the individual as petty or insignificant.

> • Ever since Jessica found a new boyfriend she's been brushing off her ex, Tony.

- *__BS__*   bullshit의 두음 문자; Bull shit.

> • My boss is full of BS.
> • That's BS – John wouldn't behave like that.

- **bubba**   형제, 촌뜨기; Brother; hick, redneck

- **buck**   달러(dollar); Money

> • My Nintendo DS costed 150 bucks.

- **buck naked**   완전히 벗은; Completely nude.

> • The man was running down the street buck naked!

- **buck wild**   거친, 통제가 안 되는, 무례한; Uncontrollable, un-civilized; wild; CRAZY

> • I'm tired of going to parties where everybody is buck wild.

- **bucket list**   죽기 전에 꼭 해야 할 일이나 하고 싶은 일들에 대한 리스트; A list of things a person wants to do before they "kick the bucket"

> • "She had what I call a 'bucket list,' and that was the last thing on it," Marjorie Carpenter said Tuesday.

- *__bucket of shit__*   허풍, 거짓말; Lies

- *bucking bronco* 성교 시 후배위 체위의 일종; The Bucking Bronco is an sex position in which the man mounts the girl from the back, and cups her boobs firmly in his hands. The girl will then proceed to buck up and down like a wild bronco.

  • I decided to try the Bucking Bronco last night on my girlfriend, and she threw me off like a monkey throwing shit!

- buckle down ~에 온 힘을 쏟다; ~에 착수하다; A slogan meant to convey 'Get to work!' or to say 'Quit lollygagging and get back to work!'

  • Smith: Lets go for a break!
  Mackenzie: I can't, our section just got the "Buckle down" speech, I have to finish this file and some P2P's.
  Smith: Oh the "Buckle down" speech?, we got that too, and we pulled 10 hours of overtime each last week alone!
  Mackenzie: Yeah I know! The Boss can lick the sack butter from my hairy pair.

- buckle under (압력에 못 이기고) 허물어지다; To succumb to pressure.

- *bud* 마리화나; Marijuana

  • That is some Indica big buds! Some good shit!

- bud 친구; Friend; short for buddy.

  • Hey, bud, what's up?

- *bud* 클리토리스; Clitoris

  • Sarah exploded when Karlie started to gently flick her tongue over the bud.

- buddy up (~와) 친구가 되다; To form small teams.

  • One year I was buddying up with Klammer, another artist.

- buff ~광, 애호가; Enthusiastic for; fan for~

- buff 근골이 늠름한; Muscular

- He is buff.

□ **buffalo** 강요하다; To intimidate or coerce, as by a display of confidence or authority.

□ **buffy** 근골이 늠름한; Muscular

□ *BUFU* 항문 성교; Butt fuck.

- She's in the wheelchair cuz mandingo bufued her last night.

□ **bug** ~을 괴롭히다, 방해하다, 귀찮게 굴다; To pester.

- Stop bugging me!
- Don't bug me, I really need to concentrate!

□ **bugaboo** 귀찮게 하는 것, 걱정거리; Overly annoying person that constantly calls or goes to your home uninvited.

- Jeremy L. is such a bugaboo!

□ **bugger** 녀석, 놈(chap); 싫은 녀석; Technically means to sodomize, but sometimes is used to refer to a person in a derogatory manner.

- That bugger stole my Holden!

□ *buggery* (남성 간의) 항문 성교; Anal intercourse.

- The perp got 5 years for committing buggery and posting on the internet.

□ **built** 좋은 체격의; Large, well built, highly muscular, great presence, huge

- He is so built.

□ *bukkake* 안면 사정 행위; A sexual practice that involves many men ejaculating on the faces of a smaller number of women (usually a single person).

- I know you love bukkake.

- **bulldoze** ~을 억지로 밀어붙이다, 강행하다, 강제로 밀어 넣다; Forcefully shoving or putting a dick in another person's mouth.

  - You best shut the fuck up before I bulldoze your mouth until you can't speak anymore.

- ***bullshit*** 형편없는, 지랄 맞은; Inferior; worthless

  - Looks like bullshit to me.

- ***bullshit*** 허튼수작; 거짓말(lie); 허풍, 과장; Nonsense or completely untrue.

  - That is nothing but bullshit. I do not believe a word of it.

- ***bullshit*** [불쾌감을 나타내어] 헛소리 마!, 집어치워!, 거짓말 마라!; Expression of sadness or dismay; something considered by the speaker to be unreasonable or improper.

  - "Oh, bullshit, Andy replied. You bullied us until we showed you what would happen the next time. She's right. You treat us like your slaves because old man Travers treats you like his. Well, I'll be damned if I'm going to be Eric Travers' piss boy. No way in hell."

- **bum** 남에게 기식하다, 빌어먹다; Beggar; To borrow. Etymology; from bums (homeless people,) who "borrow" money, cigarettes, etc.

  - Poor Charlie had to go on the bum.

- **bum** 고장, 엉망; Out-of-order, malfunctioning

- **bum** 떠돌이, 부랑자; A homeless person or beggar.

  - When he came back from the backpacking trip, he looked like a bum.

- **bum** 게으름뱅이, 건달; A lazy person.

  - Get off your butt, you bum!

- ***bum*** 엉덩이; Buttocks, butt, ass

53

• She has a real hang-up about his big bum.

□ **bum around**   빈둥거리다[빈둥거리며 돌아다니다]; To be lazy.

• I love just bumming around watching the tube.

□ **bumbass**   바보, 멍청이; One who has both lazy and retarded qualities.

• Why don't you stop watching television and study a little bit for once, you bumbass.

□ **bumfuck**   시골, 촌구석; An imaginary place where all the residents are hicks, rednecks, or otherwise backwards.

• He's from Bumfuck, Nebraska.

□ **bummed out**   낙담한, 허둥거리는; Depressed

• I'm really bummed out.

□ **bummer**   실망, 불쾌한 경험, 불유쾌한 일; Expression of sadness or dismay.

• You gotta go? Oh bummer!

□ **bump**   없애다, 없던 일로 하다, 없애다; Like "forget that", used to express dislike. (bump you!)

• You know what? Bump you, I'm leaving.

□ **bump off**   ~를 제거[살해]하다; To kill.

• Despite being bumped off two previous flights, he finally got his chance.

□ **bumping**   바글바글하다. 와글와글하다; Full of people. Typically used to refer to a party, a dance club (disco), etc. Usually pronounced as "bumpin."

• That party was bumping!

54

□ **bumps and grinds** (쇼의 댄서 등이) 허리 부분을 쑥 내밀고 비트는 [돌리는] 동작; The stereotypical dance of a stripper, including the swindling and thrusting of the pelvis.

- One boy was up close to a girl's back, bumping and grinding to the pounding beat of the music.

□ **bun** (이성)친구; A boyfriend or girlfriend.

- That's my bun!

□ *bun* 엉덩이; A buttock. Usually used in the plural.

- Nice buns.

□ *bun-buster* 해결하기 힘든 문제; An extremely difficult or unpleasant problem.

□ *bung hole* 항문; Anus

- I need TP(toilet paper) for my bunghole.

□ *buns* (특히 남자의) 엉덩이(buttocks); 여성의 성기; Buttocks

- Nice buns.

□ **burn rubber** 타이어에 불이 날 정도로 속도를 내다; To accelerate quickly in an automobile, such that the tires don't get traction with the ground and spin freely.

- To run away from him, she burnt rubber.

□ **bush league** 질 낮은, 아마추어인; Amateurish; MINOR LEAGUE

- Your silly use of statistics and political rhetoric is bush league.

□ **bushed** 몹시 지친; Tired

- The next day I was completely bushed.

□ **bushpig** 촌놈; An unattractive person from the Bush, i.e. the country-side of Australia.

• You bush pig.

□ **bushwhack** 매복하다; To lie in wait; to ambush; to assault. Broadly, it means to launch a surprise assault from a hidden place, especially if the victim is unarmed.

• Afghan officials say Taleban fighters who bushwhacked two convoys carrying members of the same family have killed at least 30 people.

□ **bust** 가슴; Breasts

• She's got a huge bust.

□ **bust** 군중을 흩어지게 하다; To cause a crowd to disperse; BREAK UP.

• The cops busted the party.

□ **bust** 단속하다; (경찰이) 급습하다, 가택 수색을 하다, 구속하다; To arrest; to be incarcerated.

• He got busted for drugs.

□ **bust** (주먹으로) ~을 치다, 때리다; To punch or hit.

• If you don't shut up I'm going to bust you in the mouth.

□ *bust [break] one's ass* 필사적으로 버티다, 열심히 일하다; To work hard.

• I busted my ass to get that job.

□ **bust a gut** 배꼽 빠지게 웃다; To laugh so hard your stomach hurts.

• I thought I'd bust a gut laughing.

□ *bust a load* 사정하다; To ejaculate.

- I busted a load in my pants.

□ **bust a nut**   전력을 다하다, 대단한 노력을 기울이다; To work hard.

- I busted a nut on that project.

□ *bust a nut*   사정하다; To ejaculate.

- I won't stop 'til I bust a nut.

□ *bust ass*   방귀 뀌다; To flatulate; FART

- Dude, did you just bust ass?

□ *bust ass*   전력을 다하다, 대단한 노력을 기울이다; To work hard.

- There are only two hours left, we should bust our ass.

□ bust on   ~을 마구 때리다; To hit, attack

- The bouncers busted on some drunken guy last night.

□ *bust one's ass*   전력을 다하다, 대단한 노력을 기울이다; To work hard.

- Dude, you'd better bust ass if you wanna finish that on time!

□ **bust one's balls**   전력을 다하다, 대단한 노력을 기울이다; To use a lot of effort to do something sometimes even in vain.

- I busted my balls making him understand me but he acted wrong anyway.

□ *bust one's buns*   전력을 다하다, 대단한 노력을 기울이다; To work hard.

□ *bust one's butt*   전력을 다하다, 대단한 노력을 기울이다; To work hard.

□ *bust one's nuts*   사정하다; To ejaculate.

- I won't stop 'til I bust my nut.

□ ***bust one's ball***   남을 아주 곤란하게 만들다; To make someone's
life difficult on purpose out of jest or with contempt, perceived or not.

• I got my balls busted last night by my wife nagging me.

□ ***bust one's buns***   남을 아주 곤란하게 만들다; To make someone's
life difficult.

□ ***bust one's butt***   남을 아주 곤란하게 만들다; To make someone's
life difficult.

□ bust out   (~로 부터) 도망치다. 탈옥하다; To leave a place;
does not have to be forcefully as the term would imply.

• Oh shit! She's waking up, let's bust out of here!

□ ***bust somebody's ass***   때리다, 괴롭히다; To beat up; to harass or annoy.

□ ***bust somebody's balls***   때리다, 괴롭히다; To beat up; to harass or annoy.

□ ***bust somebody's butt***   때리다, 괴롭히다; To beat up; to harass or annoy.

□ busted   고장 난; Broken, not correctly functioning, doesn't work.

• This radio is busted.

□ busted   돈 한 푼 없는; With no money left.

□ busted   피곤한; Tired

□ bust-up   싸움, 심한 언쟁; A fight.

• Sue and Tony had a bust-up and aren't speaking to each other.

□ bust-up   실패, (일의) 망침; A failure.

□ ***butt***   궁둥이, 엉덩이(buttocks); Ass, buttocks

58

- "Let's go help Allie along," Shelly said when she regained her breath. "I think two mouths on her nipples and a tongue in her butt should do it."
- Shelly would put a finger up Allie's tight little butt.

□ *butt fuck*　　　　항문 성교; Anal sex.

- Sheryl almost died when Tom asked her if she wanted to butt fuck.

□ butt in　　　　~에 참견하다, 주제넘게 나서다; To meddle in another person's private business.

- John told his brother not to butt in when he was talking to his girlfriend.

□ *butt love*　　　　항문 성교; Butt sex.

- Did we just make butt love?

□ *butt one's ass*　　　　남을 곤란하게 만들다; To make someone's life difficult.

□ butt-buster　　　　난제; 해결하기 어려운 문제; An extremely difficult or unpleasant problem.

□ butter up　　　　아부하다; To flatter, especially for future gain.

□ buttercup　　　　순진한 소녀; A cute, innocent female.

- Don't cry, my little buttercup.

□ *butterface*　　　　얼굴만 빼고 전반적으로 매력적인 여성(대개 몸매가 훌륭하나, 얼굴은 못생긴 여성의 경우에 사용); Chick with a hell of a nice body, but the face is ugly.

- She looked real good… but her face (butterface).

□ butterfingers　　　　[단수 취급] 물건을 (손에서) 잘 떨어뜨리는 사람; 부주의한 사람, 서투른 야구 선수; 서투른 사람; A clumsy person, especially one who tends to drop things.

- It was you who dropped it, butterfingers.

59

- *butterhead* 얼굴만 빼고 전반적으로 매력적인 여성; A woman with everything looking good but her head.

  - Everythang look good, butterhead(but her head).

- *butt-fuck* (~와) 항문 성교를 하다(assfuck); To be on the giving end of anal sex.

  - She got butt fucked.

- butthead 바보 같은[꼴 보기 싫은] 녀석; Person who thinks with his ass, as opposed to his brain as most normal human beings do.

  - That guy's a member of the Young Republicans… what a butthead.

- *butthole* 항문; Anus

  - Her motions became frenzied and Derrick found his whole finger buried in Jenny's butthole.

- buttinski 말참견하는 사람; A meddler; someone who intrudes or interferes.

  - Get out of here, Buttinski. You weren't invited into this talk.

- buttload 많은 양; An extremely large quantity of anything that takes up space.

  - I drank a buttload last night and had to get my stomach pumped from the resulting alcohol poisoning.

- Button your lip! 입 닥쳐!; Shut Up!

- buy the farm 살해되다, 죽다; To die, especially in combat.

  - They knew that if their father were to buy the farm they would have to sell the farm.

60

step. 03

C

□ **c' word** Cunt(여성 성기)에 대한 완곡어법; Cunt

• Interestingly enough, so far there haven't been any reports of angry Tea Party protesters shouting the "c" word at female lawmakers.

□ **cabbage** (~을) 훔치다, 슬쩍 하다; to steal; to borrow without asking.

• I cabbaged my roommate's beer from the fridge last night.

□ *cabeza* 펠라티오; Head, blowjob, face, dome⋯ (in Spanish literally means head) pronounced as "cuh-bay-sa"

• Yo, dude, that hot Latin chick in my Spanish 2 class gave me some cabeza! Dude⋯ me gusta mucho⋯.

□ *caboose* 엉덩이; Buttocks

• She got one damn fine caboose.

□ **cadge** 구걸[걸식]하다; To get items by sponging or begging.

• Can I cadge a Ciggy?

□ **call it Christmas** 문제에 대한 좋은 해결책; A good solution to a problem.

• We'll just get some beer and call it Christmas.

□ **call shotgun** (10대 사이에서) 차[트럭]의 조수석에 먼저 타려고 하다; To claim the (front) seat next to the driver in an automobile. Derives from the "old west" when stagecoaches routinely had an armed guard (typically with a shotgun) seated next to the driver on top.

• Steve: I can give you guys a lift if you want.
  Bob: I call shotgun!
  Andy: Darn Bob, you already sat in front last time!

□ **call the shots** (상황을) 지휘[통제]하다; To be the leader.

• This is my party, I call the shots!

□ *cameltoe*   여성이 옷을 타이트하게 입어 앞부분이 선명하게 보이는 것; The outline of a human female's labia majora, as seen through tightly fitting clothes; The visible cleft of the outer labia under tight clothing. (A "frontal wedge" on a female.)

• "Do you know what a camel toe is?" "Of course. Jesus, I'm not nine. I know all the dirty words and nicknames, too."
• That girl had some nasty cameltoe at her ballet recital.

□ can   해고하다; 끝나게 하다, 버리다; 중지시키다; To fire or get rid of someone.

• They won't can me; I'm the only one who knows what's going on in this place.

□ can   감옥; Jail or prison.

• I'm a need both of you to do me a favor. And by what I mean by that is, I need you to do what I say. Or else I'll leave your asses in the can tonight.

□ can   화장실; The restroom.

• Where's the can?

□ candy-ass   소심[비겁]한 사람; 계집애 같은 사내(sissy); Wimpy, weak-willed, overly meek and mild, pusillanimous.

• He is such a candy-ass when it comes to these things.

□ Capisce?   알아들었어?; Do you understand me?

□ capish   이해하다(보통 의문문으로 사용. 이탈리아어 방언에서 유래); To understand. Used as a question. Pronounced colloquially as "ka-PEESH", and frequently misspelled as capish, capeesh, kapish, etc.

• Joey expects his money by Monday. Capish?

□ carp   훔치다; To steal; to take something without permission.

• While the cashier's back was turned, I carped a hat from the rack.

□ **case of the Mondays** 월요병; General malaise felt on the first day back to work after the weekend.

• Sounds like you've got a serious case of the Mondays.

□ **cash in** 죽다; To die.

□ **cash in** 경제적으로 성공[번창]하다; (돈 따위를) 벌다; To make a profit.

□ **cash in *one's* chips** 가게를 걷어치우다; 죽다; To die; kick the bucket; perish; depart this life.

• In that terrible accident you might cash in your chips right before your wedding ceremony.

□ **catch** 좋은 결혼 상대자; 횡재한 물건; A person who would make an excellent significant other.

• Yeah, we're both single, lonely people. I mean, she said I was a catch.

□ **catch (*one's*) drift** 말을 알아듣다; To understand. usually used aggressively.

• Have the money by Tuesday, or bad things will happen. You catch my drift?

□ **catch on to** 이해하다; To understand.

□ **catch *somebody* with his/her pants down** 범행 현장에서 잡다; Arrest in the very act of a crime.

□ **catch some z's** 잠자다. 눈 좀 붙이다; To sleep.

□ **catch with a hand in the cookie jar** 범행 현장에서 잡다; Arrest in the very act of a crime.

□ **catch with a smoking gun** 범행 현장에서 잡다; Arrest in the very act of a crime.

□ **catch[or get] hell**   크게 혼나다, 심한 꾸중을 듣다; Saying used to describe the hell raising you get when you do something fucked up and get caught by someone.

- Man, my pop found out I skipped school yesterday and I caught hell.

□ **cat's chance in hell**   전혀 희망이 없는; Hopeless

□ **cave in**   굴복하다: To succumb to pressure.

□ **charity case**   자선사업 대상자; A case for a welfare worker.

- I'm going to his formal dance, but he's just a charity case.

□ **chatter-box**   수다쟁이; A person who won't shut the fuck up.

- A: Hey you!   B: Me?
  A: Yeah, you!   B: What?
  A: Shut the fuck up!   B: Why?
  A: Cause you're being a chatter-box, and it's annoying the shit out of me.
  B: Cunt.

□ **cheapo**   싸구려, 값싼 물건; Cheap quality or just something rubbish.

- I will forego the use of paper plates for months till they go on sale for 20 cents off. Some call me a cheapo. I call it pure genius.
- That is some cheapo handbag.

□ **cheapskate**   구두쇠; A stingy person.

- You only got me a half pint - you cheapskate!

□ **Check!**   좋다!, 알았다!, 확인!; Ok, or yes. Acknowledgment of an item from a checklist.

- Let's go to the club next weekend. Check.
- Q: Gas in the tank?   A: Check.
- Q: Suitcases in the trunk?   A: Check.

□ **check it out**   여기 좀 봐. 한번 봐; Pay attention.

- Check it out. So at the club last night, there was this dude….

□ *cheeks*   궁둥이, 엉덩이; Buttocks

- Shelly was certain that Karlie just wanted her to finger her butt but she had other plans. She knelt forward and used both of her hands to part the girl's cheeks.

□ cheerio   안녕, 잘 있어; Goodbye

- Well, I best be off, cheerio.

□ cheese   매력적인 여성; Attractive female.

- I'm going to the party to find me some cheese.

□ cheeseball   싸구려의, 저급한; Cheesy; corny

□ *cheesecake*   성적 매력이 있는 여성; 여성의 섹스 어필, 곡선미, 각선미; Legs of a woman… especially the portion on the inside of the thighs.

- Man, will you look at her CHEESECAKE?

□ cheesy   값싼, 싸구려의; Lacking in taste; lame; corny; of poor quality; shoddy

- His clothes are so cheesy, but hey, I dig clothes from the seventies anyway.

□ cheesy   진부한; Corny

□ *cherry*   처녀막, 동정; A membrane in a woman's vagina, known more properly as a hymen.

- I popped my girlfriend's cherry while I fingered her.

□ cherry-tops   (경찰차 안의) 경찰; Police, usually in cars. From the flashing red light (the same color as red cherries) on police cars.

- Jimmy was doing 90 and got chased by the cherry-tops.

66

C

- **Chevy**　　　　　쉐보레(Chevrolet) 자동차의 애칭: A Chevrolet automobile. Pronounced as "shevy".

  • Hank sure has a nice Chevy.

- **chew _one's_ ass off**　　비난하다; To attack verbally.

- _**chick flick**_　　　(여성 관객을 겨냥한) 여자들 영화; A movie primarily of interest to females, often due to content love, friendship, emotional scenes) or cast (primarily females).

  • My girlfriend couldn't go out tonight because she's watching chick flicks with her friends.

- **chicken**　　　　겁쟁이, 비겁자; 겁먹다; A coward.

  • Michael: Why does everybody think that I'm scared of girls?
    George: Because you're a chicken.
  • What's the matter, are you chicken?

- **chicken**　　　　겁을 먹고 (~을) 그만두다[(~에서) 꽁무니를 빼다];
  To be afraid; to be scared.

- _**chicken dick**_　　　겁쟁이; Scared or coward person.

  • You Chicken Dick or Don't be a Chicken Dick.

- **chicken feed**　　　하찮은 것[사람]. 적은 양; Small amount.

  • It's impossible to live on such a chicken feed salary.

- **chicken head**　　　바보, 멍청이; Stupid; jerk

- _**chicken head**_　　　펠라티오를 자주 하는 여자; A female who performs
  fellatio frequently.

  • That girl is a chicken head – she's blowing everyone on this street.
  • Those girls are chicken heads.

- **chicken out**　　　겁을 먹고 (~을) 그만두다[(~에서) 꽁무니를 빼다]; To decide at the last moment not to do something you said you would do, because you are afraid.

67

- You're not chickening out, are you?

□ **chicken-hearted**   겁 많은, 소심한; Timid, Liable to fear.

□ **chicken-shit**   겁쟁이; 쓸모없는; 사소한 일; (경멸할) 실없는 이야기; 거짓말; Feeble; unimportant; cowardly.

- That chickenshit can't kill a fly.

□ **chill**   (계획 따위가) 완벽한; 좋은, 굉장한(cool); Great, awesome; COOL

- My boyfriend's new Mustang is way chill.

□ **chill**   진정하다; To calm down.

- You need to chill before you're completely pissed.

□ **chill**   흥미진진한; Exciting

□ **chill out**   (사람이) 냉정해지다, 침착해지다; [명령형으로] 침착해!, 마음 편히 가져!; To relax, to become calm.

- Dawg, you need to chill out.

□ **chilled out**   차분한, 진정된; Calm

□ **chilling**   흥미진진한; Fun or exciting.

- That movie was chilling.

□ **Chinaman's chance in hell**   가능성이 전무한; No chance at all.

- The evil elf Kucinich hasn't got a Chinaman's chance of winning the nomination.

□ **chinwag**   잡담하다, 수다 떨다; To converse with others. Commonly used in Australia.

- Today I went and had a bit of a chinwag with my mate!

68

- chinwagger   말이 많은 사람, 수다쟁이; A man who talks a lot.

> • That guy wouldn't shut up about how his Viking character died in Dungeons and Dragons. What a chinwagger!

- chipper   원기 왕성한; 명랑한; Feeling exuberantly happy.

> • I'm feelin' real chipper today! I just stole a cookie and didn't get caught!

- *chiquita banana*   매력적인 여성; An attractive female.

> • Look at that chiquita banana over there.

- chock-a-block with   꽉 들어찬, 꽉 찬: Filled to capacity or beyond.

- *chocolate cha-cha*   항문 성교; Anal Sex.

> • Hey man, wanna do the chocolate cha-cha?

- choke *something* off   (긴장하거나 해서) 망치다[실패하다]; To stop in midstream, to end suddenly.

- **chow down**   먹다; 식사하다; To eat.

> • Chow down, guys. The food is getting cold.

- chuck   게우다; To vomit.

> • I think I'm going to chuck.

- chuck out   쫓아내다; To send away.

- *Chuck you, Farley!*   엿먹어라! 제기랄!; A contemptuous dismissal; Fuck you!

> • Chuck you, Farley, I'm not having anything to do with it.

- chucklehead   바보, 모자라는 사람, 멍청이; An unintelligent person.

> • Shut up, you chucklehead. Boy, Bob sure is a chuckleheaded idiot. He's so stupid he forgot to friggin shut up his mouth.

#
A
B
C
D
E
F
G
H
I
J
K
L
M
N
O
P
Q
R
S
T
U
V
W
X
Y
Z

□ **chum**　　　　　친구, 벗, 옛 친구; A good friend; pal; buddy; chummy

　• They are old chums.

□ **chump**　　　　바보, 멍청이, 얼간이; A stupid or gullible person.

　• You chumps don't have a clue what this guy is up to.

□ **chunk**　　　　몸이 딱 벌어진 사람; A large obese Chinese person. Usually offensive. Comes from the word Chink.

　• Yo, check out John Kim over there. He ain't a chink. He a chunk!

□ **churn out**　　　대량 생산하다; Mass production, to have large scale of manufacturing.

　• Asian factories will be churning out larger panels for LCD TVs.

□ **chutzpah**　　　뻔뻔스러움, 철면피, 후안무치(厚顔無恥); Audacity; spirit.

　• John: I just smacked my teacher.　Mary: That took a lot of chutzpa.

□ **CI**　　　　　비밀 정보원; Confidential informant.

□ **ciao**　　　　안녕하세요; 잘 가[있어], 안녕, 그럼 또 만나; Goodbye; hello. Pronounced "chow." Italian.

　• Ciao bella. (means Hello/Goodbye girlfriend)
　• Ciao bello. (means Hello/Goodbye boyfriend)

□ ***circle jerk***　　　(3명 이상 사이의) 상호 수음(mutual masturbation); A masturbation party; can be with guys or girls. Everyone usually sits in a circle and jerks off in the company of other people.

　• I am planning a circle jerk next week if any of y'all are interested.

□ **clam up**　　　입을 다물다; 답변을 거부하다; To suddenly keep unusually quiet, often in regards to the divulging of information.

　• I clammed up during the presentation.

70

□ Clam up! 입 다물어!; Shut Up!

□ *claptrap* 쓸데없는 말; pretentious, pompous, nonsensical and or empty language.

• I've had enough of your claptrap.

□ clean *somebody* out [남에게서] (돈을) 빼앗다, (도박 불경기 따위가) [사람을] 빈털터리로 만들다; To take all of a person's money.

• The Ponzi scheme I invested in cleaned me out.

□ clean up 거금을 벌다; To make a large profit.

□ *clean up one's shit* 개과천선하다

• He cleaned up his shit.

□ cleaned out 돈을 다 털린; With no money left.

• You guys have cleaned me out!

□ clear off 달아나다[가 버리다]; To leave; to run away.

□ **click** (이성과) 뜻이 맞다, 의기투합하다; To connect, relate; hit it off with someone.

• When I first met her, we just clicked, and we're best friends now.

□ click (불현듯) 딱 분명해지다[이해가 되다]; To understand.

• Suddenly it clicked. We'd been talking about different people.

□ **clincher** (논쟁, 시합 등을 매듭짓는) 결정적인 사실, 결정타; Sure thing.

□ clip 한 번에, 단숨에; At one clip; at a clip.

□ clip 질주하다, 빨리 날다; To speed.

- We were going at a good clip.

□ **_clit_**　　　음핵(陰核), 클리토리스; Clitoris

- Lick my clit.
- The tip of his finger split her lips and he caressed her clit gently.

□ clobber　　　완패시키다; To defeat.

□ clobber　　　~을 사정없이 때리다, 때려눕히다; To strike with
great force.

- His car got clobbered by a freight train.

□ clod　　　얼간이, 바보; Someone gullible.

- That clod is so gullible, I told him Iraq won the war. Ha.

□ clonk　　　~을 치다; To hit with a dull thudding force.

- You clonked me in the din.

□ **close call**　　　위기일발, 구사일생(close shave); When something
almost happens. Especially something bad, like a collision or social mishap.

- Jerry experienced a close call when he was sailing on his boat and a
strong gale knocked down his mast and missed his head by a hair.

□ close _one's_ barn door　　　바지 앞 지퍼를 올리다; Close one's
zipper(fly) on the pants.

□ close shave　　　위기일발, 구사일생(close call); Risky situation.

- The car almost hit me. The was a close shave.

□ clout　　　(특히 손으로) 세게 때리다; To hit someone.

- I got clouted by that guy.

□ cluckhead　　　멍청이; Fool

□ **clunk**   쿵 하고 치다, 때리다; To hit.

□ **clunker**   심각한 실수; A person, speech, product or other item that is a complete flop.

□ ***clusterfuck***   엉망진창; An event or process which is totally disordered and discombobulated, resulting in a situation of extreme difficulty, and manifesting a state of intense frustration, even anger.

> • "If we get into dealing with 50 or 100 employees, I'll think about jumping off a bridge," Adam lamented. "Jesus Lord, we just have the one and look at the clusterfuck we've wandered into."
> • Hey, what is that clusterfuck on your desk?

□ **clutch**   위기, 절박한 경우; The crucial moment that comes between winning and losing; a difficult or trying time.

> • Big-time players deliver in the clutch.

□ **c-note**   미화 100달러 지폐; $100 bill. Origin: The Roman numeral for 100 is C.

> • Do you have change for a c-note?

□ **cock**   혼자 우쭐대는 사람, 독불장군; An extremely over-confident male who acts like he knows everything.

> • A cock would say or think like, "what would you guys do without me?"

□ ***cock***   음경(陰莖); Penis

> • Adam found his zipper down and his cock out before he even knew what hit him.
> • He's practically got a Saturn V rocket for a cock.
> • I know who's mad for cock! That chap who runs the sauna.

□ ***cock tease***   몸만 달아오르게 하는 여자(성관계를 원하는 듯 유혹하면서 끝내 허락하지 않는 여자); A girl who is attractive that visually teases you because she knows you can't have her.

> • She is such a cock tease.

□ *cock up* 실수하다, 엉망으로 만들다; To mess something up. Used primarily in England.

• It's my ass on the line and I don't want a cock up!

□ *cocksucker* 더러운 인간(보통 남자에 대한 대단히 심한 욕); Jerk; fool; A despicable person. Literally: one who sucks "cock"

• Man, my English teacher is a cocksucker.

□ coke 코카인(cocaine). 마약[코카인]에 취하게 하다(up); Cocaine

• I've tried pot and coke. I even tried crystal meth once.

□ cold cash 현금; Ready money.

• I got the cold cash to pay for that car.

□ **cold feet** 겁, 공포; 달아나려는 자세; To lose desire or nerve to do something.

• Sometimes the bride or groom might not show up to their wedding because they've gotten cold feet.

□ *coldcock* (주먹이나 몽둥이로) 실신할 정도로 때리다; To attack unexpectedly; blindside

• The SOB coldcocked me ⋯ I never saw it coming.

□ *colitas* 마리화나 봉오리; Marijuana buds.

• Warm smell of colitas, rising up through the air. ⋯ "Hotel California", The Eagles.

□ **come** 정액(精液)을 사정하다(ejaculate); To ejaculate.

• She came all over me.

□ come across (with) [금전 따위]를 지불하다, 넘겨주다; To pay.

□ **Come again?**　　　뭐라고(요)? (상대방의 말을 못 알아들었을 때 다시 한 번 말을 해달라는 뜻으로 씀); Could you repeat that?

- FRIEND: Guess What! On the weekend I ···and···(Mumble Mumble)··· pink spotty pineapple···.
  YOU: What the fuck! Come again?

□ **come apart at the seams**　　　분노가 폭발하다, 감정을 억제하지 못하다; To have a mental breakdown.

□ **come down (on) a peg**　　　높은 콧대가 꺾이다, 체면을 잃다; To become humiliated.

□ **come through with** 갚다; To pay.

□ **come unglued**　　　미치다; To have a mental breakdown.

□ **come unstuck**　　　미치다; To have a mental breakdown.

□ **come up roses**　　　썩 잘 돼 가다; To make good progress.

□ *come-on*　　　유혹의 몸짓, 유혹하는 것; A gesture or remark which someone, especially a woman, makes in order to encourage another person to make sexual advances to them.

- She was definitely giving him the come-on.

□ **commie**　　　공산당원(의), 빨갱이; Derogatory name for a Communist.

- In the 1950's, McCarthy wanted to destroy those that he called 'Commies'.

□ **comp**　　　(입장권, 음식 등의) 무료, 증정; Received without charge; complimentary

□ **con**　　　사기의, 속이는; To swindle or scam.

- She believed the con artist's story hook, line, and sinker.

□ **con**　　　죄수(convict); 전과자(ex-convict); A convict.

• He was labeled a con.

□ **conk**　　　　머리를 세게 때리다; To hit.

□ **conk out**　　　멈춰 서 버리다, 고장이 나다; To stop functioning.

□ **conk out**　　　잠이 들다; To fall asleep.

□ **conked out**　　못 쓰게 된, 아주 망가진; Broken, not functioning.

□ **conniption**　　히스테리(의 발작); 울화통, 발끈함; A bad tantrum. Also "conniption fit". One "has" a conniption or conniption fit.

• He had a conniption over the dent in the car.

□ **convulse**　　　포복절도하다; laugh in an uncontrolled way.

□ ***coochie***　　　여성의 성기; Women's vagina.

• Man, I wanted some of that coochie but she wouldn't give it to me.

□ **cook *someone's* goose**　　큰 문제에 빠지다. (마치 남의 집 오리를 죽인 것처럼); To be in trouble.

□ **cook the books**　　회계 장부를 속이다; To tamper with, especially with accounting information.

• He was arrested for cooking the books.

□ **cooked**　　　녹초가 된, 망가진; Broken

• Well, you drove without any oil. Why do you think your car is cooked?

□ ***cookie***　　　여성의 음부; Female genitalia; vagina

□ **cooking (with gas)**　　일이 잘 풀리는; Doing very well; to perform an action quickly or efficiently.

□ **cool**　　　멋진, 근사한, 훌륭한; (사교적으로) 세련된, 스마트한; Very good, excellent, wonderful, interesting, fun, etc.

- That's a cool car.
- That new bike is cool.
- Cool!

▫ **cool**   [열정 분노 따위를] 식히다; [사람을] 달래다, 진정시키다;
Laid back, relaxed, not freaked out, knows what's going on.

- After the argument, Bill asked Andrew, "We cool?", and Andrew replied, "Ya, we cool."

▫ **cool it**   냉정해지다; 말려들지 않는다; 속도를 줄이다; Loosen
up and stop being uptight.

- Don't get too hot-blooded; cool it!

▫ **cool million**   엄청나게 많은 돈; A large but unspecified amount
of money.

▫ **cool out**   냉정해지다[하게 하다], 침착해지다[하게 하다]; To
calm down.

- Yo, my man, cool out, son!

▫ **cop**   ~을 훔치다; To steal or walk out of a place with.

- I went to the dealership and copped me a pimped-out Suburban for 40 G.

▫ **cop**   ~을 잡다, 획득하다; ~을 체포하다; To get; receive;
purchase; steal, or have

- Yo, I'm about to cop a drink, want one?

▫ **cop**   경찰; A police officer, derived from the word "copper", which is what police officers were slangly called when their badges
were made of copper.

- Damn cop gave me a ticket, I fucking hate him.

▫ **cop a feel**   (몸을) 몰래 더듬다; To unwantedly grope a person;
feel up.

- I was having fun dancing with that guy until he tried to cop a feel.

□ **cop out**   (약속 따위를) 어기다, 배신하다; (책임 따위를) 회피하다; To take the easy way out of a sticky situation; to place blame on something else to make things easier.

• Saying you're sick just because you want to avoid a big test that you're prepared but scared for is a cop out.

□ **cop some z's**   잠깐[선잠] 자다; To sleep a little.

□ **copacetic**   훌륭한; 틀림없는; 아주 만족스러운; Excellent, first-rate

• Henry: If any of this is making you uncomfortable.
  Ron: Not at all, no, no···. I'm totally copacetic.

□ **copy that**   (무전) 알았다; To understand.

• Captain Tidwell: I do copy that.

□ *cornhole*   항문; Anus

• I banged her cornhole last night.

□ *cornhole*   항문 성교하다; To have anal sex.

• After I cornhole you, you won't shit right for a week.

□ **cost an arm and leg**   아주 비싸다; Very expensive.

• A: Our clients have gone to all other stores.
  B: But everything in there cost an arm and a leg.

□ **cotton on to**   이해하다; Understand or realize something after some difficulty, especially without people telling you about it.

□ **couch potato**   오랫동안 가만히 앉아 텔레비전만 보는 사람; A lazy person who does nothing but sit on the couch and watch television.

• Please don't lie around like a couch potato. Get up and do something productive.

- **cougar**　　　젊은 남자와의 연애나 성관계를 원하는 중년 여성; A middle-aged woman who seeks out much younger men for romance or physical intimacy.

  - Let's go cougar hunting tonight, boys.
  - Hey, now you're single, I'm single, and it's like, "Look out, world! Two cougars on the prowl."

- **cough up**　　　(돈)을 마지못해 주다; To give money to pay for something especially when you would prefer not to.

  - Come on, cough up. It's your turn to pay.

- *cow girl*　　　여성 상위 체위; A female that likes to literally ride up and down a man's penis, or something resembling the male genitalia.

  - Briana Banks loves riding the cock, she's a true cow girl.

- *cow pie*　　　쇠똥; A large pile of cow shit.

  - Watch out for that cow pie.

- **Cowabunga!**　　　만세, 해냈다; 자, 간다(surfer가 파도 마루에 올라 탔을 때의 외침); How exciting! (An exclamation of rejoice from the early 1990s.) Usually uttered by teenagers wearing neon colors. Brought to popularity by the ever-so-famous Teenage Mutant Ninja Turtles.

  - Leonardo: The pizza just got here! Michaelangelo: COWABUNGA dude!

- **cowboy**　　　무모[무책임]한 사람; 위험한[어려운] 일을 쉽게 떠맡는 사람; Wild, impulsive, living on the edge and taking risks without worrying about the consequences.

  - That cowboy sure did leave a mess behind, didn't he?

- **cowboy up**　　　용기를 내다; To quit bitching and be a man when it gets tough start playing hard.

  - Before the big game against our rivals, someone said "Cowboy up" to the pessimistic pussies.

- **crack**　　　시도[도전](의 기회); An attempt.

- She hopes to have another crack at the world record this year.

□ **crack**   미치다; To go insane.

□ *crack*   크랙, 정제 코카인(흡연용); The freebase form of cocaine that can be smoked.

- I've stayed away from crack and heroin but I've taken X and other pharmaceuticals.

□ **crack down on**   ~에 단호한 조치를 취하다; ~을 엄히 단속하다, 탄압하다; To make punishments for a crime or violation more severe.

- The crack down on drug abuse means that fewer addictions will occur.

□ *crack head*   크랙[코카인] 상용[중독]자; A person who does too much crack.

- Hey Mr. Johnson sold his car for 20 dollars, He must be a crack head.
- Deci is a crack head.

□ crack *somebody* up   ~를 몹시 웃기다; To make someone laugh out loudly.

- Gill's so funny, she just cracks me up.

□ **crack the whip**   채찍을 휘두르다[사람들을 들볶다]; To be demanding of work. Originally used in slavery and horse training.

- Man, my old lady is really cracking the whip on me to get the lawn mowed.

□ **crack up**   (~을) 크게 웃(기)다; To burst into loud laughter.

- That movie was great! I couldn't stop cracking up.

□ **crack up**   (중압감을 못 이기고 정신적으로나 육체적으로) 무너지다[쓰러지다]; To become insane.

□ **crackerjack**   뛰어난 사람, 일류 인사; 뛰어난 것; Excellent, first-rate, someone very skilled or proficient.

- John was a crackerjack of a mechanic: he could make a Mustang hum going in reverse.

80

- **crackers**   (~에) 푹 빠진[about, over]; 미친; Crazy, nuts, extremely foolish.

  • Our English teacher is crackers.

- **crackin'**   멋진, 최고의; Exciting and/ or cool and/ or ecstatic

  • The party's crackin' tonight!

- *crackpot*   머리가 돈, 제정신이 아닌; Crazy or eccentric.

  • That girl comes up with so many crackpot ideas.

- *Cram it!*   입 닥쳐!, 알게 뭐야!, 될 대로 되라지; Shut Up!

- *crap*   잡동사니, 쓰레기; Worthless junk and/or pointless things.

  • What the hell is this crap all about?
  • You are a serious piece of crap.

- *crap*   똥(shit); (a ~) 용변, 배변; 설사; A pile of shit.

  • I crap my pants all the time.

- *crap*   허튼소리; Nonsense; full of lies.

  • I guess it's just a load of crap what everyone says about her.

- *crap around*   1. 바보 같은 짓을 하다 2. 농땡이 부리다; To waste time.

- *crap out*   실패하다, 망쳐 놓다; 못쓰게 되다; To stop operating properly; to ruin.

  • Freakin' controller crapped out.

- *Crap!*   (불신 불만 불쾌감을 나타내어) 쳇, 우라질; What one says when one is afraid to say shit.

  • Oh crap!

□ *crapola*　　　　　말도 안돼!; An expression of the word crap; double shittiness when something goes wrong.

　• Crapola, my car stereo is gone!

□ *crappy*　　　　　더러운, 불결한; 불쾌[지독]한; Bad or displeasing;
inferior; worthless

　• Bailey: A mysterious lady with a shotgun.
　　Stark: Yeah, who knows? Maybe she's just a crappy neighbor.

□ crapshoot　　　　위험하여 예측 불가능한 일, 불확실한 일; (주사위) 도
박; A toss up, roll of the dice, or a gamble; anything could happen.

　• That team has been up and down lately but I got a good feeling about
　　tonight. At the least it's a crapshoot.

□ **crash**　　　　　멈춤, 작동 정지, 고장; To shut down; cease to work;
applied to a computer or program.

　• My computer crashed.

□ **crash**　　　　　자다, 무료로 묵다; To sleep.

　• I was so tired after work. I just crashed.
　• You can always crash at one of our places.

□ **crash and burn**　　잡쳐 버리다; To have a spectacular failure or fall
from grace.

　• Dude, if you don't stop doing crack, you're going to crash and burn.

□ crater　　　　　　떨어지다, 실패하다; To fall as if from a great height,
hit the ground with a significant impact, and end up below ground level.
Used figuratively to describe a severe downturn in popularity, reputation,
value, etc.

　• My stock portfolio cratered during the tech sector implosion a few years back.

□ crazy about　　　~하는 데 푹 빠져 있다; Overly excited or enthusiastic about something.

□ **crazy as a catshit**　　미친; Crazy

□ *creampie*　　　　　질 내 사정; A genre of pornography that features ejaculation inside the man's sexual partner; ejaculating inside sexual partner.

• I gave her a creampie.

□ **creampuff**　　　　(줏대나 기개가 없는) 물렁이; Someone who's soft, and gets mistaken for a girl first time.

• You are a creampuff.

□ ***creep***　　　　　싫은 녀석, 불쾌한 사람; An annoying person.

• Tell your brother to go away. He is such a creep.

□ **creep out**　　　(공포 따위가) ~을 엄습하다; To make someone feel fear or discomfort.

• My 14-year-old daughter is pretty creeped out about it.

□ **creep *somebody* out**　　　　공포에 떨게 하다; To make uncomfortable or afraid.

□ **creeper**　　　기는 것[사람]; 곤충, 파충류 동물; A weird or disturbed person. From "creep"

• Look out, creeper!

□ **creeps**　　　오싹한[근질근질한] 느낌, 전율; 혐오감; A feeling of discomfort (scared or queasy) greater than the willies or the jitters, but less than being freaked out or even grossed out.

• Looking at that homeless guy over there gave me the creeps.

□ ***Cripes!***　　　　[놀라움을 나타내어] 이크, 그것참, 우라질, 제기랄! (또는 Cripe!); Used to express annoyance, anger, or dismay. Used to express annoyance, anger, or dismay; An alteration of "Christ."

- Cripes, I forgot my keys again!
- Cripes! I forgot my bloody dagger in the church!

□ **croak** 죽다; To die.

- Apparently, he croaked when they got to the hospital.

□ **crock** 거짓말, 허풍; 실없는 소리, 난센스; 도움이 안 되는 것; Bullshit, nonsense, something that is a lie.

- True beauty is on the inside? What a crock!

□ **crock of shit** 거짓말, 허풍; 실없는 소리; Something that is false, misleading, full of lies, etc.

- The assertion that your car is exceptional is a crock of shit.

□ **crowd** 공간을 침범하다; To invade someone's personal space.

□ **crud** 쓸모없는 것, 불쾌한 것; Euphemism for crap.

- Oh shi… cra… crud! I left my homework at the library!

□ **cry uncle** 항복하다, 패배를 인정하다. 자비를 청하다; To beg for mercy.

- I'm going to make my examination cry uncle.

□ **crying** (나쁜 일 따위가) 심한. Crying shame, a crying need의 구와 같이 사용

□ **cum** 사정하다; To ejaculate.

- He hated to cut her short but he knew he was going to cum and cum hard any moment.

□ **cum** 정액(精液)(come); Semen

- He then squirted his warm load of cum right down my throat.
- Clean your cum off of the bed.

84

□ *cunnilingus*　　　쿤닐링구스(입술이나 혀로 여성의 성기를 애무하는 행위); Oral sex performed on the vulva of a female.

• I performed cunnilingus on her until my tongue couldn't move anymore, she appreciated it very much.

□ *cunny*　　　여성의 음부[성기]; A diminutive of cunt derived from the Latin word, cunnis.

• She felt her cunny jump, burning with its own great fire.

□ *cunt*　　　여성의 음부; Female genitalia.

• She has a nice cunt.
• Sarah took Adam's wrist and gently guided it to the folds of her own cunt.

□ *cunt*　　　(성교 대상으로서의) 여자; [경멸적] 계집; Derogatory term for a disliked female; bitch

• You fucking cunt!
• My ex-girlfriend is a fucking cunt.
• See that girl? She's a cunt.

□ **cup of tea**　　　(자기 취미/기호에 맞는) 일[화제, 사람, 물건]; Something one enjoys; (ONE'S) THING.

• That movie wasn't really my cup of tea.

□ cupcake　　　연인을 부르는 말; Form of reference for a loved one.

• Hey, cupcake!

□ curtains　　　끝, 최후, 종말; 죽음; 해고; When something is over; dying

• If u fuck with me it's gonna be curtains.

□ cushy　　　(일/자리 따위가) 편한(easy); 즐거운; Extremely comfortable.

• Her figure made her look really cushy, so we decided to call her that.

□ cut *one's* own throat   1. 자기 목을 찌르다 2. 자멸을 초래하다; 자살하다; To cause problems for oneself.

□ *cut some*　　　　섹스하다; To fuck around.

- Cut some!

□ *cut somebody a new asshole/one*　공격하다; To attack.

□ cut *somebody* dead ~를 딱 못 본 척하다; To reject, to ignore.

□ **cut the crap**　　호들갑 떨지 말고 진실을 말해!, 헛소리 마!; To tell someone to stop talking.

- A: "Where's my money, Marv?"
  B: "Yo, hey, I've been meaning to call you, something came up, and I, uh…."
  A: "Cut the crap, douche bag, where's my money?"

□ **cut the shit**　　　그만둬! 장난치지 마!; To tell someone to quit play-ing; to knock it off.

- You: What were you doing last night?
  John Doe: You….
  You: Cut the shit; what were you doing?

step. 04

D

□ **dab hand**   (무엇을 아주 잘하는) 명수, 달인; To be good at something, to be an expert in a specific field.

- That Paul's a dab hand with PCs – he always manages to solve my problems.

□ **daddy of all**   거대한; Large

□ *daisy chain*   난교(亂交), 그룹 섹스; A group sex formation involving multiple partners, with the participants lying in a circle, putting their mouth to the genitals of the next person.

- The shoot ended with a six-girl daisy chain. Derrick thought it might be the hottest thing he'd ever seen.

□ **daisy dukes**   길이가 아주 짧은 데님 반바지; Extremely short denim shorts, as worn by the character Daisy on the television program "The Dukes of Hazard."

- She had on some Daisy Dukes.

□ **damn**   빌어먹을, 제기랄(실망/짜증 등을 나타내는 욕설); Expression of surprise, contempt, outrage, disgust, boredom, frustration

□ **Damn and blast!**   빌어먹을, 제기랄(실망/짜증 등을 나타내는 욕설); Expression of surprise, contempt, outrage, disgust, boredom, frustration

□ **damn it**   빌어먹을, 제기랄(실망/짜증 등을 나타내는 욕설); Expression of surprise, contempt, outrage, disgust, boredom, frustration

- Lana: Damn it, we're never gonna find Benoit!
  Archer: … and we might if you two would stop being bitches for five seconds!
  Leslie: Three years of investigations, phone calls, Freedom of Information Act requests, and still, I had nothing…. Until a wellplaced bribe to a gentleman at Baskin-Robbins revealed…. Ron's birthday is on Friday.
  Ron: Damn it. I was so careful.
  Leslie: Well, you blew it. All for a free scoop of rum raisin.

□ **Damn it to hell!**   빌어먹을!; A remark to show one's dissatisfaction, which can often replace the remark "Fuck!"

- Damn it to hell! My old lady got drunk and fucked Wayne!

□ **Damn it!**　　　　빌어먹을!; An exclamation of displeasure.

□ Damn skippy　　　그것 좋지; A term of approval or excitement.

□ **damn straight**　　그래 맞다; An affirmation, usually to a proceeding statement. Origin: Australia.

> • Person 1: Wow, this band is awesome!
> 　Person 2: Damn straight!

□ **Damn!**　　　　　빌어먹을, 우라질(짜증스러움을 나타내는 욕설); Expression of surprise, contempt, outrage, disgust, boredom, frustration

> • Damn! I hate him.

□ damn-all　　　　　아무것도 아님; Nothing at all.

□ damned　　　　　빌어먹을, 제기랄(실망/짜증 등을 나타내는 욕설); Damn

□ damnedest　　　　빌어먹을, 제기랄(실망/짜증 등을 나타내는 욕설); Most

□ dang　　　　　　Damn의 완곡한 표현; Equivalent of damn.

> • Oh dang, I'm flat out broke.

□ **darn**　　　　　Damn의 완곡한 표현; Used to express frustration or anger. Origin: euphemism for damn.

> • We've missed the bus? Darn!

□ darnedest　　　　빌어먹을, 제기랄(실망/짜증 등을 나타내는 욕설); Most

□ dead　　　　　　완전히; Completely; 'dead broke, dead right'와 같은 방법으로 사용

□ **Dead sure!**　　　틀림없다; Certainly, Definitely

□ decider　　　　　결정자, 결재자; A person in a leadership role, usually of limited intelligence and lacking keen self-awareness, who stubbornly insists on making all the decisions that often end in abject failure with dire consequences for others.

- I hear the voices and I read the front page and I know the speculation but I'm the decider and I decide what is best and what's best is for Don Rumsfeld to remain as the Secretary of defense.

□ **deck** ~을 때려눕히다(knock down); To punch someone very hard, knocking them to the ground in some cases.

- Johnny decked Tim, and he fell to the floor with his face bleeding.

□ **deep doo-doo** 아주 난처하게 되어, 곤경에 빠져; Euphemized version of deep shit, doo-doo being a baby word for "shit."

- "We're in deep doo-doo now," said Bush the Elder as the election returns came in.

□ **deep pockets** 충분한 자금력, 강력한 자금원; A rich family or making lots of money from job. Being wealthy.

- I heard Johnny's pockets run deep. You should ask him out!

□ *deep shit* 몹시 골치 아픈 일; To be in trouble.

- I shot the wrong asshole, now I'm in deep shit!

□ *deep throat* 펠라티오; Deep fellatio.

- When she performed deep throat on me, it made me forget all other blowjobs.

□ **deep-six** (계획 등을) 포기하다; To abandon, to get rid of, to ignore, or to bury something. It comes from the six feet depth of a grave.

- I'm sick and tired of the deal we made. It's time to deep-six that shit.

□ **delicate** 생리 중인; On monthly period.

- I'm feeling delicate.

□ **deliver (the goods)** 약속을 이행하다; 기대[요구]에 부응하다; To meet the promise, to satisfy the expectation.

- She always delivers on her promises.

□ **desk jockey**   사무직원; Someone whose primary means of employment involves a desk. This can be anything from someone who is just above cubicles to a receptionist to a glorified receptionist.

- The twins got jobs as desk jockeys at an RV rental place, so they explain rental contracts in both of Canada's national languages.

□ *dick*   음경(陰莖); Penis

- And every day from 3:00 to 5:40 p.m. Karlie would suck a dick, give a handjob or get her pussy licked.
- Adam's dick jumped of its own volition.
- Agatha: Kick their asses, Mont! Punch 'em in their dicks!

□ *dick*   사내, 녀석; 얼간이; An adjective to describe a guy who is a jerk or does mean and stupid things. A general insult; jerk; asshole

- That guy is such a dick for calling me that!
- Wilfred: That motorcycle dick is ruining the neighborhood. You need to put that asshole in his place.
  Ryan: What's the point of a confrontation? I'd just get my ass kicked.

□ *dick around*   빈둥거리며 돌아다니다, 시간을 소비하다; To waste time; to lose focus; to lack seriousness of purpose.

- I don't even think I got anything done all Tuesday. I just skipped class and dicked around.
- We finished the treasure hunt while the other team was still dicking around with the map.

□ *dick face*   꼴 보기 싫은 놈, 녀석; When someone is being an ass to you or the people around them. Rude person.

- I can't stand when Tim is Being a Dick Face.

□ *dick flick*   남자 관객 대상의 남성 위주 폭력 영화; Movies that appeal more to males; they typically include bloody violence and/or machismo displays of strength, and sometimes brain-dead humor. Ex: Clerks, Saving Private Ryan, Robocop; counterpart of Chick Flick.

• Don't invite any girls to go with us; it's strictly a dick flick.

□ **dick wad**   비열한 놈; 바보, 멍청이; Asshole; stupid person; moron.

• Don't be such a dick wad.

□ *dickhead*   바보; Asshole; stupid person; moron.

• He is such a dickhead.

□ *dickwad*   비열한 놈; 바보, 멍청이; General insult; jerk; asshole

• Magician: Those yokels out there get what they deserve. I give them pure magic, and they respond like a bunch of slack-jawed cattle.
Sam: Yeah, well, maybe they respond that way because you're such a total dickwad.

□ diddle   사기 치다; To cheat or swindle.

• He diddled me out of that job.

□ *diddle*   자위하다; Masturbate, jerk off, Female masturbation.

• It was rare for her to diddle her pussy without also fingering her asshole. She loved the way she could feel the dual intruders through the thin membrane that separated her ass from her cunt. The results were always very satisfactory.

□ diddle around with *something*   시간을 낭비하다; The act of not doing anything very productive fucking around.

• All they did at the mall was diddle around.

□ diddley-shit   아주 적은 양, 쓸모없이 적은 양; A small or worthless amount.

□ die laughing   우스워 죽다; To find something extremely funny.

□ **dig** 이해하다; To perceive and comprehend the nature and significance of; grasp; gather.

- A: Ya dig?
  B: Yeah, I can dig it.

□ **dig** ~을 좋아하다; 즐기다; To find attractive, pleasant, to enjoy.

- A: Did you hear that cd?
  B: Yeah. I dig it.

□ **dig it** 알다. 이해하다; To understand.

- Can you dig it?

□ **Dig me?** 알아들어?; Do you understand me?

□ **dig on** 즐기다; To enjoy.

- Right now, I'm really diggin' on that new Erykah Badu song.

□ *dig out* 성관계를 갖다; To have sex with someone.

- I'd like to dig her out.

□ *dildo* 모조 남근, 남근 대용품(artificial penis); A sex toy for women.

- You are going to wake up with my Derrick Driller dildo in your asshole.

□ *DILF* 매력적인 유부남; Acronym for "dad I'd like to fuck" ; a heterosexual female's version of a MILF.

- That father is quite a DILF, if I do say so…

□ **dime** 10센트 동전; A US coin worth ten cents.

- Deposit a dime and dial your number.

□ **dime**　　　　　　　아주 매력적인 사람; A very attractive person; a perfect ten. Frequently, attractiveness is rated on "a scale of 1 to 10." In the United States, a dime is worth 10 cents. Hence, a "dime" is one whose attractiveness rates 10 on the scale. Also dime piece.

• He's a dime piece.
• He's a perfect dime.

□ *dime bag*　　　　　10달러 분량의 마약; $10's worth of an illegal drug. From "dime"+"bag".

• Dealer: How much you need?
  Client: Just a dime bag.

□ *dime piece*　　　　아주 매력적인 여성; An attractive female; "10". From a dime being worth 10 cents.

• Halle Berry is a straight dime piece.

□ **dime-a-dozen**　　아주 흔해서 가치가 없는; Something so common that its value is little or nothing.

• Rappers like Ja Rule, Chingy, and Benzino are a dime a dozen.

□ **dimwit**　　　　　　멍청이, 얼간이; an unintelligent person.

• Your new boss is kind of a dimwit, isn't he?

□ **dinero**　　　　　　돈, 현찰(스페인어로 돈의 의미임); Money(from the Spanish word for money)

• I don't really need extra dinero when I have a life to live.

□ **ding-a-ling**　　　　바보, 얼간이; 괴짜, 미치광이, 별난 사람; Synonym for "dingbat" or "crazy person" or "nutbar". Usually used to signify someone who's crazy or incompetent, silly or dumb.

• He shit the sheets. He's a real ding-a-ling.

□ *ding-a-ling*　　　　남자의 성기; Penis

- The little boy was withering on the ground because, his ding-a-ling got hurt by the baseball.

□ **dingbat**　　　바보, 멍청이; Someone who is moron/stupid, or acts without common sense.

- Tiffany is the biggest effing dingbat I know!

□ **ding-dong**　　　바보, 멍청이; Someone that has no idea what they are doing or they are dumb, stupid etc.

- All those ding-dongs are causing trouble around this neighborhood.

□ *dinky*　　　남자의 성기; Penis

□ **dinky**　　　작은; Small

- There's no way your dinky car will make it up the mountain.

□ *dip one's wick*　　　성관계를 갖다; To have sex.

□ **dipshit**　　　굼벵이, 쓸모없는 사람, 한심한 사람, 재주 없는 사람; An unintelligent person; moron; dimwit; idiot

- The guy's a complete dipshit.

□ *dipstick*　　　남자의 성기; A penis.

□ **dirt cheap**　　　아주 싼, 싸구려의; Extremely inexpensive.

- In Italy, the peaches are dirt cheap.

□ **dirtbag**　　　싫은 놈, 더러운 놈. (또는 dirtball); A dirty, grimy, sleazy, or disreputable person.

- She is a dirtbag. She works as a hooker in Reno.

□ **dis**　　　~을 경멸[멸시]하다; 업신여기다, 깔보다; An insult or instance of disrespect.

- Are you dissing me?
- That was a really big dis.

□ **dish**   ~에 대해 수다 떨다; To gossip.

- The girls dished about his sexual habits.

□ *dish*   예쁜 소녀, 성적 매력이 있는 여성; An attractive female. (Possibly related to the phrase, "She looks good enough to eat.")

- That's one hot little dish!

□ **dish out**   (일반적으로) ~을 분배하다, 아낌없이 제공하다, [뉴스 정보 따위를] 제공하다; To give something out to large numbers of people or in large amounts.

- He dished out some major complaints to his mother.
- She's always dishing out advice, even when you don't want it.

□ *dishy*   매력적인; Physically attractive.

- Everybody else will love those scenes starring dishy dreamboat Mark Ruffalo as Garner's true love.

□ **ditch**   ~을 버리다, 처분하다; ~와의 관계를 끊다; To leave behind.

- My friends ditched me at the library.

□ **ditz**   바보, 얼간이; 괴짜, 별난 사람; An unintelligent female.

- Kim and Cher are such ditzes!

□ **dive**   (지하실의) 싸구려 술집; 도박장; 나이트클럽; A dump (bar).

- The barman at the dive they frequented didn't find it quite as amusing and he called the cops on the pair of idiots.

□ **DL**　　　　　　　비밀로 함; Short for down-low, which basically means to keep things under-wraps, to keep a secret or lay low.

- I'll tell you this, but, you gotta promise to keep it on the DL.

□ **D-list**　　　　　아주 등급이 낮은 유명인; A very minor celebrity.

- That actress is a D-list.

□ **do a 180**　　　　왔던 방향으로 되돌아가다. 처음으로 다시 가다; To go back on a promise or statement.

- But since then, he's "done a 180" on the issue.

□ *do a line*　　　　(흡입하려고 가늘게 만들어 놓은) 코카인 한 줄을 흡입하다; To inhale cocaine.

- The weird woman is doing a line of coke.

□ **do a number on**　~을 해치우다, 면목을 잃게 하다; 철저히 비판하다; To mistreat.

- Sun and pollution can really do a number on your skin.

□ **do away with**　~를 죽이다/자살하다; To kill.

- We must do away with all inefficient practices.

□ **do it**　　　　　성관계를 갖다; To have sex.

□ **do number on**　~을 해치우다, 면목을 잃게 하다; 철저히 비판하다; To defeat.

□ **do _one's_ damndest**　사력을 다하다; To exert effort.

□ *do one's head*　　구강성교를 하다; To perform oral sex.

□ **do _somebody_ out of**　속이다. 사기 치다; To cheat or swindle.

□ **do the full monty**   벌거숭이가 되다. 갈 데까지[끝까지] 가다; To go all the way, to finish something.

• What did you have in mind, a patch-up job or the full monty?

□ **do the heavy lifting** 어려운 일을 하다(중량 운동을 하는 것에서 파생되어); To exert effort.

□ **do the trick**   효과가 있다; To be effective.

□ **do unto others**   남에게서 바라는 것만큼 남에게 해줘라; To obey the golden rule; to treat others as one would wish to be treated. Basic religion of whatever faith teach the golden rule e.g. do unto others.

• I have nothing against religion but I'm more of a do unto others type instead of restricting free thought.

□ **Do you catch my drift?**   무슨 말인지 이해하니?; Do you understand me?

□ **Do you read me?**   무슨 말인지 이해하니?; Do you understand me?

□ **DOA**   (병원) 도착 시 이미 사망; Dead on arrival. *의사 용어; Abbr. dead on arrival. used to describe patients pronounced dead upon arrival at the hospital.

• Not only is President Bush's Iraq plan DOA in Congress, much of his domestic agenda is, too.

□ **DOB**   출생 년 월 일; Acronym for "date of birth."

• What's your DOB?

□ **doctor**   [문서 따위를] 위조[조작]하다; ~을 속이다; To alter with the intent to deceive, e.g. a document, food, or drug.

• He was accused of doctoring the figures.

□ **dodgy**   교묘하게 몸을 피하는; 둘러대어 발뺌 잘하는; 교활한, 교묘한(tricky); 위험한, 을 수 없는; Unreliable; risky; suspicious; shady

• That deal sounds rather dodgy.

□ **Does a bear shit in the woods?**   당연하지. 당연한 걸 왜 물어봐?; Is Pope the Catholic?; Sarcastic rhetorical question in response to a question whose answer is obviously "Yes."

□ *Does it look like I give a damn?*   나는 하나도 상관 안 해. 나는 전혀 상관없어; I don't give a damn.

□ *Does it look like I give a fuck?*   나는 하나도 상관 안 해. 나는 전혀 상관없어; I don't give a damn.

□ *Does it look like I give a shit?*   나는 하나도 상관 안 해. 나는 전혀 상관없어; I don't give a damn.

□ *dogass*   쓸모없는 것, 불쾌한 것.; Worthless, inferior

□ doggone   빌어먹을, 망할 놈의(짜증스럽거나 놀랄 때 씀); Aggravated exclamation. Euphemism of god damn.

• My dad worked at a doggone poultry farm his whole life.

□ *doggy style*   후배위 성교 자세; Male/female sex in which the male penetrates the female from behind, while she is on hands and knees.

• I did her doggy style.

□ do-gooder   (공상적) 박애주의자; People who do things which they think will help other people, although you think that they are interfering.

□ dog's chance   아주 희박한 가망성; No chance at all.

□ *dogshit*   개똥, 쓸모없는 것; Worthless, inferior

□ doink   바보. 멍청이; Idiot; moron

• Man, you are such a doink for believing that!

□ *doink*	섹스하다; To have sex.	

• I doinked her.

□ *doinker*	남성의 성기; A large object such as a PENIS.	

• I have a huge DOINKER.

□ dollop	소량, 약간; small amount.	

□ done for	1. 몹시 지쳐; 다 써 버려, 탕진한 상태로; 결딴나서 2. 죽어서, 다 죽어가는; 1. tired 2. doomed	

□ *dong*	음경; Penis	

• She has tried to put that monster dong in her pussy and it wouldn't fit.

□ **Don't make a peep!**	찍소리도 내지 마라!; Shut Up! Don't many a sound!	

□ **Don't mind if I do!**	그거 좋죠!; Expression of acceptance of something offered to the speaker.	

□ **Don't sweat it**	(상대방에게 하는 말로) 속 태우지 마!; Don't worry about it!	

□ *doodly-shit*	전혀 없음. 전혀 아님; Nothing at all.	

• I don't give a doodly-shit.

□ doo-doo	개똥(dog excrement); Feces; poop	

□ doo-doo head	멍청이, 얼간이; Very stupid person	

□ doofus	얼간이, 얼뜨기; An unintelligent person; IDIOT; MORON.	

• Dave is such a doofus at times.

□ doohickey	장치, 물건; 거시기(이름이 확실하지 않을 때의 대용어); Loose descriptive term for any object.	

• Hey, could you hand me that do-hickey over there?

□ **dookie** 똥; Feces

• Don't step in that dookie!

□ *dookie love* 항문 성교; Anal sex.

• I'm not into dookie love.

□ **doormat** 학대받아도 가만히 있는 사람; A person who is easily abused by others.

• The director treated the actor like a doormat.

□ **doozy** 아주 어렵고 특별한 문제; Something very complicated or difficult.

• "How do you get yourself involved in these messes?" Peg asked. "Come on, Mom. How many messes, exactly, do I get myself involved in?", "OK. Not many." Peg smiled. "But this one appears to be a doozy."

□ **dope** (믿을 만한 소식통으로부터 받은) 정보, 내보(內報); 예상; Reliable information; inside story; scoop

• What's the dope on the new boss?

□ **dope** 마약; Drugs, especially marijuana.

• He takes dope; in fact, he's high on dope now.

□ **dope** 얼간이, 바보; An unintelligent person.

• Why do you have to be such a dope?

□ **doper** 마약 상용자; A person who takes illegal drugs, or takes prescription drugs in a manner not prescribed.

• I hate cheats! That's all the dopers are.

- **dork**   유행에 뒤진 사람, 촌뜨기; 바보, 얼간이; Someone who is bookish, antisocial, etc.; nerd; geek

  • What else has you thinking about marrying that dork?

- **double-quick**   매우 급한, 매우 급하게, 아주 빠르게; Very fast.

- **douche bag**   싫은 [시시한] 놈; A derogatory term, used most often to describe males; jerk, asshole

  • "Fuck you, douche bag," Adam said. "If she wanted you to have her phone number, she would have given it to you last week when you showed up."
  • Gary: What do you think, coach?
  Coach: Interesting idea. A live wolf on the sidelines would make a pretty strong statement to the other teams. Wolf-costumed mascot: Forget it, douche bag, we already have a mascot.

- **dough**   돈(money), 현찰; Money

  • Dad works at a lumber mill. Mom answers phones at a radio station nearby. Neither of them was rolling in the dough.

- **down**   (계획에) 동의하는; In agreement with a plan to do something. Also down for; down with.

  • I'm down for that.
  • I'm down with that.

- **down in the dumps**   우울한; Depressed

- **down low**   비밀로 함; To keep quiet. Secretive. Also known as the "D.L."

  • Keep this on the Down Low.

- **down the road**   장래에; At some future time.

  • That is a discussion for down the road.

- **down-and-out**   빈털터리인, 노숙자 신세인; With no money left.

- **drag king** 남장 여성; A (usually homosexual) female dressed in man's clothing.

- **drag queen** 여장(女裝)을 (좋아)하는 호모(남성 동성애자); A (usually homosexual) male dressed in women's clothing.

  • He told me he just likes to go out and score the occasional blowjob from a street hooker and he had no idea that drag queens did their business over by Macarthur Park.

- **dreamboat** 멋진 사람[것], 이상적인 연인; An attractive person, usually male.

  • I hope he asks me to prom. He's such a dreamboat.

- **drive nuts** 미치게 하다; To make crazy.

  • That guy's voice is driving me nuts. Make me want to kill myself!

- **drop in the bucket** 아주 적은 양. 간에 기별도 안 감. 새 발의 피; Something with little effect because – compared to everything else – it's very small.

- **droppings** 똥; Animal feces.

  • It is made of fallen leaves, animal droppings, and rotting plant matter.

- **druggie** 마약 상용자; A habitual drug user.

  • She lost her desk job because her spouse Darrell is a druggie lowlife.

- **dry heave** 헛구역질; To attempt to vomit, but to expel no liquid.

  • If even one of you thinks about dry heaving in my car, you're all walking home.

- *dry hump* 옷을 입은 상태로 성행위 흉내; To simulate sex activity, without the removal of clothes.

- *dry sex* 옷을 입은 상태로 성행위 흉내; Simulated sex, without the removal of clothes.

• They had dry sex.

□ **ducats** 돈; Money

• Hey man, you got any ducats I can borrow?

□ **dude** 녀석, 놈; [부르는 말로] 당신, 자네; A male.

• Dude! Randy said. "Are you like on 'roids or something?"
• He's a weird dude.
• Relax, dude.
• That dude over there is pretty cute.

□ **duds** 의류, 옷; Clothes

• Nice duds.

□ **dufus** 바보. 멍청이; Fool

□ **duh** 흥, 첫(당연한 것을 말하는 것을 비웃을 때 사용); A sarcastic exclamation used when someone states the obvious.

• Person A: Don't run that red light.
  Person B: Duh!
• Person A: I bet it hurt when you got shot in the chest.
  Person B: Duh.

□ **dumb bastard** 바보, 멍청이; A stupid person.

□ *dumb fuck* 바보, 멍청이; A stupid person.

• Don't be such a dumb-fuck.

□ *dumb shit* 바보, 멍청이; A stupid person.

□ *dumbass* 바보, 멍청이; A very unintelligent person.

• What kind of dumb-ass talks back to the teacher?

□ **dumb-bell** 바보, 멍청이; An unintelligent person.

□ **dumbbutt**   바보, 멍청이; An unintelligent person.

□ **dumbhead**   바보, 멍청이; An unintelligent person.

□ **dumbsize**   (회사가) 업무를 제대로 할 수 없을 정도로 감원하다; To reduce the number of people employed in an organization or company to the point that there are no longer enough to carry out the work effectively.

□ **dummy**   바보, 멍청이; An unintelligent person.

• That's not the right answer, you dummy!

□ **dump**   황폐한[지저분한] 거리, 초라한 장소; An unappealing location due to dirtiness or dilapidation.

• Man, your house is a dump.

□ **dump**   ~을 해고하다, [애인을] 버리다; [계약을] 해지하다; To end an intimate relationship with someone.

• How can you dump me for another man?

□ **dumps**   우울, 의기소침; A dull, gloomy state of the mind.

□ **Dunno**   몰라; I don't know.

□ **durndest**   최선, 베스트; 최대 한도, 극한; Most

□ **dusting**   구타; A beating.

□ **dustup**   소동; 싸움, 주먹다짐; 논쟁; A disagreement or fight.

□ **dweeb**   샌님, 꽁생원; A person who is bookish, antisocial

• Let's leave before the dweeb gets here.
• You're just upset that you're not dealing with some spineless dweeb anxious to get out of his Mommy's basement.

□ *dyke*	여성 동성애자, (남자역의) 레즈비언; A lesbian.
□ **dynamite**	발군의, 뛰어난, 최고의, 놀라운; Especially fine, ex-
cellent	

• That new restaurant is dynamite!

□ **dynamo**	정력이 넘치는 사람; An energetic and aggressive
person.	

step. 05

E

□ **eager beaver**   아주 열심인 사람, 일벌레; An earnest and hard-working person.

  • Shit, he's such an eager beaver when it comes to getting laid.

□ **ear candy**   듣기엔 좋지만 깊이가 없는 음악; Something pleasing to listen to, especially music-related.

  • Tonight's program was ear candy and a credit to all.

□ **easy mark**   잘 속는 사람, 봉; Gullible person.

  • Maybe I just look like an easy mark.

□ **easy on the eyes**   보기 좋은; Extremely attractive.

  • She may be easy on the eyes but she is totally conceited.

□ **easy touch**   (특히 돈을 우려먹기) 쉬운 [만만한] 사람; Gullible person.

  • Unfortunately, my father is no easy touch.

□ *eat*   [이성에게] 구강성교를 하다, ~의 성기를 핥다; Lick someone's vagina.

  • Yo girl, I'm about to get waxed cuz Styles gonna eat tonight!

□ *eat a dick*   젠장 할! 헛소리 마!; A generic yet abrasive come-back to a verbal attack.

  • My girlfriend was complaining that we don't spend enough time together and I disagreed by saying "EAT A DICK!"

□ *eat crap*   굴욕을 참다; To become humiliated.

□ **eat crow**   굴욕을 참다; The anguish of humiliation at having to admit to wrongdoing or Failure; to become humiliated.

108

> • I say I'm a great cook. Then you eat my food and it is no good. I sit there and eat crow.

□ **eat dirt**　굴욕을 참다; To become humiliated.

□ ***eat hair pie***　[이성에게] 구강성교를 하다, ~의 성기를 핥다; To perform cunnilingus.

□ **eat humble pie**　잘못[실수]을 인정하다; To apologize for and face humiliation for a serious error.

> • It was the governments turn to eat humble pie.

□ **eat it**　실패하다. 패하다; Fail

> • Oh, man, Tony Hawks did a triple flip & landed on his face – he totally ate it!

□ **eat my shorts**　빌어먹을!, 뒈져라!, 이 바보야!; Insult used by cartoon character, Bart Simpson, from The Simpsons.

> • Principle Skinner can eat my shorts.

□ ***Eat off!***　꺼져라!; Go away! Euphemism for "fuck off!"

□ ***Eat shit***　똥이나 씹어라!; An expression of extreme dislike or anger when used in the imperative, i.e. go fuck yourself.

> • You THINK I'm the selfish one in this relationship, Jack? Well, eat shit and die!

□ ***eat shit***　굴욕을 참다; To become humiliated.

□ ***Eat shit and die!***　똥이나 씹어라!; A contemptuous dismissal.

> • That mother-fucker just cut me off! Hey you! Eat shit and die!

□ **eat *something* up**　믿다; To believe unquestioningly.

- Those newbies eat up rumors about his hobby.

□ **eat up**　　　　[이성에게] 구강성교를 하다, ~의 성기를 핥다; To perform oral sex on a female.

- I ate up Sarah like a bowlful of Jell-O.

□ **edgy**　　　　신랄한, 가시 돋친; Socially dangerous or daring; intellectually provocative; tending to induce unease or stress in viewers. Especially used to describe artistic and intellectual work.

- "Alamo Bay" was an edgy movie on immigration.

□ **Eep!**　　　　놀람의 감탄사; An exclamation of surprise.

- Eeep! You scared me.

□ **effing**　　　　빌어먹을, 제기랄(fucking 대신 쓰는 욕설); Censored (bowdlerized) version of "fucking". Also "f'ing"

- I hate that effing Stern.

□ *effing*　　　　엄청난, 굉장한; Extreme; extremely; very

- What took you such an effing long time?

□ **egghead**　　　　인텔리, 지식인; An overly intellectual person; someone who thinks too much.

- Charles can't order lunch without using an algebraic formula … what an egg head!

□ *eight ball*　　　　1/8 온스의 코카인; A quantity of cocaine or crystal that weighs an eighth of an ounce, hence an "eight ball", which is equivalent to 3.5grams.

- We did an eight ball of blow and danced until ten the next morning.

□ **end of the line**　　　　한계, 종말; The very end, the definite end.

- It was the end of the line for the urban farming experiment.

110

□ **epic fail** 크나큰 실패; A large failure.

• Woman, to man hitting on her: But, hey, if you're cool with your delusion, congratu-fucking-ations.
Roman: Woof. Epic fail.

□ **escort** (돈을 받고) 사교 모임에 동반해 주는 여자. 고급 콜걸을 의미함; A term for a woman paid by the hour, not the act, but usually for sex. a prostitute. Often, higher quality and cost compared to street scrag.

• I hired a fine escort last night - she blew me away.

□ **even the score** (자기에게 해를 입히거나 속임수를 쓴 자에게) 복수하다, 응징하다; To exact revenge, to exact retribution.

• He tried to even the score but did consider what the full outcome might be.

□ **everything but the kitchen sink** (필요 이상일 정도로) 많은 것들; 생각나는 모든 물건; Everything.

• However, he said that the Bill covered almost everything but the kitchen sink.

□ **ex** 전남편, 전처, 전 애인; A person with whom one is no longer in a relationship. From ex-boyfriend, ex-girlfriend, ex-husband, ex-wife, etc.

• Ryan: My ex, Paula ··· she's getting married. Wilfred: How'd she dump you?
Ryan: Actually, I dumped her. Wilfred: Yeah, right.

□ **exec** (기업의) 경영자; Executive

□ **eye candy** 눈으로 보기 좋은 것, 매력적인 사람; An attractive person.

• That guy was complete eye candy.

□ **eyeball** (무례할 정도로) 눈을 동그랗게 뜨고 쳐다보다; To stare.

□ **eyewash** 허풍; 거짓 약속; False promise; words intended to
confuse.

F

- **f' word**   욕설(fuck을 대신해서 쓰는 말); Fuck

 • Barney Frank (D-Mass.), an openly gay congressman, was called the 'f' word.

- **facepalm**   자신의 손바닥을 얼굴에 갖다 댐으로써 창피함, 놀람, 분노, 절망 등을 표현; The physical gesture of placing one's hand flat across one's face or lowering one's face into one's hand or hands. The gesture is found in many cultures as a display of frustration, embarrassment, shock, or surprise.

 • In fact the Today Show and MSNBC seemed to be reveling in Cramer's very public facepalming.

- **face time**   감옥에 수감되어 형을 살다; To serve time in jail.

 • My brother faced time for smoking weed.

- **face-off**   대결; A fight

 • Both teams are ready to face off.

- **facial**   얼굴에 사정하는 성행위, 안면 사정; The sex act of ejaculating on a person's face.

 • There's a good facial scene in this movie.

- **fag**   (남성) 동성애자(의); Derogatory term for a homosexual.

- **fag**   (경멸적) 자식, 새끼; General disparaging term for anyone, though usually males.

 • I done a good one with Violet for those fags at Dazzle.

- **faggot**   남성 동성애자; A male homosexual. Extremely offensive.

 • That Elton John is such a faggot!

- **faggot**   (경멸적) 자식, 새끼; A general insult.

• That guy is such a faggot.

□ **fake out**   속이다, 기만하다; To trick somebody; to deceive.

□ **fall down on the job** 일을 제대로 하지 않다; To fail.

□ **fall flat**   완전히 실패하다[아무런 호응을 얻지 못하다]; To fail completely.

□ **fall flat on _one's_ face** 완전히 실패하다; To fail completely.

□ **fall for _something_**   ~에게 홀딱 반하다[빠지다]; To be attracted to something.

□ **fall guy**   (남의 잘못을 뒤집어쓴) 희생양; A person who is blamed for something bad.

• He is such a fall guy.

□ **fall head over heels for**   홀딱 빠지다; To be attracted to something.

□ **fall off the wagon**   (금주를 그만두고) 다시 술을 마시기 시작하다, (일반적으로) 금욕을 깨다, 절제를 잃다; To resume drinking alcohol or drugs after a period of sobriety.

• I had this other thought, that was: what better way to distract myself than to fall off the wagon?

□ **fall on _one's_ ass**   엉덩방아 찧다. 실패하다; To fail completely.

□ **fancy schmancy**   최고급의; A derisive recognition of a high class.

• Well, have fun at your fancy schmancy meeting! I wish I could come, but I'm not freakin' good enough!

□ **fancy _somebody_**   (성적으로) 끌리다; To like someone in a sexual way; to want to be with them.

• Is there someone else you particularly fancy?

- **fandom**   (스포츠, 영화 등의) 팬층, 팬들; A group of fans for a specific show/book/movie etc.

> • The Harry Potter fandom is huge!

- **fanfic**   팬픽. 영화나 TV쇼의 팬이 쓴 이야기; "Fan"+"fiction". Works written by a fan of a particular work of fiction.

> • He's really into Star Trek fanfic.

- **fanny**   엉덩이; The buttocks.

> • I'm going to swat you on the fanny, young man.

- *fanny*   여성의 성기 (주로 영국); British slang for pussy.

- **fart**   (특히 소리가 크게 나게) 방귀를 뀌다; An instance of flatulence; "the passing of gas."

> • That was a pretty nasty fart, dude.

- **fart**   어쩐지 싫은 녀석; An annoying person; a fool.

> • He's a crazy old fart.

- **fart around**   빈둥거리다; To waste time, to mess around.

> • WITH her heavy workload, one could never accuse KATY PERRY of farting around.

- **fart around with *something***   시간을 낭비하다; To spend time not doing anything productive.

- **fashionista**   패션 리더(항상 최신 유행대로 옷을 입는 사람); A person obsessed with fashion.

> • The Mercer has its super-hip lobby crammed full of New York's premier fashionistas.

- **fat cat**   배부른 자본가, 많은 정치자금을 내는 부자의; A rich person.

□ **fat chance**   가망 없음, 매우 희박한 가망성; Little or no chance.

• Fat chance of getting a raise this year.

□ **fat mouth**   (행동은 하지 않고) 말만 많은 사람; Very talkative person.

□ *fat-ass*   뚱뚱한 (사람); An overweight person.

• Is this how you spend your free time, fat-ass? Lying half-naked on a bed in black socks at 11:30 in the morning?

□ **fathead**   얼간이, 바보; Fool

□ **fatty**   뚱뚱한 사람; A fat person.

• Britain is fast becoming a nation of fatties.

□ **fed**   연방 정부의 관리, (특히) 연방 수사국(FBI)의 수사관; 연방 정부; A member of the federal government.

• Don't let the feds find out about your cash business.

□ **fed up with**   질리다, 물리다, 식상하다; Tired of.

• I'm fed up with your shit!

□ **feed** *somebody* **a line**   (환심을 사기 위해) 남에게 허풍 떨다, 거짓 말하다, 아첨 떨다; To deceive; to flatter.

□ *feedbag material*   매력적인 여자; Attractive female.

□ **feel like a million bucks**   몸의 상태가 매우 좋다; To feel great.

• Since I got my hair cut, I feel like a million bucks.

□ **feel like a million dollars**   몸의 상태가 매우 좋다; To feel great.

• Since I got my hair cut, I feel like a million dollars.

□ *feel like ass*   기분이 더럽다; To feel terrible.

• Man, I feel like ass today. Must've been all the stuff I drank last night.

□ *feel like crap*   기분이 더럽다; To feel terrible.

• He feels like crap because he can't find a job.

□ **feel like shit**   기분이 더럽다; To feel terrible.

• He felt like a shit after he dumped her.

□ feel up   (특히 원치 않는 사람의) 몸을 만지다[더듬다]; To feel another person's body, in a sexual way, with one's hands.

• Haley: It looks like you were felt up by that creepy guy around the corner.
Alex: Ew! Why him?
Haley: 'Cause he's got, like, freakishly tiny hands.

□ feel weak at the knees   무릎에 힘이 빠지다; To feel like falling down at any moment because of a strong fear or other emotion.

□ **feisty**   혈기 왕성한, 거침없는; Tough, independent, and spirited.

□ **fella**   남자, 남자친구; "Fellow", i.e. a man. a particular group of male friends.

• Where are the fellas tonight?

□ *fellatrix*   펠라티오(남성 성기에 하는 오럴 섹스)하는 여자; A female performing fellatio, deep-throating.

• She was a good fellatrix.

□ **fence**   장물아비; A person who purchases known-stolen goods to re-sell them. To sell stolen goods. An old organized crime term.

• So wait, they're gonna fence all that stuff and then pay us for it?

□ **fender-bender**   (자동차의) 가벼운 사고; A non-serious motor vehicle accident. i.e. the fenders may be bent, but that's about it.

• I've already had a fender-bender this morning, which is not a good sign
for the way things are likely to turn out today.

□ ferret out   ~을 캐내다[찾아내다]; To find out.

□ few beers short of a six-pack 약간 정신이 뒤떨어지다; Stupid; Retarded

□ few cents short of a dollar   약간 정신이 뒤떨어지다; Stupid; Retarded

□ few fries short of a happy meal 약간 정신이 뒤떨어지다; Stupid; Retarded

□ few peas short of a casserole 약간 정신이 뒤떨어지다; Stupid; Retarded

□ few pecans short of a fruitcake 약간 정신이 뒤떨어지다; Stupid; Retarded

□ few sandwiches short of a picnic 약간 정신이 뒤떨어지다; Stupid; Retarded

□ few slices short of a loaf   약간 정신이 뒤떨어지다; Stupid; Retarded

□ few spokes short of a wheel 약간 정신이 뒤떨어지다; Stupid; Retarded

□ fiddle with   (마음에 들지 않아서 자꾸 이리저리 바꾸며) 만지작[주
물럭]거리다; To mess with.

• I've been fiddling with this thing all day, and it still doesn't work.

□ fiend   ~광; An addict.

• You shouldn't smoke so much - you're becoming a fiend.

□ *fifth base*   항문 성교; In the "sex as baseball" metaphor, anal sex.

□ filch   좀도둑질을 하다; To steal something small or of
little value.

• To filch from friends and relatives is the mark of a coward.

□ **FILF** 성적 매력이 있는 중년 남성. MILF의 남성형; Father I would like to fuck; an attractive older man. Abbreviation for "father I'd like to fuck."; male version of MILF.

• Have you ever been to her house? Her dad's a total FILF!

□ **filthy rich** 더럽게 부유한 (엄청나게 부자인); Extremely rich.

• Look at Posh and Becks who are filthy rich.

□ **filthy with** 더럽게 많은; Having a very large amount of.

□ **finger** (범인을 경찰에) 찌르다, 밀고하다; To identify to the authorities the perpetrator of a crime.

□ *finger* (~의) 성기를 손으로 애무하다; Finger fuck.

• Karlie had never kissed another girl. Then again, she had never had two other girls finger her pussy either.

□ *finger bang* (~의) 성기를 손으로 애무하다; Finger fuck.

□ **finger licking good** 굉장히 맛있는; Extremely tasty.

• Those burgers were finger licking good.

□ *finger-fuck* (~의) 성기를 손으로 애무하다; The stimulate of the female genitals with one's fingers.

• That was a good finger-fuck.

□ **fink** 일러바치다, 배신하다; To inform on another person or group to authorities.

□ **fired up** 노한, 격분한; 열광한, 흥분한; Excited; energetic; wild; out of control.

• He had a few drinks. Now he's all fired up.

120

□ **firefight**   공식적인 업무에 우선하여 시급한 업무를 처리하다; "Putting out fires" (last-minute disasters) instead of performing one's official job."

• Month by month, our national health services are merely firefighting.

□ *fist*   (성기에) 손을 집어넣다; To insert the fist into the rectum or vagina for sexual purposes.

• I'm a big fan of fisting.

□ *fist fuck*   (성기에) 손을 넣는 행위; To insert the fist into the rectum or vagina for sexual purposes.

□ **fitted**   잘 맞는 옷을 입은; Dressed well.

• That boy is fitted!

□ **fix *somebody's* wagon**   보복하다; To seek revenge.

□ **fizzle out**   흐지부지되다; To fail or to end in a weak or disappointing way.

□ **flake**   약속을 어기다; To not show up or call or do whatever you were supposed to be.

• "Probably someone flaked for the morning," Allie said with a nod. "So the company is in dire straits unless they find someone else to fill in."

□ **flame**   악플을 날리다. (전자 우편 따위로) 매도하다, 욕설을 퍼붓다; To post a message to an internet forum intended to insult and provoke; an instance of "flaming."

• "I got a bad review from one of Daystar's producers who asked for an 'after-hours' performance for himself," Allie explained. "When I turned him down, he flamed me."
• "After I wrote on the message board that Hondas are the best cars, a bunch of people sent me flames."

□ **flash**   (사람 앞에서) 성기[유방, 팬티 따위]를 슬쩍 보이다; To happily expose one's naked or partially naked.

- "If I had to guess, he probably likes Shelly's boobies best," Rachelle said. "Every time I've seen him tonight he's been sneaking a peek. I wish she would just flash him and get it over with."

☐ **flasher**　　　　　　(길거리에서 여성들을 향해 성기를 드러내 보이는) 노출증 환자; A person who exposes their genitals to unsuspecting strangers in public.

- There's a flasher who ties sausage to his willy.

☐ **flat broke**　　　　　완전 거덜 난[쪽박을 차게 된]; Completely broke.

☐ **flat-out**　　　　　　속도가 최고인(top), 전속력의; 전력을 다한; 완전히; At full capacity, at maximum speed, totally, thoroughgoing

- Then I found out the girl he wanted me to work with does escort work so I flat-out turned him down.

☐ **flatten**　　　　　　때려눕히다; To crush an object down from a greater size to a smaller one.

☐ **flea short of an infestation**　　　(머리가) 약간 모자란; Stupid; Retarded

☐ **fleece**　　　　　　바가지를 씌우다; To be ripped off; to pay for something and get inferior or no product.

☐ **flick**　　　　　　　영화 (한 편); 영화; A movie.

- A: What did you do on your date last night? B: We had some dinner and caught a flick.

☐ **flip off**　　　　　　가운뎃손가락(중지)을 들어 보이다; To raise only the middle finger in someone's direction. An offensive gesture.

- Leslie gave Walt the finger, of course. It was rare for 20 minutes to go by without her flipping off someone. Sometimes she did it for no apparent reason.

☐ **flip *one's* lid**　　　　1. 발끈 화를 내다 2. 정신이 돌다, 미치다; To lose one's temper.

122

- Your dad is going to flip his lid when he sees what you did to his car.

☐ flip *one's* wig   1. 발끈 화를 내다 2. 정신이 돌다, 미치다; To lose one's temper.

☐ **flip/give/shoot somebody the bird**   중지를 들어 올리다. (욕설의 몸짓); To hold up the middle finger to another; to make a rude sign at somebody with your middle finger.

- He expected Karlie's face to redden but she only flipped him the bird, catching him completely off guard.
- That guy almost hit my car so I flipped him the bird.
- Adam flipped them both the bird, a double shot, one for each, so they didn't have to share.

☐ floor   (특히 스포츠 경기에서) 때려눕히다; To knock a person off of his/her feet, or to stun (exaggeration).

☐ **floor it**   가속 페달을 힘껏 밟다; To hit the acceleration pedal (or, in the US, gas pedal) to such extremities that it is parallel to the floor of a car. i.e. Hit maximum speed as quickly as physically possible.

- That fucker's getting away, FLOOR IT!

☐ flop   완전 실패하다; To fail miserably.

☐ *fluffer*   도색 영화 남성 주인공 발기 지속 담당자; A person on the crew of a pornographic film whose job is to make the leading male erect, when required.

- I mean they were blackballed. No one would hire them as a fluffer even.

☐ flummoxed   당황한, 혼란스러운; Confused or perplexed.

☐ **flunk out**   (~에서) 성적 불량으로 퇴학당하다; To have to leave school or college because your marks/grades are not good enough.

☐ flunky   (요리사 등의) 조수; A person that does anything to be accepted or appreciated.

123

- He got his flunky to pick up his package!
- Now you've heard the terms. Be a good little flunky and pass them along.

□ **flush**　　　　　　　(돈을) 많이 가진; Rich, having money.

- He/she is flush.

□ **fly**　　　　　　　바지 지퍼; The zipper on bottom-wear.

- The fly of your jeans is open.

□ **fly by the seat-of-one's pants**　　(계기에 의존하지 않고) 직감으로 [손으로 더듬어] 조종하다; 구체적인 계획 없이 직감으로 행동하다; To act based upon intuition rather than a concrete plan

□ **fly in the ointment**　옥에 티; Something which ruins or spoils everything else; a nuisance or problem; an unpleasant or disagreeable detail.

- One fly in the ointment – who pays for it.

□ **fly off the handle**　버럭 화를 내다; To become enraged.

- My dad flew off the handle when he found out I was pregnant.

□ **fly the coop**　　　~에서 달아나다[날다]; To escape.

□ **fly-by-night**　　　빨리 한몫 잡을 생각만 하는, 금전적으로 믿을 수 없는, (빚에 몰려) 야반도주하는 사람, 믿을 수 없는 사람; An unreliable organization, especially a business.

- Health care and education are too important for politicians to use for their own fly by night political ambitions.

□ **FOFL**　　　　　너무 웃겨서 바닥을 뒹구는 (채팅 영어); "Falling on floor, laughing"

□ **fool around**　　　(할 일을 안 하고) 노닥거리다; To waste time.

□ **fool around**　　　(이성과) 놀아나다; Flirt between man and women, but they don't have the serious relation.

124

• Chris and I fool around in his car before he drops me off.

□ *foot job*　　　　　여성이 남성의 성기를 발로 애무하는 행위; A sexual act where the genitalia are stimulated by someone's feet.

□ **for a song**　　　　헐값으로[싸구려로]; For very little money.

□ **For Christ's sake!**　제발; 하느님 맙소사; Oh! No!

• For Christ's sake! How could you already have another parking ticket?

□ **for crying out loud**　세상에[맙소사](화가 나거나 놀랐음을 나타냄); Exclamation of frustration.

• His father in-law studies TB for the CDC for crying out loud.

□ **For crying out loud!** 제발; 하느님 맙소사; Oh! No!

□ **For God's sake!**　세상에[맙소사](화가 나거나 놀랐음을 나타냄); Oh! No! exclamation of anger or frustration.

• For God's sake, why won't this work?

□ **for nothing**　　　공짜로[거저]; For free.

□ **For Pete's sake!**　제발, 부디; 도대체, 대관절; Oh! No! an exclamation of displeasure.

• Oh, for Pete's sake! Could you please turn down your stereo? I'm trying to study.

□ **For sure!**　　　　(의심할 여지없이) 확실히[틀림없이]; Certainly

□ **Forget it!**　　　　생각도 하지 마! (no의 뜻을 강하게 나타냄); Strong statement of "no."

□ **Forget it!**　　　　잊어버려! (호의에 대한 답례를 하려는 상대방에게); You don't need to feel obligated.

□ **fork out/over**　　(특히 마지못해) (~에) 돈을 들이다; To pay for.

four-letter word (네 글자로 된) 욕설, 육두문자; A swear word. Phrase that refers to any number of "bad" words, often seen in forum posts. Can mean shit, fuck, damn, and even other non-four-lettered-words such as ass and bitch.

• Bob got fired from his job because he said a four letter word to a customer.

fox 속이다; To deceive.

fox 여우 같은 사람. 매력적인 사람; An attractive person.

• She is quite the fox.

foxy 성적 매력이 있는, 섹시한; Attractive. Usually used only to describe females.

• Damn, she's foxy!

freak 기겁을 하다[하게 만들다]; To become angry.

freak ~에 열광한 사람, ~광; A person very enthusiastic about a thing or activity.

freak 아주, 굉장히; Very; really; extremely.

• That is freak expensive.

freak 괴짜, 기형; A person who is strange or different. A term of derision, typically used to dismiss someone outside of one's social clique. Also used as a playful tease.

• He is such a freak!

freak 변태 성향을 갖고 있는 사람, (성적인) 변태; A person with odd sexual proclivities.

• That boy is a freak.

freak out 자제력을 잃다[잃게 하다], 흥분하다; To react with extreme or irrational distress or composure.

126

- Do what he says! I'm freaking out! I'm freaking out here!
- Sam: If I'm ever gonna have a chance with Andi, I gotta come clean.
  Sock: Oh, she's gonna freak out, man. She's gonna think you're off your nut.

□ **freak out**   겁먹게 하다, 겁먹다; To cause fear; to feel fear.

□ **freak out**   미치다; To become insane.

□ **freaked out**   겁먹은; To be afraid; to be scared.

□ *freaking*   가혹한, 호된, 지독한(명사 또는 형용사를 강조), 지독한; Extreme; extremely; very.

- Bailey: Yeah. Uh, so we'll probably talk to, uh, some neighbors. Stark: Yeah, if we can find any. This place is a freakin' ghost town.

□ *freaking*   빌어먹을 (fucking 대신에 쓰는 욕설); Far less vulgar replacement for "fucking."

- I could tell he was bringing some serious hardware. But he was super shy. It took me all freaking day to get him alone.
- It's freaking huge.

□ **freaky**   해괴한, 기이한; Frightening, disturbing

- That horror movie was freaky!

□ **free lunch**   공짜; lunch received without charge; usually used in "There's no (such thing as a) free lunch."

- There's no (such thing as a) free lunch.

□ **free ride**   무임승차; 불로소득; Riding without paying; earnings without working.

- I've had an opponent every time. I've never had a free ride. I've had to fight.

□ **freebie**   공짜; Something given away for free.

- Jeanie got promotional freebies at a new spa and asked us if we wanted to go get manis, pedis, and massages.

□ **freeze *somebody* out**　　(일부러 쌀쌀맞게 굴거나 곤란하게 하여)
~를 (~에서) 몰아내다[(~을) 못하게 하다], 따돌리다; To prevent somebody
from being part of a group or taking part in an activity, business, etc. by
being very unfriendly or making things very difficult for them.

□ **freeze the blood**　　오싹 소름이 끼치게 하다, 등골이 오싹해지게 하다;
To cause fear.

□ **freeze up**　　(걱정이 되어) 얼다; To become afraid.

□ **French kiss**　　짙은 입맞춤; Kiss with an open mouth, usually
placing one's tongue in the other person's mouth.

> • They were outside French kissing.

□ *fricking*　　빌어먹을 (fucking 대신에 쓰는 욕설); Fucking

> • Get off my lawn, you frickin' kids!
> • This test was so frickin' horrible!

□ **fried**　　고장 난, 망가진; Non-functioning, in reference to
electronic devices.

> • That phone is fried.

□ *frig*　　Fuck의 대용어; Alternate version of "fuck"

> • What the frig are you doing?

□ **frig**　　자위하다; To masturbate.

> • I was at this girl's house last night and after we were kissing I gently got
> my fingers into her pants and frigged her.

□ *Frig!*　　Fuck!의 완곡어법; Euphemism for fuck.

□ **frigging**　　Fucking의 완곡어법. Frigging은 "masturbating" 또
는 "intercourse"의 의미, Extreme; extremely; very.

> • Holy Christ it's Frigging hot as sin in here.

- frighten the living daylights out of   깜짝 놀라게 하다, 겁주다; To cause extreme fear.

- *front bottom*   여성 성기; Childish name for the female genitalia.

- fry   부수다, 망가트리다, 파괴하다; To destroy an electronic device with heat or electrical current.

  - Yeah, I spilled some Coke into my monitor and fried it.

- *FUBAR*   엉망인; 손댈 여지가 없는; Utterly botched and confused. Acronym of "Fucked up beyond all(any) recognition"

  - That project is totally fubar.

- *fuck*   성교하다; To have sex (with). The use of this term may imply a lack of romance or intimacy; contrast with "make love."

  - I fucked her last night.

- *fuck*   씨발, 제기랄, 젠장, 우라질; Derogatory dismissal.

  - Aw, FUCK!

- *fuck*   씨발, 일반적인 욕설이나 무시; A general insult or insulting retort.

  - Fuck, that hurts.
  - Get the fuck out my face!
  - He said that! Well, fuck him!

- *fuck*   damn 대신에 쓰는 강의어(强意語); Interjection used for emphasis; Very, extremely

  - What the fuck are you doing here?
  - I think I am your fucking perverted fucking bitch.
  - Fuck, that's a lot of money.

- *fuck*   비열한 녀석; A really stupid/despicable person.

  - You stupid fuck!

□ **fuck**　　　　가혹하게 대하다, 학대하다; 속이다, 이용하다; To take advantage of, cheat, trick, deceive, kid

- Are you trying to fuck with me?
- Are you fucking me?
- The car dealer really fucked me.

□ **fuck around**　　　　빈둥거리다; To waste time, to mess around.

- He just fucks around on the computer all day.

□ *fuck around with something* 빈둥거리며 돌아다니다, 시간을 소비하다; To spend time not doing anything productive.

□ *fuck hole*　　　　여성의 성기; Female genitalia.

□ **Fuck it all!**　　　　우라질!, 제기랄!; Expression of surprise, contempt, outrage, disgust, boredom, frustration.

□ **Fuck it!**　　　　제기랄!, 젠장!, 닥쳐!, 꺼져!, 알게 뭐야!; Expression of surprise, contempt, outrage, disgust, boredom, frustration.

□ **fuck me**　　　　이런 제기랄; An exclamation of extreme displeasure; "oh shit"

- Fuck me, we're surrounded!

□ **fuck off**　　　　꺼져버려; An intense way of telling someone to get lost or go to hell.

- Kyle: [You] sound like a clown. Not even nymphos would go for that.
  Roman: Fuck off! Nymphos would go for that.

□ *Fuck off and die!* 꺼져버려; A contemptuous dismissal.

□ **Fuck off!**　　　　꺼져버려; A contemptuous dismissal.

□ *fuck one over*　　　　먹이[밥]로 삼다; To take advantage of.

- I'm pretty sure the mechanic fucked me over.

130

□ *fuck over*   ~을 이용해 먹다; To take advantage of.

□ **fuck <u>somebody</u> up**   ~의 신세를 조지다; To severely injure (a person) or damage or ruin (a thing).

> • He really fucked that guy up!

□ **fuck *something* up**   ~을 개판으로 만들다[조지다]; To severely injure (a person) or damage or ruin (a thing).

> • Thanks for fucking up my car.

□ **fuck up**   ~을 개판으로 만들다[조지다]; To severely injure (a person) or damage or ruin (a thing).

□ *fuck with*   ~를 가지고 놀다[~에게 수작을 부리다]; To mess with.

> • You better not be saying what I think you're saying. I'm not the kind of guy you want to fuck with.

□ **Fuck you!**   엿 먹어라!; A contemptuous dismissal.

□ **Fuck!**   씨발, 제기랄, 젠장, 우라질; Vulgar expression used to emphasize displeasure with someone or something.

□ *fuck-all*   전혀 없음(nothing); Nothing at all.

> • These instructions make fuck all sense to me.

□ *fuck-ass*   바보, 멍청이; Another word for idiot, moron, etc.

> • You stupid fuck-ass, you broke my shit.

□ *fuckbunny*   난잡한 젊은 여성; A promiscuous person. Usually used to refer to females. Probably refers to the mating habits of rabbits.

> • She's such a fuckbunny.

□ *Fucked if I know!* 정말 아는 바 없다; I don't know.

□ **fucked up**   [사물 · 상황이] 엉망인, 몹시 혼란한; 심란한, 큰 충격
을 받은; Messed up, botched; Damaged; poorly manufactured; injured

- Did you hear Ramsey dumped his girlfriend because she was getting too fat? That's pretty fucked up.
- You're pretty fucked up!

□ **fucker**   바보 같은 놈, 싫은 사람, 녀석, 놈; A general insult.
When directed at someone who is present, often prefixed with "little"

- He's just a fucker.
- You little fucker.

□ *fuckhead*   바보, 얼간이 (특히 남성); Somebody who is stupid,
careless, or inconsiderate.

- That stupid fuckhead pulled in front of me.

□ *fuckin' A*   "Fucking Affirmative"에서 온 말로 강한 긍정을 나타
냄; An exclamation of satisfaction or happiness; Expression used to denote correctness; "Fucking affirmative". Originated in US army.

- Person A: Hey dude, I got the beer. We're all set.
  Person B: Fuckin' A, man!
- You're fuckin' A right. You're going to pay for damages.

□ **fucking**   1. 괘씸한, 지독한, 지긋지긋한, 완전한 2. 대단히, 지독
히; 1. Displeasing, despicable, etc. 2. very; really; extremely.

- Are you fucking kidding me?
- None of you live here. Your daughter doesn't live here. The sign says 'Resident Parking Only.' I am a resident. So move this fucking rust bucket somewhere else or by God I'll stuff your asses in the trailer and move it myself.

□ **fucking A**   "Fucking Affirmative"에서 온 말로 강한 긍정을 나타
냄; An intensifier. The "A" is a long A. "Fucking ay, aye!"; Expression of
acceptance of something offered to the speaker.

□ **fucking well <auxiliary verb>** 씨발 ~(화를 내며 하는 명령이나
진술을 강조); Intensifier, surely, definitely

• We fucking well should!

□ *fuckup*   실수만 하는 사람, 얼빠진 사람; A person who messes up; a screw up.

    • He got fired because he was a fuck-up.

□ *fuckwit*   바보, 얼간이; An unintelligent person; MORON; DIM-WIT; IDIOT

    • Don't trample that dog crap into my house, fuckwit!

□ fudge   속이다; [비용 등을] 부풀리다, 과장하다; 우유부단하다, 꾀부리다; (약속 등을) 어기다, 지키지 않다; To falsify.

    • Politicians are often very clever at fudging the issue.

□ full monte/monty   (필요한) 모든 것; 발가벗은 알몸뚱이; Nakedness; everything you need.

    • They'll do the full monty if you pay them enough.

□ **full of baloney**   실없는 소리, 허튼소리, 엉터리, 거짓말; To be dishonest, full of lies.

□ **full of beans**   실없는 소리, 허튼소리, 엉터리, 거짓말; To be dishonest, full of lies.

□ *full of bullshit*   실없는 소리, 허튼소리, 엉터리, 거짓말; To be dishonest, full of lies.

□ *full of crap*   실없는 소리, 허튼소리, 엉터리, 거짓말; To be dishonest, full of lies.

□ **full of piss and vinegar**   기운이 철철 넘치는; Full of energy.

□ **full throttle**   거침없이, 완전히 어떤 일을 하는; To do something, completely, without restraint.

    • Man, that was one full throttle party.

□ funk   의기소침, 실의, 낙담; Mental depression.

- I guess I don't want to see you go into a funk if Cassie works with you tomorrow and then does a scene.

G

- **gabber** 수다쟁이; Talkative

- **gadzillion** (상상 속의) 무한대의 숫자; Indefinite and fictitious number; inexact term of indefinite size, used for comic effect, for exaggeration.

- **gaga about/for/over** (너무 좋아서) 거의 제정신이 아닌; Crazy

  • My daughter is just gaga about entertainers.

- **gang up on** ~을 집단으로 공격하다; To join together in a group in order to overpower someone else.

  • The girls had promised not to gang up on Adam but they had broken that vow the night before.

- **gangbang** (한 여성을 상대로) 난교(亂交)하다; 윤간하다; 윤간에 끼다; A session of sex involving multiple men and a single female. Sometimes used in the context of rape.

  • I would love to be in a gangbang with that chick.

- **ganja** 마리화나; Marijuana

  • Let's go smoke some ganja.

- **garden tool** 난잡한 젊은 여성; Promiscuous female.

- **gas bag** 말이 많은 사람; A person who makes many empty statements.

- **gash** 여성의 성기, 여성을 낮춰 부르는 말; Slang for vaginal passage. Often used in describing an undesirable woman, or man who is acting less than manly.

  • She had a lovely gash.
  • That bitch ain't nothin' but a gash.

- **gay** 동성애자, 게이; A homosexual person.

> • Child: Mom, Dad, I have something to tell you. I'm gay.
> Parents: We will love you no matter what your sexual preference is.

□ **gazillion**   엄청난 수; A very large number. gadzillion

> • When they submitted their idea to the Pepsi Refresh project, it got a gazillion votes.

□ *gazonga*   젖, 유방; A breast. Usually used in reference to a large breast.

> • Man, she's got some huge gazongas!

□ **gee (whiz)**   (놀람/감탄을 나타내어) 야; (짜증스러움을 나타내어) 에이; Exclamation to emphasize a reaction or remark.

> • Ah gee, Steve, you are so ignorant.

□ **geek**   행복한 표정을 짓다; To display an embarrassing amount of happiness; to act like a geek (nerd).

> • She geeked when he asked her out.

□ **geek**   괴짜. 어느 한 가지 분야에만 몰두하는 괴짜; Nerd; a person who is intensely interested in a subject or thing.

> • Are you telling me, in this town full of super-geeks, you can't find one person who can do a simple math problem?

□ **get (*one's*) groove on**   즐겁게 춤추다; To have fun dancing. Also get (one's) swerve on.

> • Yeah, I was at that party; I really got my groove on.

□ *get (one's) rocks off*   사정(射精)하다, 성교하다; To enjoy in a sexual sense.

> • You are into some weird porn. But… whatever gets your rocks off man.

□ **get a bang out of**   ~에 흥분하다. ~에서 쾌감을 얻다; To enjoy.

- **get a fix**   마약을 한판 하다; To ingest a drug.

  • I need to get a fix.

- **get a kick out of**   ~에 흥분하다. ~에서 쾌감을 얻다; To enjoy.

  • I got a kick out of persuading people to buy things.

- **get a life**   (명령형으로 쓰여) 정신 차려라. 따분하게 굴지 마; Change your life radically! (get real!)

  • Dude, you need to get a life.

- **get a line on**   ~에 대한 정보를 얻다; To secure information about.

- **get a load of** *somebody/something*   ~ 좀 봬[들어 봬]; To take a look at, examine

  • Get a load of that!

- **get a move on**   (명령문으로 쓰여) 빨리해[서둘러]; To start a task; to move quickly.

  • She had to get a move on if she wants to go home before midnight.

- **get along**   (일이) 되어가다, 진척되다[with]; To make a progress.

- **get an eyeful**   (흥미롭거나 특이한 것을) 유심히 보다; To obtain a full view of.

  • Walk down the average city street and you'll get an eyeful of modernist architecture.

- ***get any***   (섹스) 좀 하다. (주로 의문문으로 사용됨); To have sex. Used as a question.

  • You gotten any lately?

138

□ **get cold feet**   (계획했던 일에 대해) 갑자기 초조해지다[겁이 나다];
To be nervous about entering into a long-term commitment, especially
marriage.

• Why do I always get cold feet before I give a presentation?

□ **get cracking**   즉시[서둘러] 일을 시작하다; To start a task.

□ **get even**   ~에 복수하다; To seek revenge.

□ **get going**   ~하기 시작하다(begin); To start a task.

□ *get head*   구강성교를 받다; To receive oral sex.

• I got some head last night.

□ **get high**   (마리화나나 환각제를 통해) 몽롱한 기분을 느끼다;
To get high via smoking marijuana or doing drugs.

• Hey man, I'm gonna get high.

□ *get in (one's) pants*   성관계를 갖다; To have sex with. Also
"get into (one's) pants."

• Guys you meet in bars, they'll say anything to get in your pants.

□ **get in on the ground floor**   (계획·프로젝트 등에) 처음부터 관여하
다; To start a task.

□ **get in *somebody's* hair**   남을 괴롭히다; To annoy someone.

□ **get it**   이해하다; To understand.

□ **get it in one**   이해가 빠르다; To succeed in grasping the issue
at hand quickly.

□ *get it off*   (남자가) 오르가슴에 이르다, 사정(射精)하다; To climax.

139

• It is very easy to get it off the internet; my secretary did so this morning with no difficulty at all.

□ **get it on**   (~와) 섹스하다; To engage in coitus.

• She's gettin' it on with that guy.
• They got it on last night.

□ **Get it?**   알았어? 이해했어?; Do you understand me?

□ **get laid**   섹스하다; To have sex.

• I'm not looking to get married, man, I just want to get laid.
• It doesn't change the fact that you made a bad decision because you want to get laid.

□ **Get lost!**   꺼져; (거절을 나타내어) 턱도 없어!; Go away!

□ **get moving**   빨리 시작하다[떠나다/움직이다]; To start a task.

□ **get off**   오르가슴에 도달하다[하게 하다]; 흥분시키다; To climax.

• Did you get off?
• She would do her best to get Adam off with her mouth, and swallow every fucking drop, or to make sure Shelly had an incomplete ride before Adam filled her little pussy with his juice.

□ **Get off my back!**   귀찮게 하지 마! 나 좀 내버려 둬!; Stop annoying me!

□ **Get off my case!**   귀찮게 하지 마! 나 좀 내버려 둬!; Stop annoying me!

□ **get off *one's* ass**   일을 시작하다; To get to work; figuratively, to stop procrastinating or to stop being lazy.

□ **get on**   열정적으로 입 맞추다; To kiss passionately; MAKE OUT.

• She got on that guy last night.

□ **get on *one's* back**   남을 괴롭히다; To annoy someone.

□ **get on *one's* nerve**   신경을 건드리다; To annoy someone.

□ **get on the ball**   빈틈없이 하다, 주의 깊게 하다; To become focused.

□ *get one's cookies*   짜릿한 쾌감을 느끼다; 오르가슴을 느끼다; To climax.

> • I'm really enjoying this and not just because I got my cookies harder than ever.
> • Sarah had plenty of time to go get her cookies.

□ *get one's ass in gear*   꾸물거리지 말고 당장 움직이다; To stop wasting time; to start a task.

□ **get *one's* foot in the door**   기회를 얻다; 잽싸게 끼어들다; To make an initial small step towards gaining entrance to something (a job, a university, a relationship).

□ *get one's head out of one's ass/butt*   멍청한 행동을 그만하다; To stop acting stupidly.

□ *get one's hump on*   섹스하다; To have sex.

> • We went back to my place and got our hump on.

□ *get one's nut off*   사정(射精)하다; To ejaculate.

□ **get *one's* own back**   ~에게 복수하다, 보복하다; To seek revenge.

□ *get one's shit together*   다시 집중하다. 인생을 제대로 정리하다; To get focused or organized; to have one's life in order.

> • I told my son if he doesn't get his shit together soon that he's got to move out.

□ **get *one's* teeth into**   ~에 열중하다. ~에 달려들어 시작하다; To start a task.

- ***get one's thumb out of one's ass/butt*** 멍청한 행동을 그만하다; To stop stupid thing.

- **Get out of my face!** 내 앞에서 꺼져!; Go away!; Leave me alone!

- **Get out of my hair!** 괴롭히지 좀 마세요!; Leave me alone!

- **Get over it!** 그건 잊어버려; Come to terms with whatever is bothering you and stop complaining; used to tell somebody that they should stop worrying about something which you think is not important or not their business.

- get owned 지다, 패배하다; To lose, to be defeated.

- get physical 싸움을 시작하다; To start a fight.

- *get physical* 성관계를 갖다; To have intimate/sexual contact.

> • Are you aware that your daughter and my son have been getting physical? I mean, can you imagine anything that inappropriate?

- ***get pissed (off)*** 화가 나다; To become angry.

- *get some* 성교하다; To engage in sexual activity.

> • I got some from that girl last night.

- ***get some booty*** 성교하다; To have sexual intercourse.

> • He got some booty last night.

- get some shuteye 한숨 자다; To sleep.

- get somewhere 조금/약간 진전을 보다; To make some progress.

- get square 복수하다; To seek revenge.

□ ***get stuffed***   꺼져; 집어치워; An angry retort; Stop!, Go away!

- I didn't like his cringe, said to him, "Get stuffed!"

□ **get the drift**   (어찌 되어 있는지 또는 남이 하는 말을) 알다, 이해하다; To understand.

- My German isn't very good, but I got the drift of what she said.

□ ***Get the fuck out!***   썩 꺼지지 못해!; A contemptuous dismissal.

- Get the fuck out of here!

□ **get the hand of**   ~의 방법을 배우다; To learn how to.

□ ***Get the hell out!*** 꺼져! 여기서 꺼져!; A contemptuous dismissal; Go away!. Leave right now.

□ **get the idea**   이해하다; To understand.

□ **get the message**   이해하다, 알아듣다; To understand.

□ **Get the message?**   알아들었어?; Do you understand me?

□ **get the picture**   이해하다, 알아듣다; To understand.

□ **Get the picture?**   알아들었어?; Do you understand me?

□ **get the show on the road**   (활동 · 여정을) 시작하다; To start.

□ **get to 1st base**   (데이트에서) 키스(에 성공)하다; To kiss, make out.

□ **get to 2nd base**   (데이트에서) 가슴을 만지(는데 성공하)다; To put one's hands up a person's shirt, with hand-on-skin contact, e.g. the fondling of breasts.

□ **get to 3rd base**   (데이트에서) 성기를 만지(는데 성공하)다; To stimulate the genitals with one's hand.

□ **get tough with**   엄한 조치를 취하다. 엄하게 다루다; To be strict with somebody whose behavior you do not like; be ready to punish somebody.

□ **get under *one's* skin**   ~를 괴롭히다; To annoy.

□ **get wise to**   ~을 알다, 알아[탐지해]내다, 눈치채다; 박식한 체하다; To understand.

□ *Get your finger out of your ass(butt)!*   더 이상 헛일 말고 제대로 된 일을 시작해라!; Stop sitting around or messing around and get ready for serious action.

□ *Get your head out of your ass!*   정신을 다른 곳에 팔지 마라!; Stop being so self-involved.

□ **get[or have] *a person's* number**   남의 정체[본심, 약점]를 알다[간파하다], 남을 꿰뚫어 보다; Get[or have] a person's weakness or true self.

- "We've got your number now," Sarah said. "We know just what you like and don't think we won't use it to our advantage."

□ **get-go**   시작, 개시, 최초; The beginning.

- He has been guilty from the get-go.

□ **gig**   (대중음악가/코미디언의) 공연; (특히 임시로 하는) 일; Any job. Derived from the musical industry sense.

- Hey, did you hear? Mark's got a new gig.

□ **gip, gyp**   1. 바가지 2. 바가지를 씌우다; To cheat, to deceive.

□ *give a flying fuck*   신경 쓰다. 상관하다; To care. Used always to imply that one doesn't care.

- I don't give a flying fuck.
- Like I give a flying fuck.

144

□ *give a rat's ass*   신경 쓰다. 상관하다(언제나 부정문의 형태로 사용);
To care. Always used in the negative, as the example sentence shows.

• I don't give a rat's ass about what you think!

□ *give a shit*   신경 쓰다. 상관하다(언제나 부정문의 형태로 사용);
To care.

• I don't give a shit about any of this.

□ give a thumper   세게 때리다; To strike someone with great force.

• I just gave him a thumper.

□ give all the way   최고의 노력을 하다; To exert effort.

□ *give face*   구강성교를 해주다; To perform fellatio or cunnilingus; GO DOWN ON.

• This girl I talked to wanted me to give her face and I said hell no!

□ *give head*   구강성교를 해주다; To perform fellatio.

• She gave him head.
• She pulled some dorky guy aside after school and gave him head at the
library.

□ give her the gun   차의 속도를 높이다; To speed a car.

□ give it a rest   (짜증스러우니) 그쯤해 뒈[그만해]; Shut up!, Shut
up and take a break from talking about this topic!

• Give it a rest! Ye talk too much.

□ **give it all** *one's* **got**   전력[혼신의 힘]을 다하다; To do one's best effort.

• Whatever you do, you must give it all you've got.

□ **give it** *one's* **best shot**   전력[혼신의 힘]을 다하다; To do one's
best effort.

- I gave it my best shot, but couldn't stand her demands.

□ **Give me a break!** 그만 좀 해!; 좀 봐주세요; A plea for help, relief, or patience in the face of difficult situation.

- Give me a break, I was just trying to help!

□ **Give me five!** 우리 손바닥 부딪쳐! 하이파이브하자!; A request for a celebratory gesture of slapping hands in the air–often above the head.

□ **Give me some skin!** 우리 손바닥 부딪쳐! 하이파이브하자!; A request greeting or celebratory gesture of slapping hands.

□ *give one's left[or right] nut to do* ~하기 위해서라면 뭐든지 하다; To do one's best effort to do something.

- I know you'd give a nut to have me again but you'll just have to wait.

□ **give over** 포기하다; To surrender.

□ **give** *somebody* **a pain in the ass/butt** 귀찮게 하다; To cause agony.

- That guy gave me a pain in the neck with his constant demands.

□ **give** *somebody* **a pain in the neck** 귀찮게 하다; To cause agony.

- He gives me a pain in the neck.

□ **give** *somebody* **an earful** 잔소리를 늘어놓다; To give excessive or animated talk.

- He gave me an earful about his boss.

□ **give** *somebody* **(holy/merry) hell** 공격하다; To attack.

□ **give** *somebody/something* **the up-and-down** 아래위로 훑어보다; To take a thorough look, to scrutinize.

□ **give** *somebody* **a bad/hard time**   ~에게 어려움을 가져오다, ~에게 어려움을 주다; To cause difficulty or make trouble for someone.

□ give *somebody* a line   속이다; To deceive.

□ **give** *somebody* **a piece of one's mind**   생각한 바를 거리낌 없이 말하다, 따끔하게 한마디 하다; To express one's opinion strongly; to voice one's disagreement or dissatisfaction, especially with another person; to scold or rebuke someone.

• She gave a piece of her mind to the students that lived in the dormitory, 'cause she was a dormitory leader.

□ give *somebody* flak 꾸중을 하다; To criticize.

• My boss gave me flak for coming late.

□ give *somebody* the business   ~를 화를 내며 꾸짖다; To reprimand angrily.

□ **give** *somebody* **the cold shoulder**   매몰스럽게 굴다; To snub, resist or reject somebody; to regard somebody distantly.

• He was given the cold shoulder in the team.

□ give *somebody* the dickens   ~를 화를 내며 꾸짖다; To reprimand angrily.

□ give *somebody* the dope   정보를 알려주다; To tell somebody all the important information they need.

□ **give** *somebody* the low down 비밀이나 내부 정보를 알려주다; To tell somebody all the inside information about something.

□ give *somebody* the once-over 한번 훑어보다; To examine; to evaluate.

□ **give** *somebody* the scoop   ~에게 특종을 알려주다; To tell somebody all the current and/or exclusively obtained information about something.

- give *somebody* the shivers   등골을 오싹하게 하다; To cause fear.

- give *someone* axe   해고하다, 쫓아버리다; To dismiss, fire, eject, or send away.

- give *someone* his/her marching orders   해고하다, 쫓아버리다; To dismiss, fire, eject, or send away.

- give *someone* his/her walking papers   해고하다, 쫓아버리다; To dismiss, fire, eject, or send away.

- **give *someone* the boot**   해고하다, 쫓아버리다; To dismiss, fire, eject, or send away.

- give *someone* the chop   해고하다, 쫓아버리다; To dismiss, fire, eject, or send away.

- give *someone* the chuck   해고하다, 쫓아버리다; To dismiss, fire, eject, or send away.

- give *someone* the gate   해고하다, 쫓아버리다; To dismiss, fire, eject, or send away.

- give *someone* the heave-ho   해고하다, 쫓아버리다; To dismiss, fire, eject, or send away.

- give *someone* the push   해고하다, 쫓아버리다; To dismiss, fire, eject, or send away.

- **give *someone* the sack**   해고하다, 쫓아버리다; To dismiss, fire, eject, or send away.

- give *someone* the shaft   해고하다, 쫓아버리다; To dismiss, fire, eject, or send away.

- give *someone* the shove   해고하다, 쫓아버리다; To dismiss, fire, eject, or send away.

- give *something* a miss   ~을 포기하다; To forego something.

□ **give the 3rd degree** 조사하다, 심문하다; To interrogate.

• She really gave me the third degree.

□ **give the elbow** (교제하던 사람을) 차다[퇴짜 놓다]; To reject, ignore

□ **give the shivers** 등골을 오싹하게 하다; To cause fear.

□ **giveaway** 공짜, 거저, 경품; Free samples; freebie

□ **glam** 미화[치장]하다, 매력적으로 보이게 하다; Glamorize

□ **glam** 글래머인; Shortened form of "glamorous."

• She is glam!

□ **GLBT** 동성, 양성, 성전환의 두음 문자; Acronym for "Gay, lesbian, bisexual, transgendered."

• Statistics of discrimination against GLBT youth are even worse.

□ **glitch** 작은 문제; A flaw.

• A glitch in the computer is stopping the printer from working.

□ **glob** 한 방울의 작은 양; A small round amount.

• The container drops to the floor and thick globs of cheese roll out.

□ **glop** (기분 나쁘게) 질척거리는 것; A mushy mess of something.

• I'll probably remember it and laugh whenever I find a massive glop of bird's leavings on my windshield.

□ **go** 시도; An attempt.

• I doubt if he'll listen to advice from me, but I'll give it a go.

G

☐ **go all the way** (~와) 갈 데까지 다 가다[성관계까지 하다]; To have sexual intercourse.

- Have you guys gone all the way yet?

☐ **go along with** ~에 동의하다; To believe; to agree.

☐ **go ape for** (~에) 열중하다, 열광[심취]하다; To feel attracted over.

☐ *go ape shit* 화가 나다; To lose one's temper, usually involving violent actions.

- Ben will go ape shit.

☐ **go at it** (결연히, 필사적으로) 싸우다 (싸우기 시작하다); To start a fight.

☐ **go AWOL** 탈영하다; 무단결근[외출]하다; To go missing without permission or explanation.

- The guitarist went AWOL in the middle of the recording.

☐ **go back to square one** 다시 원점으로 돌아가다.; To backtrack to the start.

- The plan of building a garbage disposal facility went back to square one due to opposition from the residents.

☐ **go back to the drawing board** 다시 원점으로 돌아가다; To backtrack to the start.

☐ **go ballistic** 분통을 터뜨리다. 화가 나서 길길이 날뛰다; To become enraged, lose one's temper; FREAK OUT.

- When she found out he lied, she went ballistic.

☐ **go bananas** 머리가 확 돌다(미친 듯이 화를 내거나 터무니없는 짓을 함을 나타냄); To go insane.

- When I told him that his girlfriend left town, he went bananas.

150

□ go batty	미치다. 돌다; To go crazy.	

□ go belly up	완전히 망하다; To die; to be ruined financially.

- Did you hear his business went belly up?

□ **go blank** "go blank."	(마음 따위가) 텅 비다; To forget; have one's mind

□ **go bonkers**	돌아버리다; To go crazy.

- He just went bonkers.

□ **go crackers**	미치다. 돌다; To go crazy.

□ go down in flames	파멸하다, 못쓰게 되다; To fail completely.

□ go down like a lead balloon	완전히 망하다; To fail completely.

□ *go down on*	구강성교를 하다; To perform oral sex.

- Although she thought Shelly, Sarah and Allie were gorgeous, she had not considered having them go down on her or going down on them.
- I think I would offer to go down on you once a month for that amount.
- She was gonna go down on me, but then I woke up and realized she wasn't there.

□ **go down the drain**	헛수고[수포]로 돌아가다, 못 쓰게 되다; (회사가) 도산[파산]하다; To fail completely.

- Years of work went down the drain.

□ go down the tubes	못쓰게 되다, 도산(倒産)하다; To fail completely

□ **go easy**	서두르지 않고[태평스럽게] 하다; Don't hurry.

□ go easy on *something*	(명령형으로 쓰여) ~를 살살 다뤄라, 너무 심하게 하지 마라]; Do not use too much of something; Do speak too much about something, etc.

□ **go flat-out**	전속력을 다하다; To go with full speed.

□ ***Go fly a kite***   꺼져! 귀찮게 굴지 말고 저리 가!; An angry retort.
Go away!

> • Person A: I don't like you.
>   Person B: Go fly a kite.

□ **go for**   ~을 좋아[선호]하다; To feel attracted over.

□ **go for broke**   (~에) 전부를 걸다; To risk everything in some endeavor.

□ **go for it**   단호히 목적을 추구하다, 사생결단으로 덤비다; To risk everything in some endeavor.

> • Sink or swim, let's go for it.

□ ***Go fuck yourself!***   뒈져 버려!; A contemptuous dismissal; an angry retort.

> • You should tell your boss he can go fuck himself.

□ ***Go fucking figure!*** 참 이해가 안 돼!; Who would have thought!

□ **go full blast**   전속력을 다하다; To go (operate) at full capacity.

□ **go great guns**   (사람이) 척척 잘해 나가다; (일이) 대성공이다; To be successful.

> • Everything is going great guns around here. We're making lots of money.

□ **go haywire**   (일이) 잘못되다[걷잡을 수 없게 되다]; To malfunction.

> • My computer went haywire.

□ **go hogging**   약간 마음에 들지 않는 여자라도 찾다; To go out seeking even less desirable girls.

- Let's give the fat girls a chance and go hogging.

☐ **go home in a box**   죽다, 살해되다; To die.

- The CSIs looked for something that made the victim go home in a box.

☐ **go like a bat out of hell**   엄청 빠르게 가다; To go very fast.

☐ **go like a shot**   엄청 빠르게 가다; To go very fast.

☐ **go like blaze**   엄청 빠르게 가다; To go very fast.

☐ **go like gangbusters**   성황을 이루다; To make good progress; to make a big hit.

☐ **go like greased lightning**   아주 빨리 (신나게) 달리다; To move very fast.

☐ **go like hell**   엄청 빠르게 가다; To go very fast.

☐ **go like the devil**   엄청 빠르게 가다; To go very fast.

☐ **go make me a sandwich**   잔말 말고 샌드위치나 만들어 와!; General insulting retort to a female.

- Female: ⟨compelling argument⟩
  Male: Whatever. Go make me a sandwich.

☐ **go number one**   쉬하다; To urinate.

- Mom, I need to go number one.

☐ **go number two**   응가하다; To defecate; poop

- Mom, I need to go number two.

☐ **go nuts**   미치다; To go crazy.

- About once a week we get this way. I mean we just go nuts on each other.

□ **go nuts about/ over**	열중하다; To go crazy over.
□ **go off** *one's* **bean**	미치다; To go crazy.
□ **go off** *one's* **head**	미치다; To go crazy.
□ **go off** *one's* **nut**	미치다; To go crazy.
□ **go off** *one's* **rocker**	미치다; To go crazy.
□ go off the deep end	미치다; To go crazy.
□ go on the lam	미치다; To go crazy.
□ go out of *one's* skull	미치다; To go crazy.
□ go over like a lead balloon	완전히 망하다; To fail completely.
□ *Go piss up a rope!*	꺼져! 귀찮게 굴지 말고 저리 가!; Go away!
□ **go postal**	몹시 화를 내다, 격분하다; To go insane.
□ *Go screw!*	꺼져 (버려)!; To leave.

• I've gotten calls for her from 'Daddy's Little Fuckhole'? which I told to go screw as soon as I heard the guy's name.

□ **go south**	(주가 따위가) 하향하다; To take a turn for the worse.

• His health has gone south.

□ **go the distance**   끝까지 해내다; To continue playing in a competition or sports contest until the end.

□ **go the extra mile**   (~을 위해) 특별히 애를 쓰다; To do something extra – more than required.

• Those who go the extra mile will get rewarded someday.

□ **go the limit** 끝까지 노력하다; To do one's best effort.

□ **go the whole nine yards** 끝까지 노력하다; To do one's best effort.

□ **go there** 특정 주제에 대해 이야기(토론)하다; To mention or ask something that a person doesn't want to talk about.

• Don't go there.

□ go through the roof 화가 머리끝까지 치밀다; To become very angry.

□ go tits-up 죽다, 작동을 멈추다; To die or stop functioning.

• The motor on my boat went tits-up today.

□ go to bat for ~를 도와주다; To take someone's side.

• I tried to go to bat for Bill, but he said he didn't want any help.

□ ***go to hell*** 거꾸러져라, 뒈져라! 지옥에나 가라!; A contemptuous dismissal.

□ go to pieces 몸과 마음이 허물어지다; To go crazy.

□ go to the mat for (~와의 언쟁에서) (~의) 편[역성]을 들다; To do one's utmost on behalf of something.

□ go up in flames 꺼져 없어지다; To fail completely.

□ **go up in smoke** (계획·희망 등이) 연기처럼 사라지다[수포로 돌아가다]; To fail.

• His career went up in smoke after a steroids scandal.

□ go weak at the knees 무릎에 힘이 빠지다; To feel weak because of fear.

□ go west 죽다; 못쓰게 되다; (돈 등이) 없어지다; To fail.

□ *gobble* <u>*one's knob*</u> 펠라티오하다; To perform fellatio.

155

- Have you gobbled his knob yet?

□ **gobbledygook**   (특히 공문서에 쓰이는 복잡하고) 이해할 수 없는 말
들; Nonsense

□ **gobs**   많은 양; A large amount.

□ **God Squad**   (특히 전도에 열심인) 기독교도들; Any group of
evangelical Christians, members of which are regarded as intrusive and
exuberantly pious.

- I'm not with the God Squad or anything like that. I am not calling to tell you
how horrible you are or get you to change your mind about what you do.
- Yes, I have heard that the 'God Squad' is finally now concerned with
green issues.

□ ***Goddamn it!***   (분노 · 당혹 · 놀람 따위를 나타내어) 빌어먹을, 제기
랄!; Exclamation of displeasure.

□ **gofer**   (회사의) 사환; A low-level worker whose primary responsibility is going and getting things. From "go for."

□ **go-getter**   (특히 사업에서) 성공하려고 단단히 작정한 사람; An
ambitious or enterprising person.

□ **gold digger**   돈을 목적으로 남자와 교제하는 여자; A woman who
is dating a wealthy man only for his money.

- Man, you need to break up with her. She's a gold digger.

□ **gold-brick**   (꾀병을 부리는) 게으름뱅이; Lazy person.

□ **golden parachute**   (직원이 회사를 떠나야 하게 될 경우 지급하기로
계약서에 명시하는) 고액의 퇴직금; An employment clause specifying that
if the employee is dismissed, they will receive a very large severance
package.

- In addition, the bill limits "golden parachutes" and requires that unearned
bonuses be returned.

□ **Golly!**   야, 와(놀람을 나타냄); Interjection of surprise.

156

◻ **gomer**	바보; Geek, nerd, or weirdo.	

• What a Gomer!

◻ **goo**　　　　　(불쾌하게) 찐득찐득한 것; Any thick, sticky substance.

◻ **goof**　　　　바보 같은 실수; A foolish mistake.

• That was actually a pretty serious goof. It might cost you your job.

◻ **goof**　　　　바보, 멍청이; A funny or silly person.

◻ **goof around**　　시간을 허비하다; To waste time.

◻ **goof around with *something***　시간을 허비하다; To spend time not doing anything productive.

◻ **goof off**　　　(특히 할 일을 안 하고) 빈둥거리다; To waste time.

• I also scheduled time for employees to just goof off together.

◻ **goof up**　　　어리석은 실수를 하다; To make a mistake.

• Am I worried that someone might goof up and get hurt? Of course.

◻ **goofball**　　　멍청이; A fool.

◻ **goof-off**　　　게으름뱅이; A lazy person.

◻ **goofus**　　　어리석은 사람, 바보; A fool.

◻ **goop**　　　　끈적끈적 들러붙는 것; A viscous thing.

◻ **goose egg**　　(경기에서) 무득점, 0점; Zero point.

◻ **gosh**　　　　이크, 아이쿠; General exclamation. Origin: euphemism for "God."

• Gosh, that was good.
• Gosh! That's incredible!

□ **Got it!**   알았다; To understand.

□ **Got it?**   알았어?; Do you understand?

□ **Got me?**   알았어?; Do you understand?

□ **Gotcha!**   잡았다; 알았어; "Got you"; To be holding onto a person physically.

> • Oh, I gotcha!

□ **gouge**   바가지를 씌우다; 값을 부당하게 올리다; To exact or extort a large amount money.

□ **GQ**   맵시 있는 남성, 멋진 남성, 세련된 남자; A man that is dressed well, attractive and well off. From the magazine GQ, originally called Gentlemen's Quarterly.

> • Man, that guy was GQ.

□ **grand poobah**   중요한 인물. 고위직; A person who is important or high-ranking.

> • The grand poobahs think we'll lose our shirt. We're not. I've been running this program for 18 months now and it outperforms every facet of our operations except for the most lucrative high-end loan division.

□ **grass**   마리화나; Marijuana

> • Henry: And how high were you during this?
> Ron: Not important. Don't do grass, get high on life.
> • Hostel guest: You hold any magic mushroom?
> Ted: Magic mushrooms? We're cops.
> Hostel guest: Then, grass?

□ **gravy**   수월한 돈벌이, 노다지판; Money or profit acquired easily, especially tips or bonuses.

> • We expect to at least make back our investment. Anything over that is gravy.

158

□ **gravy train** (노력을 하지 않고 이득을 얻을 수 있는) 좋은 입장[지위, 일]; 부당 이득; A lucrative endeavor that requires little work.

> • They would be responsible for a portion of my fees and the general upkeep of everything you own or will own. It's not just a gravy train for them to hop onto. They will be responsible for a set percentage of your debt and liabilities, too.

□ **Greek sex** 항문 성교; Anal sex.

□ **green** 돈, 지폐 (greenback); Money (Paper currency in the United States is green in color.)

> • But if they buy euros instead, the greenback could collapse.

□ **green** 마리화나; Marijuana (Marijuana is green in color.)

> • We will smoke our green today.

□ **green bud** 마리화나; Marijuana

□ **greenback** 미 달러화 지폐; Currency of United States dollars.

> • That will set you back a few greenbacks.

□ **greenhorn** (속기 쉬운) 풋내기; A novice.

□ **greens** 마리화나; Marijuana

□ **griper** 불평하는 사람; Complaining person; grumbler

□ **grit** 투지, 기개; Spirit; courage

□ **grommet** 신참 서퍼(surfer); A young, typically pre-pubescent surfer. 1960s slang.

> • Wally's brother Beav, is a grommet down at Huntington Beach.

□ **gross out** ~를 역겹게 하다; To sicken.

159

- That food really grossed me out.

□ **Gross!**　　　　징그럽다; Disgusting

- A: He ate it with mustard.
  B: Oh, gross!

□ **grossed out**　　역겨운; Disgusting

□ **grotty**　　불쾌한; 저급한; Cheap, fifth-rate, nasty, unpleasant

- It was a really grotty little convenience store.

□ **grouchy**　　불평이 많은, 잘 투덜거리는; Very bad-tempered and complaining a lot.

□ **groupie**　　가수를 따라다니는 소녀 팬; A person who follows (or travels with) a music act from performance to performance, and who hangs out with the band. Usually implies a female who makes herself available to band members for sex.

- Other bandmates prefer to concentrate on bedding groupies rather than concentrating on the music.

□ **grub**　　구걸하다; To scrounge; to beg.

□ **grumpy**　　성격이 나쁜; Bad-tempered and miserable.

□ **grunt**　　병사, 보병; A person with little or no authority in some organization; UNDERLING, SUBORDINATE; An infantryman.

- They were the grunts of the society.

□ **GTFO**　　믿을 수가 없다! (주로 채팅에서 사용); Acronym for "get the fuck out", an expression of disbelief. Used frequently in text-based Internet communication.

- You flew to Hong Kong for $400? GTFO!

□ **guck**　　미끌미끌한 것; Slimy matter; gunk

☐ **gudgeon**	잘 속는 사람; Gullible person.	

☐ **gulp down** (남의 말이나 의견을) 믿어 버리다; To believe; to agree.

☐ **gun for _somebody_** ~을 죽이려고[해치려고] 찾아다니다; To seek someone for a showdown confrontation; to attempt to defeat.

☐ **gun _somebody_ down** ~를 쏘아 쓰러뜨리다[죽이다]; To shoot somebody, especially so as to kill or seriously injure them.

☐ **gung-ho** (특히 싸움/전쟁 등에 대해) 너무 열광하는; Enthusiastic; eager, energetic and focused toward a goal.

• Azinger's father, Ralph, was a lieutenant-colonel in the US Airforce; the son likes a bit of 'gung ho' military attitude.

☐ **gunk** 끈적끈적[찐득찐득]한 것[오물]; Any sticky or greasy substance.

• Those bolts have gunk all over them.

☐ **gut feeling** 직감, 육감(六感); An instinct or intuition.

• I have a gut feeling that he is not the murderer.

☐ **gutless** 배짱이 없는; A weak character and lack courage or determination.

• Cameron is a pretty gutless little man.

☐ **guts** 용기, 기력, 배짱, 근성; 인내력; Courage

• You didn't have the guts to confront Cyril.

☐ **guts** 요지, 핵심 내용; The essence of something.

☐ **gutsy** 배짱 있는, 대담한; Having courage or determination.

□ **gutter punk**　　　(집이 없는) 조무래기, 똘마니, 풋내기; A younger punk who is homeless or pretends to be homeless.

H

- **hack**   (돈 때문에) 무엇이든 하는 사람, (문필가의) 조수, 삼류 작가; An untalented professional.

> • He's just some consulting hack.

- **hack into**   해킹하다; To use computer skills to gain unauthorized access to files or networks.

- **hair of the dog**   해장술; 숙취일 때 마시는 술; A drink of alcohol in the morning - of the same type one was drinking the previous night - to ward off or stop a hangover. From the phrase "hair of the dog that bit (one)."

> • That's some hangover you've got there, Bob. Here, drink this. It's a hair of the dog that bit you.

- ***hair pie***   음문(陰門); Vulva

> • I'm having some hair pie for lunch.

- **half sandwich short of a picnic**   (정신 상태가) 덜 떨어진; Stupid; retarded

- **half there**   (정신 상태가) 덜 떨어진; Stupid; retarded

- ***half-assed***   저능한, 어리석은; 엉터리의, 제멋대로의; 불충분한; 현실성 없는; Incompetent, poorly executed; Shoddy or poor workmanship. Screwed up or done half way.

> • There is a valid reason for the way some of the talent is treated. We show up late. We act like jerks. We expect to be catered to and fawned over. Then we give them a half-assed effort.
> • You did a half-assed job on this building.

- **half-baked**   섣부른; Incompletely thought out.

> • He's full of half-baked ideas.

- ***handjob***   수음(手淫); The stimulation of another person's penis with the hand, typically until ejaculation.

164

- hand *somebody's* head on a plate   때리다, 괴롭히다, 죽이다; To beat up; to harass or annoy; to kill.

- **handful**   다루기 힘든 사람; A person hard to handle or deal with.

  • Her children can be a real handful.

- *handjob*   수음(手淫); The stimulation of another person's Private Parts – penis with the hand, typically until ejaculation.

  • That little slut Amy was giving hand jobs to every guy on the swim team last night!

- *Hang it!*   제기랄!; Exclamation of displeasure.

- hang loose   차분하다, 평정을 유지하다; 무사태평하다; Stand by, and take it easy or relax while doing so.

  • Weekends are important: time to hang loose and take stock of things.

- hang loose   잘 지내!; Goodbye!

  • Hang loose, dude!

- hanging loose   차분한; Relaxed

- *happy as a pig in shit*   아주 행복한; Extremely happy.

- happy camper   즐기는 사람; 기분이 좋은 손님; A happy person.

  • That man who just got rear ended in the car accident does not look like a happy camper!

- hard cash   현금; A large sum of money consisting of coins.

- **hard core**   핵심의, 절대적인, 무제한의, 단호한, 철저한, 본격적인, (사회의) 최하층의, 만성 실업의, (포르노 영화, 소설 등) 극도로 노골적인; 극단적인; Having an intense (often excessive) interest in or enthusiasm for some particular activity, pastime or hobby.

- I can't believe he went to a strip club at 12:30 in the afternoon. That's pretty hard core.

□ **hard nut**   다루기 어려운 사람; A stubborn, cynical person, especially an employee or colleague who resists efforts to improve.

□ **hard stuff**   중독성이 강한 마약; Hard drug.

- I've seen too many girls who would fuck a rancid dick for a hit and I never wanted to be that girl. So I've stayed away from the hard stuff too.

□ **hard up**   (특히 짧은 기간 동안) 돈에 쪼들리는; Not having enough cash, money; broke

□ *hard-ass*   융통성 없는 (사람); 냉혹한 (사람); Very hard; a stubborn person.

- That was one hard-ass exam.
- The shop teacher is a real hard-ass.

□ **hardhead**   융통성 없는 사람, 고지식한 사람; A stubborn person.

□ *hard-on*   (남자 성기의) 발기; An erect penis.

- She used some of the soap from her body and started to stroke Adam's hard-on again.
- That babe's giving me a hard on.

□ **has-been**   한물간 사람; A person who was once famous or successful, but is no longer.

- That guy used to be so cool! Now he's just some has-been.

□ **Hasta la vista, baby!**   "See you later"를 의미하는 Standard Spanish 구문인 hasta la vista와 baby가 연결된 형태. Jody Watley가 1987년에 발표한 'Looking for a New Love'라는 노래에서 처음 유행되었으나, 1991년도 Arnold Schwarzenegger가 주연한 영화 'Terminator 2: Judgment Day'에서 Terminator에게 말을 가르치는데 쓰여 더 유행하였다. Schwarzenegger는 이후 주지사가 되는 과정에서 이 말을 자주 사용하였다; Farewell, baby.

166

□ *haul ass*　　힘들여서 어떤 일을 하다; To work very hard.

□ **haul ass**　　서두르다; 급히 떠나다; To move at a rapid speed.

> • I saw him ten minutes ago, haulin' ass up Broadway to get here on time.

□ haul *somebody* over the coals 엄하게 야단치다; To reprimand angrily.

□ have (got) it made　　성공을 확신하다; To be in a situation in which success is guaranteed.

□ **have a ball**　　신나게 즐기다; To have a great time.

> • Don't you guys worry, I have a gift with dogs, okay?
> Wilfred's gonna have a ball.

□ *have a box lunch*　　(여성에게) 오럴 섹스를 하다; To perform cunnilingus; GO DOWN ON.

□ *have a case of the ass*　　화가 많이 나다; To feel extremely annoyed.

□ have a conniption fit　　화를 내다; To feel extreme anger.

□ **have a crush on**　　~에게 홀딱 반하다; To have a infatuation with someone.

> • The word around the plant was that he has a crush on her.

□ **have a field day**　　(특히 남들이 좋게 보지 않는 것을) 신나게 즐기다; To have a great time.

> • The health-scare 'experts' are having a field day with their Doomsday predictions.

□ **have a fit**　　(심한 충격 · 분노 등으로) 졸도할 지경이 되다; To become very excited or angry.

□ *have a go*　　섹스하다; To have sex.

- □ **have a go at *something***   ~을 해보다; To give it a shot or try. Take a chance.

> • "Have a go." said one soccer player to the next, referring to taking a shot at goal.

- □ **Have a good one!**   잘 가요!; A way of saying "goodbye" and "have a nice day" at the same time.

- □ **have a meltdown**   굉장히 화내다; To become extremely angry.

> • I almost had a meltdown when I wrecked my jeep.

- □ **have a screw loose**   머리가 돌다. 미치다; To go crazy.

- □ ***have a shitfit***   엄청 열 받다. 화나다; To throw a tantrum, to have an angry outburst.

- □ **have a short fuse**   성미가 급하다, 걸핏하면 화를 낸다; Liable to anger.

- □ **have a soft spot for**   ~에 약하다[~을 좋아하다]; To be moved by, to have tender feeling for.

- □ ***have a stick up (one's) ass***   과도하게 형식적이고 딱딱하다; To be overly formal or humorless.

> • This guy really does have a stick up his ass.

- □ **have a thing about** (이상할 정도로) ~을 아주 좋아하다; To have a very strong feelings about.

- □ **have an itch for**   ~이 탐나서 못 견디다; To have a very strong desire for.

- □ ***have balls***   용기가 있다; To have courage.

- □ **have butterflies in *one's* stomach**   마음이 조마조마하다; To feel extremely nervous.

> • He had butterflies in the stomach when he was on the stage for the first time.

□ have chutzpah	대담하다; To be audacious.	

□ have chutzpah　　대담하다; To be audacious.

□ have cojones　　용기가 있다; To have courage.

□ **have cold feet**　　무서워하다, 주눅 들다; To suffer from fear or timidity.

• I can't give my speech now. I have cold feet.

□ have gall　　용기가 있다; To have courage.

□ **have guts**　　용기가 있다; To have courage.

□ have moxie　　용기가 있다; To have courage.

□ **have nerve**　　용기가 있다; To have courage.

□ have *one's* ass in the sling　　곤경에 처하다; To be in trouble.

□ have *one's* back　　뒤를 봐주다; To look out for one's interests or well-being.

• Nobody has my back.

□ have *one's* foot in the door　　(입회가 어려운 클럽 따위에) 들어갈 기회를 얻다, 잽싸게 끼어들다; To reach the initial stage in accomplishing something.

□ have *somebody* cold　　불법을 행하는 현장에서 잡다; To have caught someone doing something illegal.

□ have *somebody* in stiches　　큰 웃음을 유발하다; To cause riotous laughter.

□ have *someone* by the balls　　~의 약점을 잡다; To have somebody at one's mercy.

• Jane has her boyfriend by the balls at last.

□ have spunk　　용기가 있다; To have courage.

□ **have the final say** 최종 발언권을 갖다; To be the ultimate decision-maker.

□ **have the last word** 최종 발언권을 갖다; To be the ultimate decision-maker.

□ **hayseed** 시골뜨기; A person from a rural area; UN-HIP, BUMPKIN.

• Anyone living outside of Manhattan is a hayseed.

□ **head honcho** 우두머리, 두목; An important person; the person in charge.

□ **head shop** 마약 복용에 관계 있는 물건을 파는 가게; A store that sells drug paraphernalia, such as bowls and bongs marijuana smoking.

• We're going over to a head shop and interviewing this guy. Does anybody still call them head shops?

□ *head-bang* 격하게 구강성교하다; To perform aggressive fellatio.

• I'm down for some head-bangin' tonight.

□ *headlights* 가슴, 유두; Breasts; boobs; tits; erect nipples.

• Man, it's cold out here. But check out those headlights.

□ **heads up** 경계, 경고, 주의; A warning.

• Yeah, none of my business, but I just thought I'd give you the heads-up.

□ **heaps** 많음; A large amount.

• I have heaps of homework.

□ **heavy hitter** 중요한 인물. 고위직; A person who is important or high-ranking.

□ **heavyweight** 중요한 인물. 영향력이 많은 인물; A person who is important or has a lot of influence.

170

□ **heck**   문장이나 단어의 강조(hell의 대용어); A non-offensive replacement for the word "hell" used to express amazement at some unlikely act or strange object.

• What the heck is he doing?
• What the heck is that thing?

□ **Heck!**   젠장, 제기랄; An interjection expressing mild to moderate displeasure.

• Heck, guys. It's just hell.

□ **heebie-jeebies**   불안 초조한 상태; The feeling of shivers down your spine, or the hair on the back of your neck rising. Usually used in reference to something scary (common usage), but can also be used in reference to something gross or stomach-churning (rare usage).

• Walking through the cemetery at night gives me the heebie-jeebies.

□ **heeled**   돈이 많은(well-heeled의 준말); Shortening of well-heeled.

□ **hefty**   크고 무거운; Heavy, bulky

□ **heist**   (상점/은행에서 금품을) 강탈하다, 강도질을 하다; To steal or swindle something from someone.

• He heisted that convenience store.

□ **helicopter parent**   극성 부모. 자녀를 지켜보며 주위를 맴도는 부모. 특히 교육 측면에서 대단한 열의를 보이는 경우를 가리킴. (helicopter mother, helicopter mom, helicopter dad도 같은 의미로 사용됨); An over-attentive parent. One who hovers over their child as a helicopter hovers.

• We hovered over every school, playground and practice field - "helicopter parents," teachers christened us, a phenomenon that spread to parents of all ages, races and regions.

□ **hell**   문장 전체의 강조, 도대체; Intensifies whole sentence.

- Hell, I wish I'd known.
- What the hell was that all about?

□ **Hell no**   빌어먹을, 안돼!; An emphatic "no."

□ **hell of a**   (말하는 내용을 강조하여) 굉장한[엉망인]; Extreme; extremely; very.

- That was a hell of a show.

□ **Hell to the no**   Hell no의 강조; An emphatic "hell no."

□ **Hell!**   제기랄, 빌어먹을; General exclamation, usually (but not always) conveying displeasure.

- Person A: What movie should we go see?
  Person B: Hell, I don't know.

□ **hella**   아주, 굉장히; 진짜로; Very, totally; lots of.

- That party was hella sketch. What with all those skanky-ass girls.

□ **hellacious**   뛰어난, 두드러진, 멋진, 무서운; 만만치 않은; 심한; Extremely large or impressive, terrible, awesome

□ **hell-bent for leather**   맹렬한 기세로, 전속력으로, 무턱대고; With full speed.

□ **hellish**   지독히 기분 나쁜; Awful, horrific.

□ **Hell's bells!**   우라질!, 제기랄!; Exclamation of surprise or delight.

□ **helluva**   대단한; Extreme; Extremely; very; Hell of a.

- That was one helluva dee-lish-uss cake!

□ **helter-skelter**   허둥지둥하는; Carelessly scattered, disordered

□ **Hershey Highway**   항문 성교; The anal cavity; usually used when speaking in a sexual manner about taking it in the ass.

172

- Hey look at Adam, he is probably about ready to go down Misty's Hershey Highway again….

▫ **heteroflexible**　　동성애 관계에도 개방적인 태도를 보이는 이성애자; A person who identifies themselves as primarily heterosexual but can find the same sex sexually appealing.

- Most girls I know are heteroflexible.

▫ **Hey, man!**　　이봐, 형씨; Hello!

▫ **hiccup**　　(약간의) 문제; A small problem or difficulty.

▫ **HIG**　　'How's it going?'의 약어

▫ **high**　　(술/마약에) 취한; Intoxicated from drugs.

- Hey man, I'm gonna get high.

▫ **high as a kite**　　(술/마약)에 완전히 취한; In an excited state, especially because of drugs, alcohol, etc.

▫ **high end**　　최고급; The most expensive of their kind.

- This is high-end tourism at its zenith.

▫ **high falutin'**　　허세를 부리는; Something being made to sound complicated or important in order to impress people.

- This isn't high falutin art-about-art. It's marvelous and adventurous stuff.

▫ **high roller**　　(특히 도박에) 돈을 많이 쓰는 사람; A wealthy person who gambles large amounts.

▫ **hightail (it)**　　꽁지가 빠지게[몹시 서둘러] 떠나다; To go or move in a great hurry.

▫ **high-wire act**　　줄타기; 아슬아슬한 행동; Very risky act.

▫ **hillybilly**　　시골뜨기; Rural dweller.

- *himbo* 외모는 훌륭하지만, 무식하거나 천박한 남자; (허우대만 멀쩡한 젊은 남자); A stupid, attractive man. Male version of BIMBO.

  • If he weren't such a himbo, I'd consider him as boyfriend material.

- hinky 수상쩍은, 의심스러운; Unusual, weird

  • She has done like 900 girl-girl scenes in the last 11 years. I'm sure one or two of them were hinky.

- **hip** (최신 유행의 사상 · 스타일 따위에) 통달한, 정통한, 진보된. 세련된, 때를 벗은, 멋있는, 흥미 있는, 마음이 내키는; Having knowledge of what is stylish, fashionable, or cool.

  • I know you are all hip over Becca Blaze and you overpaid to get her. But her scene was lackluster.

- hired gun 살인청부업자; A person hired for their expertise.

  • They are hired guns and no amount of jingoism will change that.

- hit 마약 1회분, 마리화나 한 대; 술 한잔; (약물 따위에) 취하기, 황홀, 도취; A single unit of an illegal drug.

  • I've seen too many girls who would fuck a rancid dick for a hit and I never wanted to be that girl.

- **hit [press, push] the panic button** (뜻밖의 일에 겁을 먹고) 허둥지둥해 버리다; To feel fear and confusion.

- hit it 섹스하다; To have sex.

  • They met at the club and went back to her place to hit it.

- **hit it big** 성공하다, 잘 되어가다, 큰 이윤을 남기다; To make a large profit.

- **hit it off** (~와) 죽이 맞다; To get along well.

  • I thought you guys hit it off really well.

- hit it raw 콘돔을 착용하지 않고 섹스하다; To have sex without a condom.

  • Can I hit it raw?

- hit *someone* where it counts 아픈 곳을 때리다; To hit.

- **hit the ceiling** (몹시 화가 나서) 길길이 뛰다; To feel extreme anger.

- hit the hay 잠자리에 들다, 자다; To go to bed.

- **hit the jackpot** 대박을 터뜨리다; Have a stroke of luck; have sudden luck.

  • Many gamblers try to hit the jackpot in Las Vegas.

- **hit the road** 길을 나서다; To leave.

  • We need to hit the road by 5.

- hit the roof (몹시 화가 나서) 길길이 뛰다; To feel extreme anger.

- **hit the sack** 잠자리에 들다, 자다; To go to bed.

  • I'm tired, I'm going to hit the sack.

- hit the skids 내리막이 되다, 파멸[영락]하다; To suffer from failure.

- **hitch** 장애, 지체, 고장, 중단; Snag, trouble

  • I'm glad we brought off the plan without a hitch!

- ho bag 매춘부; Prostitute

  • I need to track down my ho-bag sister.

- hob-knob 교제하다, 어울리다; To mingle, usually with the upper class of society.

  • After the opera, we hobnobbed with the foreign heads-of-state.

□ hoe	창녀; A general insult, usually applied to females.

• She is such a hoe.

□ hoist	훔치다; To steal.
□ hoity-toity	거들먹거리는, 거만한; Someone getting uppity or snobby with a person.

• Don't get hoity-toity with me.

□ hokey	유난히 감상적인.; Corny

• Most set ups are hokey and contrived. This one was good. I mean, it wasn't new but the acting was a lot better than what I expected.

□ Holla!	안녕하세요; A greeting.
□ holler uncle	졌다고 말하다, 항복하다; To cry uncle.
□ *Holy fuck*	아이고, 저런, 빌어먹을; Expression of terror, awe, surprise, shock, etc., often at something seen for the first time or remembered immediately before using this term.
□ *Holy shit!*	아이고, 저런, 빌어먹을; Expression of terror, awe, surprise, shock, etc., often at something seen for the first time or remembered immediately before using this term.

• Holy shit, that car just exploded!

□ home run	섹스하다; In the "sexual contact as baseball achievement" metaphor, means sexual intercourse.

• Person 1: Did you get to 3rd base? Person 2: Actually, I hit a home run!

□ home run	성공; A success.

• I think we're going to hit a home run with this new album.

□ homie [homey]	고향 친구; 함께 뭉쳐 다니는 친구; A close friend.

176

□ **homo**　　　　　　　동성애자; A homosexual person.

• He knows what he'd like to do to "queers" and "homos".

□ honcho　　　　　　책임자; A leader.

• So I called to tell them what's what. All I get is the head honcho telling me I'm not the sort Dazzle will be working with anymore and that my contract didn't specify anything past what they paid me.

□ honker　　　　　　코; Nose

• She has a huge honker. I love it.

□ hooch　　　　　　(아주 독한) 술(특히 밀주); Liquor, especially home-made liquor (e.g. moonshine.)

• Pass the hooch.

□ *hoochie coochie*　　섹스. 섹스하다; Sex or sexual play.

□ **hood**　　　　　　불량배; 망나니; 깡패, 갱; 범죄자; A criminal or de-linquent. Perhaps shortened from "hoodlum."

• That guy is a hood.

□ hoodwink　　　　　속이다; To deceive by underhanded methods.

• The car salesman hoodwinked me into buying a lemon.

□ hoof it　　　　　　(빨리) 걸어가다; To walk fast.

• I saw'em comin' and hoofed it home.

□ hook　　　　　　훔치다; To steal.

□ hook up　　　　　성관계를 갖다; Sexual activity, though typically not coitus. Usually implies more than kissing or "making out." Making out+touching breasts would qualify as a "hook up."

• They hooked up last night after the party.

□ **hooked**   (~을) 대단히 즐기는, (~에) 빠져 있는; Addicted

• He's hooked on prescription painkillers.

□ **hooker**   창녀; A prostitute.

• Hookers look for customers near the big hotels.

□ **hooker**   여성의 비하(창녀 같은 년); A general insult.

• You stupid hooker!

□ ***hooter***   (여자의) 가슴; A breast. Usually used in the plural.

• Did you see the size of the hooters on her?

□ **hope in hell**   가능성(희망)이 전혀 없는; Having no chance at all.

□ **hopped up**   흥분한, 흥분하게 만드는, (자동차 등이) 마력을 높인, 마약을 사용한; On drugs.

• Sorry about that weird voice mail. I was hopped up on Nyquil when I left it.

□ **horesfeathers**   난센스, 허튼소리; Nonsense

• Oh man, you are talking complete horsefeathers.

□ **horked**   고장 난, 망가진; Broken

• I had to take my computer to the shop - it was horked.

□ ***horny***   성적으로 흥분한, 발정한; Sexually aroused.

• I am so horny I just need fucked. Can we do that? I want to feel your cock clear in my throat from this end this time.

□ ***horse's ass***   바보, 멍청이; Idiot; jackass

□ ***horseshit***   1. 실없는 소리, 거짓말, 허풍(경멸/혐오감 따위를 나타내어) 헛소리하지 마, 바보 같으니. 2. 허튼소리를 하다; Blatant nonsense, more likely stemming from ignorance than any intent to deceive.

178

• Don't you realize that's horseshit?

□ **hose** ~을 속이다, 속여 빼앗다; ~을 죽이다, 해치우다; To seriously injure or kill. To take advantage of.

• Let's hose these assholes!

□ **hose** 부수다, 망가트리다; To break, ruin, or destroy.

• Thanks for hosing my computer.

□ **hosed** 망가진; Broken.

• The computer is hosed.

□ **hot and bothered** (성적으로) 흥분한; Aggravated; sexually aroused.

□ **hot diggety** 이것 좋은데! 좋아!; Exclamation of excitement or agreement. Also hot diggerty and hot diggety dog.

• Speaker: Do you want to go to the party?
  Response: Hot Diggety!

□ *hot dog* 콘돔 없이 섹스하다; To have sex without a condom.

• I like to hot dog my chicks!

□ **Hot dog!** 좋아! 대단해!; Delighted agreement; exclamation of excitement.

□ **hot for** ~에 열중한; Attracted to.

□ **hot potato** 뜨거운 감자, 난감한 문제; Something no one wants to handle or accept responsibility for.

• The abortion issue in the USA is a political hot potato.

□ **hot seat** 곤경(에 빠져); Trouble

□ ***hot shit*** 대단한 것, 훌륭한 사람, 거물; 좋았어, 잘했군, 물론 이지; A person who is extremely attractive, "cool," talented, etc. Almost always used sarcastically, especially to refer to someone who "thinks they're hot shit." That is: someone who is has an extremely elevated self-image.

• That would-be Marilyn Monroe thinks she's hot shit.

□ hot spot 분쟁 지대; Area in trouble.

□ **hot stuff** 섹시한 사람; An attractive person.

• The kid is hot stuff!

□ hot to trot 섹스를 밝히는; Sexually eager.

• That girl is hot to trot.

□ hot water 곤경, 고생; Trouble

□ **hot-shot** (특정 직종이나 스포츠에서) 아주 잘 나가는 사람; Impressive, expert

• He's some hot-shot lawyer.

□ hottie 성적 매력이 있는 사람; An attractive person.

• I am definitely down with that chick, she's a hottie.

□ How's it hanging? 잘 지내?; A greeting, usually between men.

□ How's tricks? 안녕?; How are you?

□ hug the toilet 변기에 토하다; To be on one's knees vomiting into a toilet.

• He's huggin the toilet.

□ **Huh?** 어? 뭐?; I don't have a clue what you're getting at.

180

□ **hulking**	(흔히 불안감을 줄 정도로) 거대한; Extremely large, heavy, or slow-moving, and seemingly threatening in some way.
□ **humdrum**	단조로운, 따분한; Boring
□ **humongous**	거대한; Huge, enormous

• They got these humongous waves in Waimea.

□ *hump*	성교하다; To have sex with.

• It looked like he was humping her.

□ *hump one's fist* (males.)	자위하다; To masturbate. (Usually applied only to
□ **hung up on**	~에 열중한, 빠진; Addicted to.
□ **hunk**	(체격 좋고) 섹시한 남자; Attractive, well-built man.
□ **hunky-dory**	더할 나위 없이 좋은; Fine, wonderful
□ **hustle**	(흔히 불법적으로) 팔다; To deal drugs.

• I hustled till dawn.

□ **hustler** illegally.	사기꾼; A person who is always working; usually

• That guy is a hustler, he always balling.

□ **hype**	(마약 주사 따위를 맞은 것 같이) 흥분한, 기운이 솟은; Excited, energetic

• The whole school was hype over the Homecoming game.

□ **hype** praise it a lot.	(대대적으로 과장된) 광고를 하다; To advertise or

□ **hyped up**	흥분한; Overly excited.	
□ **hyper**	들뜬, 흥분한; Short for hyperactive.	

step. 09

I

□ **I could care less!** care at all.	전혀 관심 없어; I don't give a damn. I don't
□ **I couldn't care less!**	전혀 관심 없어; I don't give a damn.
□ **I don't buy it!** don't believe it(you).	난 받아들이지 않아. 나는 믿지 않아; I
□ *I don't give a crap* damn.	나는 전혀 상관 안 한다; I don't give a
□ *I don't give a damn* damn.	나는 전혀 상관 안 한다; I don't give a
□ *I don't give a flip* damn.	나는 전혀 상관 안 한다; I don't give a
□ *I don't give a fuck* damn.	나는 전혀 상관 안 한다; I don't give a
□ *I don't give a rat's ass* damn	나는 전혀 상관 안 한다; I don't give a
□ *I don't give a shit* damn.	나는 전혀 상관 안 한다; I don't give a
□ *I don't give a bull*	나는 상관 안 한다; I don't care at all.
□ **I don't have the foggiest** idea.	전혀 짚이는 데가 없다; I don't have any
□ **I don't know the beans about it**	전혀 알지 못한다; I don't know.
□ icky	(특히 끈적끈적하게) 기분 나쁜; Gross, unappealing

• Cooked carrots are icky.

□ iff and only if.	(수학에서) if and only if (필요충분조건을 나타냄); If

- Iff using variety of meat, place each in a separate bowl.

☐ **iffy** 불확실한; Having doubts.

- I'm not sure if I want to go; I'm a bit iffy about it.

☐ **iffy proposition** 불확실한 제안; Risky proposal.

☐ **I'll drink to that.** (상대에 동의하여) 그렇다, 동감이오, 찬성이다; I agree with you.

- A: My conclusion is that we need to respect each other for our accomplishments more.
  B: I'll drink to that.

☐ **in (deep) doo-doo** 곤경에 빠져; To be serious trouble.

☐ **in a bind** 곤경에 처한; To be in a bad situation; in trouble.

- Fuck! Killing this hobo put me in a bind.

☐ **in a flutter** 설레는; Agitated

☐ **in a funk** 침울한; Depressed

☐ **in a hole** 곤경에 처한; To be in trouble.

☐ **in a tizzy** 초조한; Distressed

☐ **in clover** 풍족한; To be in a pleasant situation; to be in ease and luxury; to be in prosperity.

- His bills were paid, his homework was done, and he was heading off on vacation: He was in clover!

☐ *in deep shit* 어려운 지경이 되어; In serious trouble.

- You are in deep shit when you come into work tomorrow.

- **in hock** 저당 잡혀; 빚을 져서; With no money left; be in debt.

- **in over[or above] *one's* head** 어쩔 수 없이; In a situation one can't cope with.

  - I can see she is a small-town kid in over her head. She wasn't raised on the mean streets of a middle-class San Diego suburb like I was. She needs a few friends and you guys are the best friends to have.

- **in *someone's* corner** ~의 편에 서서; In someone's side or support.

- **in the bag** (성공 · 당선 따위가) 확실하여; 보장되어; Guaranteed, made certain.

  - I knew that random hot chick would make sex w/ me··· I had it in the bag.

- **in the black** (경영이) 흑자로; Business term meaning a positive amount of money.

  - James is an amazing sales agent, so he helps keep the company in the black.

- **in the buff** 옷을 하나도 안 걸친, 알몸의; To be nude.

  - Strippers are in the buff.

- **in the can** (계약 따위가) 체결되어; Finished, completed

- **in the catbird seat** 유리한 입장에 있다; In a privileged position.

- **in the dumps** 낙담한; Depressed.

- **in the money** 주가가 액면가보다 높은 상태에 있는; (FINANCE) When a financial derivative has intrinsic value to the person who holds it.

  - Sweet! My call options are back in the money. Now I'd better exercise them.

- **in the red** 빚지고; 적자로; 적자 상태로; Business term meaning having a negative amount of money.

186

- James is horrible at selling things. If everyone were like him we'd be in the red in no time.

☐ **in whack** 정상(상태)에; In good working condition. The opposite of "out of whack"

- KJ: "Hey man, my car is all out of whack."
  GP: "Don't worry. I can get it in whack."

☐ **In your dreams!** 꿈 같은 소리! (가망 없는 꿈을 꾸고 있다는 뜻), 꿈 깨!; To express denial, to refuse a proposal. Same as "I don't even think about it" or "Fuck you, I won't do it!"

- Daniels: One day, I'll be mayor of this city!
  Smith: In your dreams! Who would vote for you?

☐ **intel** (군사) 정보; Intelligence

- What's the most recent intel on troop movements?

☐ **Is the Pope Catholic?** 뻔한 이야기를 묻지 마시오, 당연하지 않은가?; A rhetorical question in response to a question where the answer is an emphatic yes. This is the answer you give when somebody asks a stupid question when they already know the answer is yes. Or it's the emphatic way of answering yes to a question.

- A: Would you like to go to the beach?
  B: Is the Pope Catholic?

☐ **It sucks to be you** 그것참 안 되었네; I don't care; That's too bad.

☐ **It takes two to tango** 손바닥도 마주쳐야 소리가 나는 법 (어떤 일에 대해 양쪽이 다 책임이 있다는 뜻); Both people involved in a bad situation are to be blamed.

☐ **It won't wash!** 믿을 수가 없다; I don't believe it(you).

☐ **itchy** (몹시 ~하고 싶어 몸이) 근질거리다; Having strong desire to do something.

□ **item**　　　　　　　　매력 있는 사람; A person whose positive attributes make them a coveted rarity.

• That girl is quite an item. Good find, man.

□ **itty-bitty**　　　　　작은, 조그만; Small, tiny

• A: I love you, sweetheart. You have the most adorable itty-bitty titties I've ever seen.
B: Gee, thanks. And you have the most adorable itty-bitty weenie I've ever seen.

□ **I've had it!**　　　　더는 못 참아; I am losing my ability to cope! Cry of frustration.

step. 10

J

□ *jack* 섹시한 남성; Highly attractive and sexually intriguing individual.

• Oh my Fucking God. I would tap a Jack.

□ *jack around* ~을 만지작거리다. (일부러) ~의 시간을 허비하다; To mess or fool with. Also used in context of keeping company with.

• To jack around with electrical wires is risky.

□ *jack it* 자위하다; To masturbate.

• Were you jacking it in the bathroom?

□ *jack off* 자위하다; To masturbate; jerk off.

• "Wanna suck him for a while?" Shelly asked, her small fist jacking Adam to full hardness.
• Her tongue danced around the purple head as she jacked him off into her mouth as best she could.
• He likes to jack off every night.

□ jack up (특히 가격을) 대폭 인상하다; To increase sharply.

• Jack up the oil prices.

□ jackass 멍청이; A stupid or idiotic person.

• Stop being a jackass, Kayla!

□ jacked up 흥분한; High on some kind of upper, coke, speed, ecstasy, etc.

• This shit is fuckin great, man, it had me all jacked up last night.

□ **jail bait** 성관계 승낙 연령 이하의 아동(성관계를 하면 본인 동의 여부와 상관없이 강간죄가 성립됨); One who is too young to have sex with. As in if you do you will go to jail.

• Speaker: That chick is hot!
  Response: Yeah, but she's jail bait.

- The first time she modeled for Edward Weston, in March 1934, Charis Wilson knew she didn't look good. At 20 she was "a piece of jailbait", a mere child, especially with the stumpy plaits into which she sometimes twisted her hair.

□ **jammed**　　빽빽한, 몹시 붐비는; Full of people; "packed."

□ **jazzed up**　　다채로운, 요란한; To be really excited about something.

- Ryan got jazzed up the night before.

□ **Jedi**　　제다이(영화 Star Wars에 나오는 신비스러운 기사단(騎士團)의 기사; 우주의 평화와 정의를 지킨다). (또는 Jedi knight); The Jedi are a fictitious order of warrior monks who play an important role in the 'Star Wars' movie series by George Lucas. They were responsible for the maintenance of peace and order in the Galactic Republic, and were skilled in various mental disciplines from domination to psychokinesis.

- The way you talked that cop out of a speeding ticket, man, that was Jedi.

□ **Jeepers!**　　맙소사, 어머나(놀람? 충격을 나타내는 소리); An expression of mild surprise or shock from '60s-'70s. Popularized by cartoon character Velma of the '70s children's show Scooby-Doo. Rarely used today, except in an ironic fashion.

- Jeepers, that's a large box of ants!

□ **Jeez**　　에이, 이크(화/놀람 등을 나타내는 소리); A general exclamation. From "Jesus"

- Jeez, that was a terrible meal!

□ **jellyfish**　　나약하고 결단성이 없는 사람; Indecisive and/or weak.

□ **jerk**　　순진한 사람, 세상 물정에 어두운 사람, 멍청이, 바보; A mean person. Idiot

- If you would meet Adam on the street or if you two boys wouldn't have acted like jerks, you would know that Adam is the sweetest, gentlest man in the world.

□ **jerk (oneself) off**   자위 행위를 하다; 빈둥거리다; 실수하
다; To masturbate; to engage in an activity which is inherently wasteful
(particularly when one is at work) and for which there isn't any tangible
compensation or reward, other than one's own mental stimulation.

> • He had jerked off in the shower often enough to know semen reacted
>   badly to water.

□ *jerk ass*   바보. 멍청이; Idiot; moron

> • Bill Clinton is a jerk-ass.

□ *jerk it*   자위 행위를 하다; To masturbate. (Usually applied
only to males.)

> • He's jerking it in our dorm room.

□ **jerk off**   자위 행위를 하다; To masturbate. Usually used in
reference to male masturbation.

> • Hey, guys, the management needs everybody to get out, because they
>   caught a guy jerking off in here and they're going to send in a crew to
>   wipe down the loads.

□ *jerk off*   시간을 헛되이 보내다; To engage in an activity
which is inherently wasteful (particularly when one is at work) and for
which there isn't any tangible compensation or reward, other than one's
own mental stimulation.

> • Five minutes before my shift ended I was jerking off playing solitaire on
>   my computer.

□ jerk *somebody's* chain   못살게 굴다; To deceive a person,
usually in a kidding manner.

□ jerk(-off)   바보. 멍청이; Fool; idiot

□ jerky   바보스러운, 멍청한; Foolish; idiotic

□ **jerry rig**   임시방편으로 처치하다; To repair something quickly
without doing it properly. (Usually involves some duct tape or panty hose).

192

• I jerry rigged the water pump, it should last the night.

□ **Jesus!**　　　제기랄, 우라질, 세상에, 이럴 수가! (놀람 · 실망 · 불신 · 공포 · 강조 등의 소리); Exclamation used by some people to express surprise, shock, or annoyance

• Jesus, that was a good meal!
• Jesus, what happened to my car!

□ jiggy　　　멋진, 근사한; Attractive; sexy

• Did you see the new guy? He's so jiggy!

□ *jill off*　　　(주로 여성이) 자위하다; To masturbate. Applied only to female masturbation. Variant of "jack of."

• I am so horny. I need to jill off.

□ jillion　　　막대한 수(의)(zillion); An extremely large number or amount.

□ jillionaire　　　엄청난 부자; An extremely wealthy person.

• Stop being a frickin' jillionaire!

□ *jism*　　　(남자의) 정액; Semen

• She watched as he spewed his jism.

□ jitters　　　초조함(특히 중요하거나 어려운 일을 앞두고 느끼는 감정); A state of nervousness.

□ jittery　　　초조한, 조마조마한; Nervy, jumpy, on edge.

□ *jizm*　　　사정하다; To ejaculate.

• He jizmed all over the place.

□ *jizm*　　　정액; Semen

• She got jizm all over her hand.

□ *jizz* 정액; 이름 모를 끈적끈적한 것; Semen; A slimy substance, especially when unidentified.

• Get that jizz off me!

□ *jizz* 사정하다; To ejaculate.

• He jizzed all over.

□ jock (고교/대학의) 힘만 센 운동선수; Someone who is good at sports. Usually implies that they're not good at academics.

• His biggest worry in high school was staying out of the way of the jocks – until he got bigger than they were.

□ Johnny-come-lately (특히 지나치게 자신만만한) 신참; A newcomer.

• She might take offense if some Johnny-come-lately thinks he can do a better job.

□ *joint* 마리화나 담배; Marijuana cigarette, usually rolled by hand.

• Pass the joint over here.

□ *joystick* 남성의 성기; Penis

• Why don't you come play with my joy stick?

□ *jug* 유방; Breast

• Hey, dude, you see that girl's jugs?

□ jughead 바보; A fool.

□ juiced 술에 취한, 마약에 취한, 흥분한; Drunk, excited

• I'm all juiced.

□ jump all over *somebody* 호되게 꾸짖다; To reprimand angrily.

□ **jump down _somebody's_ throat**　　갑자기 공격하다; To attack unexpectedly.

□ **junk in the trunk**　　엉덩이가 아주 큰 여자; A woman with a large rear
end.

• That chick's got a lot of junk in the trunk.

□ **junkie**　　열성 팬; A tremendous enjoyer of.

• I'm a college football junkie.

□ **junkie**　　마약 중독자; A drug addict.

• His younger brother is a smack junkie.

step. 11

K

□ kapow	때리다, 치다; To hit.	
□ kaput/kaputt	고장 난, 망가진; Broken, not functioning.	
□ karena	순수하고 귀여운 여자애; A pretty girl.	

• She is such a karena!

□ **keep a tab on**	주시하다; Watch with vigilance.
□ **keep on trucking**	버티다. 끈기를 갖고 하다; To persist.

• Really hope to see ya, all right. Love ya. Just – no, that – miss ya. You know what? You just keep on truckin'.

□ keep *one's* eyes peeled	계속 경계하고 있다; To stay visually alert.
□ keep *one's* pants/shirt on	침착하다, 냉정함을 유지하다; To not overreact.

• Keep your pants on. It was only a minor accident.

□ keep tabs on tor continuously.	주시하다, 지켜보다; Watch with vigilance; to monitor continuously.
□ **kegger**	맥주 파티; A party at which draft beer is provided.

• It has almost become a tradition for college students to attend "keggers" every weekend.

□ **kervoka**	매력적인; Attractive
□ **keyed up**	(중요한 행사를 앞두고) 긴장한; Very excited or nervous before an important or dangerous event.
□ kibbitz	(노름을 구경하며) 참견하다. 훈수 두다; Unwanted advice. When a person is talking too much and wouldn't want to hear no more.

• I don't wanna hear no more kibitz.

□ kibitzer	(노름을 구경하며) 참견, 훈수; Unwanted advice. When a person is talking too much and wouldn't want to hear no more.

□ **kick** (강한) 쾌감, 스릴; Something thrilling; Something enjoyable.

> • That was a kick!

□ ***kick (one's) ass*** 누군가를 혼 내주다; To be victorious.

> • Our football team kicked their ass this weekend!

□ **kick back** 긴장을 풀다[쉬다]; To recline, as in a reclining chair.

> • Kick back and put your feet up.

□ **kick in** (할당된) 돈을 내다, 헌금하다; To contribute.

> • Can you kick in a few dollars for dinner?
> • I have about $2,000 and my scholarship kicks in June 1st.

□ **kick in** 효과가 나타나기 시작하다; To begin taking effect.

> • I think that Advil is finally starting to kick in.

□ **kick it up a notch** 한 단계 높이다; To increase the intensity of something.

□ **kick off** 죽다; To die.

> • He kicked off last night.

□ ***kick one's ass*** 벌을 주다; 혼내 주다; To beat someone in a competition, fight, or other situation.

> • "Fuck", Adam said. "I honestly thought I was going to have to kick their asses. Your Dad is a real piece of work."
> • You will kick his ass with your improved serve.

□ ***kick somebody's ass/butt*** 이기다. 혼을 내주다; To defeat.

□ **kick *someone* where it counts** 아픈 곳을 차다; To hit where it most hurts.

□ **kick the bucket** 죽다; To die.

> • She kicked the bucket.

□ *kick the crap out of* <u>somebody/something</u> 이기다. 혼을 내주다; To beat somebody up.

□ kick the tires　　品質을 살펴보다, 검사하다; To examine, to check out before making a purchase.

□ *kickass*　　아주 좋은, 굉장한; Very good, excellent; cool; awesome

• The Canadian Olympic Hockey team is kickass!

□ kick-back　　킥백, 리베이트, 뇌물; Money paid generally to an official for covertly assisting an organization, individual, or initiative.

• The congressman received a ten-percent kick back for supporting the legislation that would give the mining company exclusive rights to the region.

□ kicker　　(때로 the~) (뜻밖의) 문제점, 불리한 점[상황]; 의외의 결말[전개]; (계약서 따위의) 부당 조항 부분; A particularly interesting point. Usually prefixed with "the."

• And, for a kicker, I can tell them you've slept with me, a fourteen years old, and you'll get statutory rape on top of it.

□ kicking back　　긴장을 푸는; Relaxed

□ kick-off　　(활동의) 시작, 개시; The beginning.

• kick-off meeting

□ kiddie　　어린애; Young person.

□ kill　　대성공을 거두다; To generally be high performing or do a task well.

• Damn, I killed that test.
• You guys killed last night.

□ killing　　대성공; An impressive success. To generally be high performing or do a task well.

□ kingfish　　우두머리; A leader of a group.

200

□ kingpin   우두머리; A leader of a group or drug lord.

> • The Kingpin wouldn't let us down in New York City at night time.

□ KISS   좀 작작해라, 이 바보야; Keep It Simple, Stupid.

> • My motto is KISS.

□ KISS (Principle)   상품 및 광고는 가능한 한 단순해야 한다는 원칙; "Keep It Simple, Stupid". A maxim often invoked when discussing design to fend off feature creep and control development complexity.

> • Alan Gardner designs on the Kiss principle – Keep it simple, stupid – and has produced perhaps the most striking small garden this year.

□ *kiss ass*   아첨하다, 아첨하는 사람; Anyone attempting to gain favor from a superior or supervisory person by blatantly false flattery or sycophantic behavior. Derived from the term "kissing ass" which refers to the act of, as opposed to the perpetrator of said actions.

> • You are such a kiss-ass, freak.

□ kiss goodbye   ~와 작별을 하다('무엇을 잃게 되거나 하지 못하게 될 것임을 받아들인다'는 뜻); To give up hope of getting something that you want very much.

□ *kiss my ass*   엿 먹어라! 나가 죽어라! 꺼져 버려!; A blunt refusal; a general angry retort.

> • He can kiss my ass!
> • Yeah? Well, you can kiss my ass.

□ kiss of death   죽음의 키스; (언뜻 도움이 될 듯하나) 종국에 파멸을 가져오는 것; Something specific that brings bad luck.

> • Her praise of my idea is the kiss of death.

□ kiss off   ~을 거절하다, 무시하다, 해고하다, 꺼지다; To say to go away. To dismiss.

> • The starlet told the paparazzi to kiss off.

- *kiss one's ass* 아첨하다; Seek favor through flattery; to be a sycophant or toady.

  • He's always kissing his boss's ass.

- ***kiss one's ass*** 엿 먹어라! 나가 죽어라! 꺼져 버려!; A blunt refusal; a general angry retort.

- kludge 조잡한 물건, 어설픈 대책; A poorly constructed (but valid) solution to a problem or task. An improvised device, usually crudely constructed.

- klutz 어설픈 사람, 얼뜨기; An uncoordinated person.

  • I dropped my tray and broke five plates. I am such a klutz!

- **knock** [여성을] 범하다, 임신시키다; To impregnate.

  • You got knocked? Who ya baby daddy?

- knock (*one's*) socks off ~에게 큰 영향을 미치다, 타격을 주다; To be very powerful or impressive(literally so much so that the recipient's socks are knocked off).

  • Wait 'til you hear this idea. It'll knock your socks off!

- knock heads together 강경한 수단으로 싸움을 말리다; To force people to stop arguing and behave in a sensible way.

- **Knock it off!** 그만해! 집어치워! 안돼!; Stop (whatever you're doing)

  • Devil: (Imitating Sam's girlfriend.) A quickie, right, Sam?
    Sam: Knock it off!

- knock off 죽이다; To kill.

- **knock off** (유명 메이커 의류 등의) 모조품, 가짜; A forgery.

  • Deangelo: Is that a Chinatown knock-off?
    Jim: That's "Toys 'r' Us" I think.
    Deangelo: No, that's definitely a knock-off.

202

- knock *oneself* out　전력을 다하다; 녹초가 되다; To exert effort.

- knock *somebody* out　때려눕혀 정신을 잃게 하다; To knock unconscious.

- knock *somebody*'s lights out　때려눕혀 정신을 잃게 하다; To knock unconscious.

- ***knock the crap out*** *somebody/something*　완전히 때려눕히다; To beat somebody up.

- ***knock the shit out*** *somebody/something*　때려눕혀 정신을 잃게 하다; To beat somebody up.

- knock the socks off *somebody*　완전히 패배시키다; To defeat completely.

- **knocked up**　임신한; Pregnant

  - She's knocked up.

- knockers　유방; Breasts

  - Check out the knockers on that chick!
  - "So I'm just supposed to ask her how big her bust is and not give her an idea of why?" Adam wondered. "Hey, Trinity, I was wondering, just how big are your knockers?"

- knockout　성공; Success

- **knockout**　뿅 가게 매력적인 사람; Rare beauty; An attractive person.

  - She is such a knock-out.

- know *something* backwards (and forwards)　속속들이 알다; To know perfectly.

- know *something* inside out　속속들이 알다; To know perfectly.

- know *something* like the back of *one's* hand　속속들이 알다; To know intimately.

□ **know the score**   사정을 알다; 사실을 알고 있다; 사정을 이해하고 있
다; To have a grasp of an entire situation with all its ramifications.

□ **know-it-all**   (뭐든 다) 아는 체하는 사람, 똑똑한 체하는 사람; A
pompous person who acts like they know everything.

□ **knuckle down**   (~을) 열심히 하기 시작하다; To start a task.

□ **knuckle under**   항복하다. 압력에 굴복하다; To give in to pressure.

• He figured there was absolutely no way he was getting out of this one
without getting whacked around. Even so, he had absolutely no intention
of knuckling under to this maggot.

□ **knucklehead**   얼간이, 멍청이; An unintelligent person.

• What are you doing, ya knucklehead?

□ ***kooch***   (여성의) 음부; Vagina

• Your kooch is filthy.

□ **kooky**   괴짜의, 멍청한; 미친; Strange, out of the ordinary; weird

• That's a kooky haircut.

□ **kopecks**   러시아의 화폐 단위, 약간의 돈; A monetary unit of
Russia and Belarus worth one hundredth of a Rubl; money.

□ **kosher**   1. 유대교 율법에 따라 만든 2. 정직한; 합법적인;
Very good, excellent; COOL; fine; okay

• Is everything kosher?

□ **kudos**   명성, 영예, 위신; 칭찬; Used as a congratulation or
to mean good job.

• Kudos to you on your winning the spelling bee.

□ **kvetch**   투덜거리다, 푸념하다; A person who complains constantly.

L

□ **la la land**　　　환상의 세계; 꿈의 나라; A metaphorical place that one goes to when one isn't paying attention.

　　• He's off in la la land again.

□ *labia majora*　　　대음순; The two outer rounded folds of adipose tissue that lie on either side of the opening of the vagina.

　　• Karlie was still looking at the lips of Shelly's cunt, seemingly entranced by how prominent the labia majora was.

□ **la-di-da**　　　고상한 체하는, 가식적인; 너 잘났다! 얼싸구(잘난 체하는 사람을 빈정대며 하는 말); Arrogant and conceited; in a pretentiously 'posh' way.

□ *lady boner*　　　여성의 성적 흥분 상태; Sexual arousal in women. A figurative erection.

　　• Jake has such a beautiful smile that I get a lady boner just by thinking about it!

□ **laid back**　　　느긋한, 태평스러운; Relaxed, calm, not anxious.

　　• My brother is so laid back.

□ **lambast**　　　~을 세게 치다, 매질하다; ~을 엄하게 꾸짖다, 호되게 비난하다; To utterly destroy everything.

　　• I really need to lambast someone.

□ **lamebrain**　　　바보, 멍청이, 얼간이; A total idiot.

　　• Scott Whitson is a lamebrain.

□ **lamer**　　　시대에 뒤처진 사람. 아무것도 모르는 사람; A geek or social loser. Also used as Lame-ass.

　　• He is such a lamer.

□ **lap *something* up**　　　~을 덥석[선뜻] 받아들이다; To believe or accept eagerly and uncritically.

□ **latch on to**　　　~을 이해하다; To understand.

□ **later**   잘 가!(젊은 사람들끼리 헤어질 때 하는 인사); Short
for see you later.

> • Ok, have a good time. Later.

□ **Later, gator!**   안녕(Good-bye), 그럼 또 봐; 'See you later, alligator!'의 축약형; See you later.

> • Later, gator.

□ **Laughing my ass off!**   배꼽을 잡고 웃고 있는 중!; Text message used to
indicate great amusement, usually exaggerated, at something.

□ *lay*   (섹스 상대로서의) 여자; 성행위; A sexual partner.
Almost always used with an adjective.

> • She's a great lay.

□ **lay it on thick**   심하게 과장하다; To exaggerate, overstate, especially said of flattery an attempt to coax.

> • Man, he sure did lay it on thick when he tried to get his girlfriend to
> come home from the party early.

□ **Lay off!**   (명령형으로 쓰여) (~을) 그만둬[해]; Stop (whatever
you're doing). Leave alone, stop being mean to.

> • Lay off me, I'm a good bloke.

□ **lay *somebody* flat**   때려눕히다; To knock somebody down.

□ **lay *someone* in the aisles**   배꼽이 빠질 정도로 웃기다; To make
people laugh uncontrollably.

□ **lazy dog**   게으른 사람; A lazy person.

> • Get out of bed, ya lazy dog!

□ *lazy piece of crap*   하등 쓸모없는 사람; A person judged to be worthless.

> • Wow! He is such a lazy piece of crap!

□ **lazy-bones**   게으른 사람; A lazy person.

□ **Leave off!**   그만해[집어치워]!; Stop (whatever you're doing)

• None of your jokes! Leave off joking!

□ **leave *somebody* holding the bay**   어려운 문제나 상황을 다른 사람에게 떠넘기다; To leave somebody else to solve or deal with a difficult situation.

□ **leave *somebody* in a lurch**   어려운 문제나 상황을 다른 사람에게 떠넘기다; To leave somebody else to solve or deal with a difficult situation.

□ **left-winger**   좌익 성향의 사람; A person who espouses left-wing political views.

□ **leg it**   달리다; 달아나다; To run away.

• Leg it - it's the police!

□ **lemon**   (제대로 되지 않아) 쓸모없는 것, 불량품(주로 자동차); A motor vehicle with many mechanical problems.

• That used car I bought last week is a total lemon.

□ **let bygones be bygones**   지난 일은 잊어버리기로 하다; To decide to forget about disagreements that happened in the past.

• Okay, Sally, let bygones be bygones. Let's forgive and forget.

□ **let her rip**   (배·차·기계 따위를) 최고 속도로 몰다; To set something in top speed.

□ **let it ride**   (간섭 말고) 되는 대로 내버려 둬라; To let it as it goes.

□ **let loose on/at**   공격하다; To attack.

□ **let one**   방귀 뀌다; To expel flatulence; to fart.

• Hey, dude, didja let one just a moment ago? Man, I could smell your cheezer a mile away!

☐ **let the dogs out**   방귀 뀌다; To flatulate.

• Who let the dogs out?

☐ *Lewinski*   구강성교; To suck one's penis. (derived from
Monica Lewinski)

• Bro. I got the best Lewinski last night!

☐ **lez**   동성애를 하는 여자(lesbian); Short for lesbian.

• Kate loves Laura, she's a lez.

☐ **lick**   (경기 · 전쟁에서) ~을 무찌르다, 이기다; 극복하다;
To beat someone up.

• I'll give you a lickin', after school!

☐ **lick**   조금, 소량; A small amount.

• I don't speak a lick of Russian.

☐ *lick (one's) ass*   남에게 굴복하다; 아부[아첨]하다; To seek favor
through flattery; to be a sycophant or toady.

☐ **lick at**   시도하다; To have a go at.

☐ **lickety-split**   급히 서둘러[서두르는]; 재빨리[빠른], 전속력으로;
Very quickly.

• I got out of that strip club lickety-split when I realized the dancer was
actually a man.

☐ **lift**   ~을 훔치다; To steal.

• I was on the tube and lifted two wallets while exiting.
• She lifted a CD from the store.

☐ **lift doesn't go to the top floor**   약간 정신이 덜떨어지다; Stupid; Retarded

- lights are on, but nobody's home 약간 정신이 덜떨어지다; Stupid; Retarded

- *like a dog with two dicks* 행복한; Happy, as a dog would be if it found it had an extra penis.

  • He was like a dog with two dicks.

- like a doormat 불쌍한, 천대(학대)를 받는; Poorly treated.

  • Why do you let her treat you like a doormat?

- *like a pig in shit* 아주 행복한; Extremely happy.

- *like ass pie* 역겨운; Disgusting

- like hell 악착같이, 맹렬히, 필사적으로; 결코 …이 아닌; Very much; to a great extent.

  • A wisdom tooth was cutting through and it hurt like hell.

- **Like hell!** 말도 안 된다('거절'을 나타냄); 퍽도 그렇겠다(무엇이 사실이 아님을 나타냄); I don't believe it(you).

  • Like hell, you're missing your sister's wedding.

- **like nobody's business** 굉장히 많이[빨리/잘 등]; A phrase that is said to show emphasis to a statement; an extreme amount.

  • That ho can shake her booty like nobody's business.
  • She gets busy like nobody's business.

- *like pigs in clover[or shit]* 매우 운이 좋은 것 같아서, 대만족하여, 아주 기뻐서; Very happy, very lucky.

  • Once you get to start doing things the right way, you'll love this. If we set it up to where you are doing two or three features a year and working with people you like and respect, you'll be like a pig in shit.

- like watching paint dry 하도 지루해서 페인트가 마르기를 기다리는 것 같다; Extremely boring.

210

- This class is like watching paint dry.

□ **lily liver**   겁쟁이; Coward

□ **lily-livered**   겁이 많은; Cowardly

□ **line *one*'s pockets**   부정한 방법으로 자기 주머니를 채우다; To accept a bribe or other illicit funds.

□ **liquidate**   [사람 · 물건을] 치우다, 없애다, 죽이다; 제거하다; To kill another human being.

- After the protection money was not delivered, Capone ordered Frank Nitti to liquidate the malefactor.

□ **live it up**   (보통 돈을 펑펑 쓰면서) 신나게 살다; Enjoy oneself; to enjoy yourself completely without worrying about anything.

- "They're living it up at the Hotel California." – The Eagles
- I decided to live it up for a while – at least until the money ran out.

□ **live wire**   활동가, 정력가; A lively, energetic person; a person who often becomes excited and aggressive over trivial things.

- Watch what you say, because he's a live wire, he gets so mad over the tiniest things, especially if you tease him about his extensive shoe collection. But if you talk about something he likes, he'll become really excited and happy!

□ **living daylights out of**   아주, 엄청난; To a great extent.

□ **living it up**   (보통 돈을 펑펑 쓰면서) 신나게 사는; 신나게 시간을 보내는; Enjoying life to the fullest.

- I was living it up at the club last night.

□ **LMAO**   배꼽 빠지게 웃다; Laughing my ass off.

□ **LMFAO**   배꼽 빠지게 웃다; Laughing my fucking ass off.

- Someone told me Michelle deserved to win Pop Idol, and I was LMFAO.

□ *load*   사정한 정액; A unit of semen; The output of one male's ejaculation.

> • Hey, guys, the management needs everybody to get out, because they caught a guy jerking off in here and they're going to send in a crew to wipe down the loads.

□ *load a fat one*   마리화나 파이프에 넘치도록 마리화나를 넣다; To load a marijuana smoking device to overflowing.

> • Hey Chris, let's load a fat one!

□ *load of shit*   허접쓰레기 같은 거짓말; Bullshit

> • 10 inches? You're joking. That's nothing but a load of shit.

□ **loaded**   아주 돈이 많은; Really rich; loaded with money

> • She's loaded… you ever see that pimped-out Ferrari she drives around in?

□ *loaded*   가슴이 큰; Large breasted.

> • Woah, that girl's loaded!

□ loaf   빈둥거리다, 놀며 지내다; Taking so much time, procrastinating or being lazy.

> • Man, you're loafing.

□ loaf   피곤하다, 휴식이 필요하다; To be tired or to rest.

> • I am way too loafed to do anything. Must loaf.

□ loaf about   게으름 피우다; To be lazy.

□ loaf around   게으름 피우다; To be lazy.

□ loafer   게으른 사람; Lazy person.

□ **lock up**   수감하다; To incarcerate; imprison.

□ **loco**   미친 사람; Someone who is crazy. From the Spanish "loco" meaning "crazy".

- What's up, loco?

□ **loo**   화장실; The restroom.

- She's gone to the loo.

□ **loony**   미친; Crazy

□ **loony bin**   정신 병원; A mental institute.

- The naughty hacker is tracked down and locked in the loony bin.

□ **loot**   약탈하다; 훔치다; 횡령하다; To rob.

- We looted the bank.

□ **lose (*one's*) religion**   욱하고 화가 나다; To lose one's temper.

- I almost lost my religion.

□ **lose it**   화가 나다; To lose one's temper, lose one's control.

□ **lose *one's* cool**   화가 나다; To lose one's temper, lose one's control.

□ **lose *one's* head**   화가 나다; To lose one's temper, lose one's control.

□ **lose *one's* head for somebody**   ~에 매력을 느끼다. 빠지다; To be attracted.

□ **lose *one's* head over** ~에 매력을 느끼다. 빠지다; To be attracted.

□ **lose *one's* lunch**   토하다; To vomit.

□ **lose *one's* marbles**   미치다; To go insane.

□ **lose *one's* nerve**   기가 죽다, 겁먹다; To become afraid.

□ **lose _one's_ shit**   미치다; To go insane.

□ loser   실패작, 불량품; A worthless person.

- Man, Cass is such a loser.

□ loudmouth   떠버리; 입이 건 사람; A person who talks a lot, especially in an unpleasant, offensive, or stupid way.

□ louie   좌회전; Left-hand turn. One typically "does", "makes", or "hangs" a louie. See also reggie.

- Hang a louie at the next light.

□ louse up   ~을 엉망으로 만들다[잡치다]; To mess something up.

□ **lousy**   몹시 더러운, 불결한; 천한, 비열한; 불유쾌한; 비참한; Awful; contemptible

- They are lousy tippers and hell to wait on.

□ lousy with   ~가 지천으로 널린, 많이 있는; So many with, so much with.

□ love handle   배의 군살. 허리의 군살; Fat on one's sides.

- I grabbed her love handles and brought her in for a kiss.

□ *love muscle*   남성의 성기; Penis

- My old lady and I do it so infrequently, my love muscle is beginning to atrophy.

□ *love shaft*   남성의 성기; Penis

□ *love stick*   남성의 성기; Penis

□ lowdown   비밀; 실정, 진상; Information about someone or something.

214

L

- LSD 엘에스디(강력한 환각제); Lysergic acid diethylamide.

- lubricated 술에 취한; Under the influence of alcohol.

  • Dancing increased once the wedding party was sufficiently lubricated.

- lug 느림보, 얼간이; An uncoordinated individual.

- lummox 재치 없고 둔한 녀석, 굼벵이, 멍청이(lump); A clumsy person.

- *lunchmeat* (여자의) 질; The vagina.

\#
A
B
C
D
E
F
G
H
I
J
K
L
M
N
O
P
Q
R
S
T
U
V
W
X
Y
Z

step. 13

M

- **mack**   뚱쟁이, 유객꾼, 매춘 알선자, 여자에게 말을 걸며 다가가다[구애하다][on]; One who is good with the opposite sex, usually a male.

• Jeff is such a mack. He gets all the girls.

- **mackable**   매력적인; Hot, attractive

• That girl is so mackable.

- **mad about**   ~에 미치다; Attracted to.

- **madder than hell**   화가 많이 난; Extremely angry.

- **maggot**   비열한 인간; Repulsive person.

• You were so maggot last night, you fucked the homeless guy.

- **magic word**   "Please"라고 붙이는 것을 빗대어 부르는 말; "Please."

• Child: Can I have a snack?   Parent: What's the magic word?

- **main squeeze**   (정해진) 걸프렌드; One's boyfriend, girlfriend or spouse.

• I spent Friday night with my main squeeze after seeing that chick I sometimes mess around with in the afternoon.

- **make a big deal**   유난을 떨다; Exaggerate the importance of.

- **make a big production**   유난을 떨다; Exaggerate the importance of.

- **make a break for it**   탈주를 시도하다; To try to escape.

- **make a bundle**   떼돈 벌다; To earn a great deal of money.

- **make a fast buck**   돈을 손쉽게[금방금방] 벌다; To enjoy a quick financial success.

- **make a federal case**   어떤 일을 마치 연방(대)법원에서 재판해야 할 정도로 중요한 것처럼 취급하는 것; Exaggerate the importance of.

218

• I think it's totally wrong to make a federal case against this.

□ **make a full-court press**   전방 압박을 하다, 전력을 다하다; To exert best effort.

□ **make a go of it**   성공시키다; 잘 해나가다; ~을 잘하다; To succeed.

□ **make a killing**   갑자기 큰돈을 벌다[크게 한몫 잡다]; To make a lot of money.

□ **make a muck of**   ~을 더럽히다, 망쳐 놓다; To make a mistake.

□ **make a pig's ear of**   ~을 엉망으로 하다[만들다]; To make a mistake.

□ **make a teddy bear**   대변을 보다; To shit.

• I gotta make a teddy bear.

□ **make it big**   크게 성공하다; To make a large profit.

□ **make it snappy**   (남에게 하는 말로) 빨리해; Hurry up.

• Could I get a refill on this Coke? And make it snappy.

□ **make mincemeat of**   (싸움·언쟁·시합 등에서) ~를 묵사발을 만들다; Defeat somebody completely in a fight, argument, etc.; completely destroy somebody's argument, theory, etc.

□ **make *one* sick**   징그럽게 만들다, 지긋지긋하다; To cause disgust.

□ **make *oneself* scarce**   빠르게 떠나다; To leave quickly.

□ **make out**   (~를[와]) 애무하다. 키스하다; To "French kiss" (i.e. kiss with tongue contact) for a period of time.

• I can't believe my dad. First he's saying that I need to respect the sanctity of marriage, and then he's making out with her on the balcony.

□ **make out like a bandit**   큰 이윤을 남기다; To make a large profit.

□ **make short work of** ~을 재빨리 이기다[해치우다]; To do or finish something very quickly; to defeat somebody very easily.

□ **make the grade** 필요한 수준에 이르다; 성공하다; To reach a high enough standard in an exam, a job, etc.

□ *man in the boat* 클리토리스; Clitoris

□ *man seed* 정액; Semen

□ **man up** 책임감 있게 행동하거나 '남성처럼 행동'할 것을 권고하는 말; The action of getting prepared to fight like a man.

• I told him he'd better Man Up if he wants to fight with me.

□ **mark** (비웃음 따위의) 표적[대상](이 되는 사람), 봉; An easy target or victim.

• You're such a mark.

□ **marshmallow** 겁쟁이; Coward

□ *Mary Jane* 마리화나; Marijuana

• Let's go smoke some Mary Jane.

□ **maul** (사람을 공격하여 살을 찢는) 상처를 입히다; To strike heavily.

□ **maven** 전문가; An expert.

□ **maxi pad** 생리대; A sanitary napkin, sanitary towel, sanitary pad, menstrual pad, maxi pad, or pad is an absorbent item worn by a woman while she is menstruating, recovering from vaginal surgery, for lochia (post birth bleeding), abortion, or any other situation where it is necessary to absorb a flow of blood from a woman's vagina.

□ **May the Force be with you!** 당신 곁에 포스가 함께 하기를; 'Star Wars Episode IV: A New Hope)'(1977)에서 Death Star battle station 직전

에 Hans Solo 역의 Harrison Ford가 Luke Skywalker와 나누는 작별의 인사말; Used to wish someone luck with a difficult endeavor.

- **measly**   쥐꼬리만 한; Unimpressive; small in number.

- **meat and potatoes**   핵심, 요체; The essence.

- **meatball**   얼뜨기; Clumsy person.

- **meathead**   바보, 얼뜨기; A muscular, unintelligent person.

- **megabucks**   엄청난 돈; A large amount of money.

  • He's making megabucks at his new job.

- **mellow out** very little.   여유롭게 지내다[유유자적하다]; To relax and do very little.

- **meltdown** system.   원자로의 용융, 심각한 위기; A serious failure in a system.

- *member*   음경; Penis

  • Adam felt a hand on his rampant member.
  • She stroked his thick pulsating member.

- **mess around** time.   1. 빈둥대다 2. 느긋하게 즐기다; To delay. To waste time.

  • Quit messing around and come down stairs. We need to leave soon.

- **mess around**   (특히 그래선 안 될 상대와) 성관계를 갖다; To engage in sexual activity; fool around.

  • We were messing around in his car when a security guard knocked on the window.

- **mess around with _something_**   ~을 (함부로) 만지작거리다[손대다]; ~를 가지고 놀며[수리하며/만지작거리며] 시간을 보내다; To not take a task seriously.

• Those mobsters don't mess around, so don't try to make any jokes.

□ **mess up**   (~을) 엉망으로 만들다[다 망치다]; To severely in-jure.

• If you cancel now, you'll mess up all my arrangements.

□ **mess with**   ~에 쓸데없이 참견하다, 간섭하다; To annoy.

• Why are you messing with him?

□ **messed**   고장 난, 망가진; Something as broken down.

• You should see Nate's old car, it's messed.

□ **messed up**   지저분한, 더러운, 고장 난; Damaged or ruined.

• He looked really out of it with his face bright red and his hair all messed up.

□ **meter maid**   주차 위반 단속 여자 경관; A city worker who gives tickets to illegally parked cars.

• I ran into the 7/11 for 10 minutes and that damn meter maid ticketed me!

□ *meth*   필로폰(methamphetamine); Methamphetamine hydrochloride. An extremely addictive drug.

• A new way to produce methamphetamine, unseen here a year ago, is becoming the preferred way for users to get a quick high and is fueling an increase in meth-related police activity after several years of decline.

□ *Mickey Mouse*   중요하지 않은, 작은; Unimportant; small

□ **middle of nowhere** 먼 시골, 복잡하지 않은 촌 동네; A remote area; backwoods; a city or town regarded as dull or unsophisticated.

□ *MIF*   보통 나이에 비해 젊어 보이거나 매력적인 아줌마; Acronym for "mom I'd fuck" - that is, an attractive older woman. Possibly from "MILF"

222

□ ***MILF***   보통 나이에 비해 젊어 보이거나 매력적인 아줌마; Acronym for "mom I'd like to fuck" or "mother I'd like to fuck". Popularized by the movie "American Pie".

• She was only 35 but that was ancient in the business. Sure, there were MILF scenes available. She got one or two offers a month from sites that featured young men (or young women) having sex with a woman twice their age.
• It's the age of the MILF, or, to put it more crassly, the Mom I'd Like to Fuck – an acronym at once repulsive and appealing. The MILF is Stacy's Mom. She's the lady in the Strippercize class. She dresses like a Jersey mob wife, her eye tilted into a perpetual wink. Is she our future?

□ mind game   심리 작전; An attempt to manipulate or confuse.

• But his preferred method of control was insidious mind games.

□ ***mind-fucker***   아주 어렵거나 기분 나쁜 문제; An extremely difficult or unpleasant problem

□ mint   많은 돈; A lot of money. Usually: "a mint".

• You hire me and Rick and you'll make a mint on this thing.

□ mish-mash   뒤죽박죽; A confused mixture of different types of things.

□ **miss the boat**   (기회를 살리기에는) 이젠 너무 늦다, 호기를 놓치다; To lose the opportunity to do or get something because you do not act quickly enough.

□ ***missionary position [style]***   정상 체위 성교 자세; A "man-on-top" sex position usually described as the act in which the woman lies on her back and the partners face each other.

□ Mister Big   (숨은) 보스, 거물; An important person.

□ **Mister nice-guy**   멋진 남자; A nice person.

□ mix it up   (~와) 다투다[문제를 일으키다]; To fight physically.

□ *MOFO*　　　　　　Mother Fucker의 줄임; Short for Mother Fucker.

・I know who you're talking about, that kid's a MOFO.

□ mojo　　　　　　(사람의 성격상의) 매력; Sex appeal.

・I've got serious mojo.

□ **Monday morning quarterback** (이미 일이 있고 난 후에) 뒤늦게 따따부
따하는 사람; A person who criticizes after having hindsight.

・I'm sick and tired of a Monday-morning quarterback like him.

□ **mondo**　　　　　　1. 완전히; 결국; 매우, 몹시 2. 큰; 멋진, 대단한;
Great; greatly; extraordinary; extraordinarily.

・That house is mondo expensive.

□ **money-grubber**　　악착같이 돈을 긁어모으는(사람); A person focused
on acquiring money.

□ **monkey around**　　~을 갖고 놀다, 만지작거리다; To mess around,
waste time.

□ *monkey fuck*　　라이터 대신에 다른 사람의 담배로 담뱃불을 붙이다;
To light a cigarette, using another cigarette instead of a lighter.

・I lost my matches, so I had to monkey-fuck my cigarette.

□ **mooch**　　　　　　빌붙다, 빈대 붙다; To obtain or try to obtain by
begging.

・He's been mooching cigarettes all night.

□ moola/moolah　　돈, 금전; Money

・Those shoes cost a lot of moola.

□ *Moose Knuckle*　　(주로) 남성 국부의 외관이 옷 위로 드러나는 것; A
slang term that refers to the outline of a human male's genitals showing
through clothes at the crotch. It is the male equivalent of cameltoe.

224

• Damn those tight pants show his moose knuckle.

□ **_mother fucker_**　　후레자식; An extremely strong general insult.

• You stupid mother fucker.

□ **mother of all**　　최대의, 가장 큰; Used before a plural noun to form a compound noun having the sense of: the greatest or largest of its kind.

• I got stuck in the mother of all traffic jams.

□ **_motherfucker_**　　후레자식; An extremely strong general insult.

□ **_motherfucking_**　　비열한, 망할, 쌍놈의, 괘씸한; Intensifier

• That was a mother fucking huge spider.
• What a motherfucking stupid idea!

□ **mow down**　　(사람들을 여러 명) 살육하다; To kill in large numbers, esp. by gunfire.

□ **moxie**　　용기, 투지; Courage

• Ashley: I do still have enough fun in me to talk to a man in a Laundromat⋯.
• Britt: Well, and enough moxie to invite a relative stranger into your home.

□ **mucho**　　1. 많은, 풍족한 2. 대단히, 굉장히; "Much" in Spanish.

□ **muck up**　　(하고 싶던 일 등을) 망치다; To ruin; mess up.

□ **muck-up**　　실수; Mistake

□ **muddle through**　　그럭저럭[어떻게 하다 보니] 해내다; To succeed in some undertaking in spite of lack of organization.

□ **muddlehead**　　멍청이, 바보; Fool; idiot

□ **_muff_**　　(여자의) 거웃이 난 자리; Female genitalia; vagina

• I bet she has a nice muff under that dress.

□ *muff dive*　　　여성에게 구강성교를 하다; To give oral sex to a girl; to go down on her; to perform cunnilingus.

• I'm going muff divin'.

□ **mule head**　　　고집 센, 완고한, 다루기 어려운; Stupid but stubborn.

□ **mum**　　　침묵; Quiet

• Mum's the word.

□ **mumbo jumbo**　　　(실은 아무 의미도 없으면서) 복잡하기만 한 말; 허튼 소리; Speech one doesn't understand - usually jargon specific to a particular field; nonsense.

• The doctor was just talking a lot of medical mumbo jumbo.

□ **Mum's the word!** (명령형으로 써서) 아무에게도 말하지 마! (너만 알고 있어!); I will not reveal the secret.

• It's a secret, OK? Mum's the word!

□ *munch on*　　　쿤닐링구스를 하다; To perform cunnilingus; eat out.

• Yesterday, I was munchin' on that chick for an hour.

□ **munchies**　　　(파티에서 술과 함께 먹는) 간단한 안주류; A snack or something sweet to eat while drinking.

• Let's go pick up some munchies.

□ *My ass!*　　　설마, 바보 같은 소리, 아니야 (강한 부정); I don't believe it(you). A way of expressing disbelief.

• Single, he told you? Single? My ass, he had six wives. One of those Mormons, ya know?

□ **my bad**　　　내 잘못이다(자기 잘못이나 실수를 인정할 때 씀); An apology.

• Sorry, man, my bad.

□ **MYOB**　　　참견하지 마, 네 일이나 신경 써; Mind your own business.

226

step. 14

N

□ **nab**　　　　　　　[특히 현행범을] 잡다, 체포하다; To arrest.

• I got nabbed the other night!

□ **nada**　　　　　　아무것도 없음, 무(無); Nothing. It means nothing in most languages derived from Latin.

• A: Hey, what's up?
B: Nada. Nothing new.

□ **Nah!**　　　　　　아니(오); No

□ **nail**　　　　　　(특히 스포츠에서) ~을 이뤄내다; Succeed; accomplish

• He nailed a victory in the semi-finals.

□ **nail**　　　　　　[거짓 따위를] 들추어내다; [부정 따위를] 찾아내다; To discover lies; to discover betrayal.

□ **nail**　　　　　　[도둑 따위를] 붙잡다; To arrest.

• The police haven't been able to nail the killer.

□ **nail**　　　　　　~을 완벽하게 하다; 해치우다; To win; to thoroughly accomplish a given task with pin-point accuracy.

• She really nailed me in the divorce settlement, I lost almost everything of value to her lawyer.

□ **nail the concept**　　(개념을) 이해하다; To understand.

□ **nail down**　　　　~을 확정시키다, 최종적으로 해결하다; To deal something successfully.

□ **name drop**　　　(친하지도 않은) 저명인사의 이름을 마치 친구인 양 팔고 다니다; To casually drop the name of a famous person who you, a friend or relative know, so as to appear cool vicariously because you know a famous person.

228

- I'm going to name drop a little bit and I hope I don't come off sounding like a snob.

□ **name of the game**   가장 중요한 점, 불가결한 것; 본질, (본래의) 목적; 당연한 일; The most important thing, essential thing.

□ **nana**   할머니 (미 동북부); Another name for grandma or granny.

- Whenever I go to nana's house she always bakes us some yummy cookies and tells us about when she lived in New York in the 1950's.

□ **narc**   마약 전담 수사관, 마약 단속 경찰; A narcotics agent.

- Others are often visited by 'narcs' posing as traders.

□ **narrow shave**   간신히, 아주 근소한 차이; Close call.

□ **narrow squeak**   아슬아슬하게 모면함; A situation where somebody only just avoids injury, danger or failure.

□ **NBD**   별일 아니다. 아무것도 아니다; No big deal.

□ **Neanderthal**   (무례하고 거칠어) 원시인같이 구는; Behaving in a very uncivilized way.

□ **near miss**   위기일발(의 상황); Close call.

- Due to an air controller's ineptitude, the two flights to LAX were in a near miss situation.

□ **Negative**   아니(오)(no); Another way of saying no.

- Jena: I know you like that bull Jerome!
  Mia: Negative. He looks like a monkey….
- Jamal: Yo, you wanna go to the the gallery.
  Jay: Negative….

□ **nerd**   1. 멍청하고 따분한 사람 2. 컴퓨터만 아는 괴짜; A clever but socially awkward person.

- Don't waste time with those guys - they're all nerds.

□ **nerdcore** 의도적인 nerd style의 음악; A lifestyle that inspired a genre of music which embraces nerd culture, a lifestyle that says you do not need to be ashamed of what you are, if you are a nerd, embrace it and stand proud, change for no one.

• Playing dungeons and dragons on a Friday night is definitely nerdcore.

□ **nerdy** 머리는 좋으나 세상 물정을 모르는; For a person typically described as intellectual, socially-impaired, and obsessive who spends inordinate amounts of time on unpopular or obscure activity.

• Nerdy but likable, Jonathan really just wants to connect with someone.

□ **nervous wreck** 신경쇠약인 사람, 너무 긴장한 사람; An extremely worried person.

• Bob: I'm allergic. Remember our first date?
  Linda: Yeah, I remember our first date. You were a nervous wreck.

□ **neutralize** 죽이다; 말살하다; To kill and put something out of its misery.

• I'm so going to neutralize that baby kitten.

□ **Never in a million years!** 절대로 ~하지 않다; By no means.

□ **newbie** 뉴비, (특히 컴퓨터 사용의) 초보자; Someone who is new to a particular group, activity, game, field of study, etc. Also newb.

• Katie, I can't believe you've never done this before. You're such a newbie.

□ *NFW* 절대로 안 돼; No fucking way.

□ **nibble** (조금 베어 문) 한 입; Small piece.

□ **nick** ~에게 (터무니없는 돈을) 요구하다, ~을 기만하다, 속이다; (~을) 사취하다; To steal something.

• Sorry, I nicked your seat.

230

- nick   [범인을] 체포하다; To arrest.

- nifty   스마트한, 멋진, 멋들어진, 재치있는, 멋[재치]있는 것[말]; 매력 있는 계집아이; Capable, appealing; to be very cool or neat; Existing in a unique, positive manner.

 • I got a nifty new sledgehammer, care to see?

- **NIMBY**   님비(새로운 개발을 찬성하면서도 그런 일이 자기 집 가까이에서 이뤄지거나 자기 생활에 방해가 되는 것은 반대하는 사람), 지역이 기주의; Never in my backyard.

- nimrod   바보, 얼간이; Originally from the Biblical Nimrod, a mighty hunter, it has come to mean socially inadequate.

 • The guy next door to my cousin is a total nimrod.

- nincompoop   멍청이; Idiot

 • Being the stubborn nincompoop that I am….

- **nine-to-fiver**   정시(定時) 근무자, 월급쟁이; A person with an office job.

 • The film begins with Forest Whitaker playing a bored and frustrated nine-to-fiver who feels stuck in his routine.

- nip slip   옷이 잘못되어 은밀한 부위가 노출됨; Accidental exposure of intimate parts caused by wardrobe malfunction.

 • Photos of nip slips when I was 13 or 14, places where my pussy lips were visible, some out of focus shots. Most of them would fall plainly in the category of child pornography.

- **nitty-gritty**   (쟁점/상황의) 핵심; In a nutshell.

 • So, let's get down to the nitty-gritty.

- nitwit   바보, 멍청이; A very unintelligent person; "moron"; "imbecile."

 • Jay is such a nitwit.

□ nix	아무것도 없음, 무; Nothing
□ nix	퇴짜 놓다, 거부하다; To reject or cancel.
□ **No big deal**	별일 아니다[대수롭지 않다]; It wasn't a major imposition. Something that is not a big deal.

• It's no big deal.

□ no biggie	중요하지 않은 것; An unimportant thing.
□ **No biggie!**	별일 아니야!, 걱정할 것 없어; It wasn't a major imposition.
□ **No buts about it!**	두말 말고 해 주게!; Without a doubt!
□ no call no show	전화도 없이 결근하는 것; Not going to work and not calling to explain one's absence.

• He got fired for one too many no call no shows.

□ **No clue**	모른다. 단서가 없다; I don't know; no awareness; no idea.
□ no diggity	정말로! 정말이지!; Roughly equivalent to "serious." Used similarly to phrases such as, "Seriously?" "Are you serious?" etc. Can also be used as a statement rather than a question, meaning "Seriously!" Popularized by R&B/rap group Blackstreet in their song "No Diggity" on the 1996 album "Another Level."

• Sally: Einstein was smart!
Bennie: No diggity?
Sally: No diggity!

□ **No duh!**	쳇 (그걸 누가 몰라!); Scornful agreement with something the speaker thinks should go without saying.

• Speaker: Don't run that red light. Response: No duh!

□ *No fucking idea*	정말로 모른다; I don't know.

□ ***No fucking way!*** 절대로 아니다; By no means.

□ ***no glove, no love*** 콘돔이 없이는 섹스하지 마라; If there isn't a condom present, don't have sex.

> • I hope your date goes well tonight. And remember: no glove, no love.

□ **no holds barred** 어떤 제약도 없이[모든 수단을 동원하여]; Without restrictions.

> • It is a war with no holds barred and we must prepare to resist.

□ ***No shit*** 당연하지. 강한 Yes의 의미; A sarcastic response used when someone states the obvious.

> • Speaker: Don't run that red light.
> Response: No shit.
> • Speaker: I bet it hurt when you got shot in the chest.
> Response: No shit.

□ ***No shit!*** 장난 아니군! 제기랄. Surprised acceptance of an unexpected truth.

□ ***No skin off my ass/butt*** 그것은 내 알 바 아니다; I don't give a damn.

□ **No skin off my nose** 그것은 내 알 바 아니다; I don't give a damn.

□ **no sweat** 힘들 것이 없는, 쉬운; Requiring little effort, easy

□ **No sweat** (상대방의 감사 · 부탁에 대한 대꾸로) 뭘 그런 걸 갖고 그래 [별거 아냐/문제없어]; Don't worry about it.

> • Person A: Thanks for everything.
> Person B: Hey, no sweat.

□ **No way!** 절대로[결코] 아니다[안 되다]; Interjection of doubt; an emphatic "no."

> • Person A: Do you want to go to the party?
> Person B: No way. My ex is going to be there.

- **No worries**   (흔히 고맙다는 말에 대한 대꾸로 쓰여) 괜찮아요;
Don't worry about it; no problem.

> • Person A: Sorry dude, didn't mean to be late. Person B: It's cool, no worries.

- **no-brainer**   손쉬운 일, 간단한 일; An easy-to-solve problem.

> • They would have my vote if the motion came up right now. Since you've been warned, it's a no-brainer.

- **non-starter**   처음부터 (성공할) 가능성이 없는 것; A plan or idea that has no chance of success.

- **noodle**   바보; A geek, weirdo

> • Don't be such a noodle!

- *nooner*   낮 시간 잠깐 동안의 섹스; Sex during the lunch break.

- **north of**   [금액이] (얼마) 이상; More than. Contrast with south of.

> • He makes north of $100,000 a year.

- *nose candy*   코카인; Cocaine

- *nose job*   코 성형 수술; Cosmetic surgery on the nose.

- **nose to the grindstone**   쉬지 않고 죽어라 일하다; A metaphorical position which implies hard work.

> • The only way to get ahead is to work hard. Just keep your nose to the grindstone.

- **not all there**   (특히 정신병 때문에) 별로 똑똑하지 못한; To think slowly because of low intelligence, illness, drugs, etc.

- **not get to the first base**   (사업 · 관계 등에서) 1단계를 넘지 못하다[순조롭게 출발하지 못하다]; To fail to make a promising beginning.

234

□ **not have a snowball's chance in hell**   전혀 가망이 없다; To have no chance at all.

> • You have a snowball's chance in hell of winning the lottery.

□ **Not in my backyard!**   '내 뒷마당에서는 안 된다'라는 이기주의적 사고를 의미; NIMBY

□ **Not in my job description!**   내 일이 아니다! 그 일은 하지 않겠다!; According to the terms of my contract, I don't have to do this, and I'm not going to.

> • Cleaning the office is not in my job description.

□ **not on (*one's*) life**   절대로[결코] 아니다[안된다]; An assertion that something will never happen.

> • Teenager: Mom, can I stay out after curfew? Mother: Not on your life.

□ **Not on your life!**   절대로[결코] 아니다[안된다]; By no means.

□ **not playing the full deck**   약간 정신이 모자란; Stupid; Retarded

□ **not the brightest bulb in the chandelier**   약간 정신이 모자란; Stupid; Retarded

□ **not the brightest light in the harbor**   약간 정신이 모자란; Stupid; Retarded

□ **not the sharpest knife in the drawer**   약간 정신이 모자란; Stupid; Retarded

□ **Nuff said!**   그만하면 알았다[됐다]; "Enough said." As in: what I have previously said should adequately demonstrate my point.

□ **number one**   쉬하다; Urination

> • Kid: I have to go to the bathroom.
> Parent: Number one or number two?
> Kid: Number one.

◻ **number two**　　　(어린아이의 말로) 응가; The act or an instance of defecation.

• Mum, I need a number two.

◻ **nut**　　　미친 사람; A crazy person.

• He's a real nut.

◻ *nut*　　　사정하다; To ejaculate.

• The first time we did it, we had extra lubricant because the guy nutted a second or two after the first inch was in.

◻ *nut butter*　　　정액 (호두 버터와 비슷해서); Semen; sweat and other excretions in the genital area of a male.

• That guy smells like nut butter.

◻ **nut house**　　　정신병원; An insane asylum.

• I'm surprised I'm not in a white straitjacket in a nut house.

◻ **nuts**　　　미친, 제정신이 아닌; Crazy

◻ **nuts about**　　　~에 열중해 있다, 홀딱 반하다; A big fan of.

• I'm nuts about this new game.

◻ **nuts and bolts**　　　기본; 요점; ~에 대한 기초적인 사실; ~의 실제적인 상세함; The essential or practical details.

◻ **nutty**　　　미친; To be funny acting or stupid; retarded; crazy, daring.

• That dude is nuttier than squirrel turds.

◻ **nutty as a fruitcake**　　　미친; Crazy

• He's as nutty as a fruitcake. Do you know what he did yesterday? He had lunch outside in the pouring rain.

236

□ **oceans** 엄청나게 많은 (양의); A large amount of something.

□ **off (*one's*) rocker** 미친, 통제가 안 되는; Crazy, out of control.

> • He's really off his rocker!

□ **off the charts** 과도한, 측정이 안 되는; Excessive, immeasurable, way too much.

> • His Christmas lights display was off the charts this year.

□ **off the hook** 아주 좋은, 굉장한; Very good, excellent; "cool". Also many variations such as "off the Heezy", "off the fa-sheezy", "off the clock", etc.

> • Whoa, that shirt is off the hook.

□ **offline** 다른 곳에서; 지금 말고 따로(이야기하자); Not now or not here. Originally, used to suggest that a discussion be moved from a public discussion group to e-mail. Now used in business meetings to forestall lengthy conversation about a topic not core to the meeting.

> • I'm not sure of the answer to that question. I'll follow up with you offline.
> • Those are all great issues. Unfortunately, we have a lot to cover this afternoon, so let's take this discussion offline.

□ **offload** (자기가 원치 않는 것을) 없애다; To get rid of it by giving it or selling it to someone else.

□ **Oh my God!** 오, 이런!; An exclamation of surprise, shock

□ **Oh, what the heck!** 에라 모르겠다!(하지 말아야 할 것을 하려고 할 때 내뱉는 말); Interjection signaling more or less reluctant acceptance.

> • It means I'll be late for work but what the heck!

□ **Oh, what the hell!** 알게 뭐야, 아무려면 어때; Interjection signaling more or less reluctant acceptance.

> • I shouldn't tell this story, but what the hell.

238

□ **old school**　　　　구식의, 전통적인; Old. Used when describing something you remember from a long time ago.

- He was real old school. He started back in the 1970s.

□ **old timer**　　　　고참자; A person who has engaged in some activity or been in some organization for a long period of time.

□ *old-fart*　　　　늙은 사람; An elderly person.

- The old fart was driving too slow.

□ **OMG**　　　　어머나, 세상에; Acronym for "Oh my God"; a general-purpose exclamation.

- OMG - this is the best pizza I've ever had!

□ **on edge**　　　　흥분하여, 안절부절못하여, 과민한; Nervous, worried or anxious.

□ **on stamps**　　　　가난하여 정부 보조 식품 할인권으로 생활하는; Broke, out of money. Relates to having to use food stamps to eat.

- I'm so broke, I'm almost on stamps!

□ **on the back burner**　　　　~을 일시 보류하다; Of low priority. Contrast with "on the front burner."

- Since we've found out the auditors are coming, the invoices are on the back burner.

□ *on the blob*　　　　생리 중인; Having one's menstrual period.

- My girlfriend is on the blob, so we couldn't have sex.

□ **on the DL**　　　　비밀인; "On the down low", i.e. secret.

- Britt: I think she's the top candidate for being Laura's source. Is she?
  Hank: I don't know, it's all on the DL.

□ **on the double** 황급히, 신속히; Quickly

• I need to get those sneakers on the double.

□ **on the dub** 황급히, 신속히; Quickly. From "on the double."

• I need to get those sneakers on the dub.

□ **on the front burner** 많은 관심을 받는, 우선순위의 일로; A priority. Contrast with "on the back burner."

• The Jones account is now on the front burner.

□ **on the house** (술집이나 식당에서 술 · 음식이) 무료[서비스]로 제공되는; (Especially of alcoholic drinks) given to a customer free by the hotel, restaurant, bar, etc.

• It's on the house. Don't worry about paying for it.

□ **on the level** 정직한, 합법적인; Honest. Possibly from the opposite of "crooked."

• I'm sure he's no crook. He's on the level.

□ **on the rag** 화가 나서; Extremely angry.

□ *on the rag* 생리중인; On menstruation. Origin: possibly from old-style pads.

• Man, stay away from Casey. I think she's on the… rag.

□ **on the roll** 일이 잘 진행되는; Successful

□ **on the warpath** 화가 나서 싸우려고[응징하려] 드는; Be angry and ready for an argument or a fight about something.

□ **once-over** 대강 훑어보기 (특히 이성의 몸매를); A visual examination, especially of a person of the opposite sex.

• Bob is always around the gym, checking the chicks out… giving them that famous once-over…

□ one brick short of a load   약간 정신이 모자란; Stupid, Retarded

□ **one hell of a**   (말하는 내용을 강조하여) 굉장한[엉망인]; Intensifier

• That was one hell of a show.

□ *one night stand*   하룻밤의 섹스; 하룻밤의 섹스 상대; A sexual encounter (which usually but does not always include sexual intercourse) after which one or both parties make no attempt to contact the other person.

• He kept calling me, but I was like, "Dude, it was just a one night stand."

□ *one's ass off*   마구, 필사적으로, 맹렬히; Used with a verb to indicate that verb is performed with vigor; To the best of one's ability.

• He got that way by working his ass off dawn to dusk on a farm his whole life. He didn't sit and play Nintendo and catch a ride to go 100 feet down the block.
• I've got a midterm tomorrow. I'm gonna have to study my ass off between now and then.
• You really ran your ass off in the marathon.

□ *one-eyed monster*   남성의 성기; Penis

□ *one-eyed snake*   남성의 성기; Penis

□ one-off   단 한 번 있는 것. 일회성의 일이나 사건; A one-time occurrence.

• His scene with Ashley Malibu brought in $400,000 to Daystar in a month. That is one month, not a year or a decade. You take all the one-offs you've done in your career and they haven't brought in $400,000.
• I'm cool with working with you even if it is just a one-off.

□ *one's* damnedest   최선(을 다하다); With one's maximum effort.

□ **Oops!**   이크, 이런(사고를 당할 뻔했거나 무엇을 깨뜨렸거나 할 때 내는 소리); an exclamation of surprise, shock.

- **operator** (특히 부정직한 방법도 마다하지 않는) 수완가; A person who is adept at making deals or getting results, especially one who uses questionable methods.

- **opt out** 탈퇴하다; To choose not to take part in something.

  • I may opt out of the organization.

- ***oral*** 구강성교; Oral sex.

  • Is she into oral?

- ***orgy*** 난교 파티, 섹스 파티. (또는 orgy); Usually used for sex involving more than 3 people.

  • You could probably suggest a bed-hopping orgy and he wouldn't blink an eye.

- ***o-ring*** 항문; The anus.

- **otaku** 오타쿠; To be excessively nerdy, anti-social, unpopular, from Japanese word meaning "house." Probably coined because of a nerd's habit of never leaving his/her house.

  • Brian will never have a girlfriend, he's too much of an otaku.

- **out of sight** 발군(拔群)의, 넘어서 있는, 훌륭한, 출중한; Excellent, outstanding, amazing

- **out of the box** 독창적으로(생각하다). 전혀 새로운 방법으로(생각하다); Corporate-speak for "in a novel way." Typically used to refer to solving a problem or task. Often used with the verb "think." Has become cliche. Also "outside (of) the box."

  • We've got to think out of the box on this one.

- **out of this world** (이 세상의 것이 아닌 것처럼) 너무도 훌륭한[아름다운]; Extraordinary; too good to be true.

□ out on *one's* ass   거리로 쫓겨난; Having been kicked out of one's residence.

□ over and out   (무선 교신에서) 통신 끝; Goodbye!

- Man in helicopter: We're five by five, both packages on board. Over and out.

□ **Over my dead body!**   내 눈에 흙이 들어가기 전에는 (안 된다); Interjection used to mean that something will not happen (until one is dead.)

- Tobias: Um, I'm going to Vegas with Kitty.
  Narrator: But Lindsay wasn't about to lose her man without a fight.
  Lindsay: Over my dead body!

□ over the hill   한물간[퇴물이 된]; Middle-aged or older.

step. 16

P

□ **_p.o.ed_** 화가 난, 성질 난; Angry, annoyed: euphemistic variant of pissed off.

□ **pack heat** (학교 등에서) 총기를 휴대하다; To carry a firearm.

• Watch out, that dude's packing heat.

□ **pack it in** 일[활동]을 그만두다; To close down work for the moment, to end a day's work at the job.

• Hey boss, I'm going to pack it in.

□ **Pack it in!** 멈춰! 동작 그만!; Stop (whatever you're doing)

□ **packed** (특히 사람들이) 꽉 들어찬; Full of.

• The bar was packed on Saturday.

□ **_packer_** 남성의 성기; Penis

• You made me look at that kid's packer.

□ **_packing_** 큰 성기를 가진; Well hung.

• Melody says you're packing more than most guys down there.

□ **_pain in (one's) ass_** 골칫거리; A nuisance. Also "pain in the ass."; An extremely difficult or unpleasant problem.

• He's a massive, massive pain in my ass.

□ **pain in the neck** 골칫거리, 문제 인물; An annoying person or problem.

• That guy is a pain in the neck with his constant demands.

□ **pain in the rear** 골칫거리, 문제 인물; An extremely difficult or unpleasant problem.

□ **panjandrum** 대장, 두목, 높으신 분, 어르신네; A pompous self-important official or person of rank.

246

• It should leave civil servants in no doubt that power has shifted from the panjandrums to the people.

□ **paper chaser**　　　돈(이익)만 쫓는 사람; Someone who runs behind money for profit.

• Greg is a paper chaser.

□ **party animal**　　　파티 광; A person who parties hard and often.

• My new roommate is a total party animal. I get no studying done in our room.

□ **party pooper**　　　좌중의 흥을 깨는 사람; A person who "ruins" fun.

• Come on, party pooper, bust a move.

□ **pass gas**　　　방귀뀌다; To flatulate.

□ **pass wind**　　　방귀뀌다; To flatulate.

□ *patootie*　　　1. 엉덩이 2. 매력 있는 여자; The buttocks, ass; an attractive girl; a girlfriend.

• Unless they want to do it themselves, I don't give a rat's patootie if they mind or not.

□ **patsy**　　　(남의 잘못을 뒤집어쓴) 희생양; Someone who takes the blame; fall guy.

□ **peabrain**　　　바보, 얼간이; Fool, idiot

□ **Peace!**　　　안녕히, 잘 가; Interjection to announce one's departure.

• Hey, I'm leavin'. Peace, y'all.

□ **Peace out!**　　　안녕히, 잘 가; Goodbye!

• I'm leaving, guys. Peace out!

□ **peach**　　　훌륭한 사람, 어여쁜 소녀, 미인; A sweet or nice person.

• The store manager, Antonio, was a peach of a guy.

□ **peachy**   좋은; 아주 멋진; Good

• Everything's peachy.

□ **peachy(-keen)**   좋은; 아주 멋진; Wonderful, excellent

□ **peanuts**   아주 적은 액수; A small number or amount; very
little money.

□ **pec**   흉근, 가슴 근육; Pectoral muscle.

• Nice pecs. Got a kicking body.

□ *pecker*   음경; Penis

• "Slight groping is permitted," Allie said. "Nothing beyond that, don't try
to finger bang Shelly or give Sean a handjob. But if you brush against
Shelly sweet little mound or Sean or Walt's pecker, that's cool."

□ **pecs**   흉근(胸筋); Pectoral muscles.

• Black must exercise his eyebrows the way Arnold Schwarzenegger flexes
his pecs.

□ **pee**   오줌 누다, 쉬하다. 오줌(piss); 오줌 누기[싸기]; To
urinate.

• I need to pee.

□ **pee** *one's* **pants**   놀라서 오줌을 지리다; To feel fear.

□ **pee** *oneself*   놀라서 오줌을 지리다; To feel fear.

□ **pee** *oneself*   오줌을 지릴 정도로 웃기다; To laugh in an uncontrollable way.

□ **pee'd off**   짜증[신경질]이 난; Pissed off.

□ **peeved**	짜증이 난; Slightly angry.	

□ **pen**	교도소; Penitentiary

□ **penny-pincher**	깍쟁이, 구두쇠; A frugal person.

□ **peppy**	원기 왕성한, 기운 넘치는; Energetic

□ **perp**　　　　　　　범인; "Perpetrator" (i.e. person who committed a crime.)

- I whip out my cuffs, and the perp ends up in FBI or police custody.
- The perp is in custody.

□ **perv**　　　　　　　변태; Pervert; disgusting

- He's such a perv.
- Luke and Manny barged into our room while we were changing the little pervs!

□ *peter*　　　　　　　남성의 성기; Penis

□ **peter out**　　　　　점차 작아지다[조용해지다 등]; To decrease or fade gradually before coming to an end.

□ **phish**　　　　　　　이메일을 통해 합법적이고 믿을 만한 기업 행세를 하며 사용자를 속여 개인 정보를 넘겨 받아 이를 신원 도용에 사용하는 것. 사기성 이메일; E-mail scams that attempt to deceive consumers into sharing personal or financial information.

- Tax officials have asking workers who receive phishing emails to report them immediately.

□ *phone fuck*　　　　　폰 섹스; To engage in phone sex.

- Dude, last night I phone fucked this crazy bitch.

□ **pick on *somebody***　트집을 잡다; To find fault with.

- Or maybe I just wanna pick on somebody because I'm having a bad day.

□ **pick up on**	~을 이해하다[알아차리다]; To understand.	

□ **picnic**	쉽게 풀리는 문제; An easy or pleasant task.	

• This problem is no picnic.

□ ***piece of ass*** (섹스 대상으로서의) 매력적인 여자; An attractive person.

• Boy! She's a real piece of ass.

□ **piece of cake** 식은 죽 먹기; Something easy.

• The test was a piece of cake.

□ ***piece of crap*** 품질이 형편없는 것. 기분이 나쁜 것; Something displeasing or of poor quality.

□ ***piece of shit*** 품질이 형편없는 것. 기분이 나쁜 것; Poor quality; displeasing.

• I can't believe you're still driving that piece of shit car!

□ **piece of work** 대하기 어려운 사람; A difficult person; a person who has one or more extreme (and usually negative) characteristics.

• He's a real piece of work.

□ **pig** 돼지 같은 사람(불쾌하거나 무례한 또는 지저분하고 욕심 많은 사람; A person who is financially wealthy and does not share his wealth.

□ ***pigeon*** 못생기고 돈 없는 여자; An unattractive, trashy, usually poor female; HOOCHIE.

• I don't want no pigeons!

□ **pile** 많은~, ~무더기; A large amount.

□ ***pile of crap*** 거짓말, 말도 안 되는 소리; Nonsense; full of lies.

250

□ *pile of shit*	거짓말, 말도 안 되는 소리; Nonsense; full of lies.	
□ piles	많은~, ~무더기; A large amount.	
□ pinch	돈에[경제적으로] 쪼들림; With no money left.	
□ pinch	위기, 유사시; Problematic situation.	
□ pinch	~을 훔치다; To steal.	

• Someone has pinched my bag.

□ *pink canoe* 여성의 음부; The vagina.

• The gynecologist examined my pink canoe.

□ **pink slip** 해고 통지서; Notice of termination from a job.

• He got the pink slip for neglecting his duty.

□ pinko 공산주의 동조자; A communist sympathizer.

□ Pipe down! (특히 명령문으로 쓰여) 조용히 해[입 다물어]; To stop talking; to speak more quietly.

□ **piss** 1. 오줌, 소변; 오줌 누기. 2. 오줌 누다; To urinate.

• I had to go piss.

□ **piss around** 멍청하게 시간을 보내다[허비하다]; To waste time.
Also piss about.

• American submarines are pissing around under our polar ice cap looking for Russians.

□ piss ass drunk 술이 많이 취한; Extremely inebriated.

• He was piss ass drunk last night.

- **piss off**　　　　　화나게 하다; To anger or annoy.

> - Eric was pissed off that Adam had embarrassed him in front of Shelly's brothers.
> - She was already pissed off at her father and mother and she didn't really feel like dealing with any more assholes.
> - The girl was so bad, I started to get pissed off.

- *Piss off!*　　　　　꺼져; Exclamation used to tell somebody rudely to go away.

> - Why don't you just piss off and leave me alone?

- piss *on somebody/something* ~를 괴롭히다; To annoy.

- *Piss on you!*　　　　엿 먹어라!; Exclamation expressing displeasure.

- piss *one's* pants　　1. 오줌을 쌀 정도로 놀라다 2. 오줌을 쌀 정도로 웃기다; 1. To feel fear. 2. To burst into loud laughter.

- piss *somebody* off　남을 성나게 하다; To cause anger.

- **pissant**　　　　　쓸모없는(시시한, 하찮은) 사람(것); 비열한 사람(것); Small, insignificant, worthless and irritating.

> - You should have heard that sorry pissant lawyer when he called back.

- **piss-ant**　　　　　무가치한 것; Small, insignificant, worthless and irritating.

> - This piss-ant science project is going to get me no more than a C.

- *pissed off*　　　　　진절머리 나는, 역겨운, 짜증 나는; Angry.

> - Pissed off hooker said her meth head boyfriend and his pal did the murder.

- *pisser*　　　　　굉장히 어려운(불쾌한) 것; An extremely difficult or unpleasant problem.

> - So it's a pisser that Anthony's probably not going to win, then.

□ *pisshead*   바보. 병신; Asshole

• Look at the pisshead over there wearing a knitted sweater.

□ **pissing contest**   (소변 멀리 보내기 경쟁) (주도권, 우위를 잡기 위한) 싸움, 말다툼; A vain argument/conflict which is only participated in as an attempt to display superiority.

• The mayor and the sheriff are engaged in a pissing contest.

□ *piss-poor*   아주 가난한, 믿을 수 없을 정도로 품질이 낮은; Very poor; of unbelievably poor quality.

□ **pit stop**   1. 피트 스톱(급유/타이어 교체 등을 위한 정차) 2. (장기 여행 중의 휴식/식사 등을 위한) 정차; A break in travelling, usually for food or use of a bathroom.

• In motorsports, a pit stop is where a racing vehicle stops in the pits during a race for refueling, new tires, repairs, mechanical adjustments, a driver change, or any combination of the above. Not all are allowed in all formulae.

□ PITA   골칫덩어리; Pain in the ass.

□ **pity party**   슬픔을 털어놓는 파티; A way of experiencing grief, in which you spend your time feeling sorry for yourself and whining endlessly about how crappy your life is. Pity parties can be just for one or for many people, such as maybe your friends and close people, who will try to comfort you or just be there for you while you keep asking yourself what did you do to deserve whatever it is that made you so sad in the first place.

• Amanda and Michael throw a pity party and no one shows up so they're very happy.

□ **plain vanilla**   단순한, 전형적인; Without adornment or extra trimmings, uninteresting

□ **plastered**   술이 많이 취한; Extremely drunk.

• Let's go get plastered!

□ **play ball** 기꺼이 협조하다; To cooperate.

• Aren't you tired of doing what everyone else want you to do? Maybe it's time you quit playing ball with them… and just play ball with me.

□ **play hardball** 강경 자세를 취하다; To be uncooperative during negotiation.

• If Reagan is gonna play hardball, so will I. All the best, Amy.

□ **play it cool** 냉정[침착]하게 대처하다; To be nonchalant.

□ *play the skin flute* 펠라티오하다; To perform fellatio.

□ **plucky** 용기 있는; Having or showing pluck, courage or spirit in trying circumstances.

□ **plush** 아주 안락한; 고급의; Expensive, luxurious

□ **PMS** 월경 전 증후군; Pre-menstrual syndrome; to be grumpy or moody.

• She's really pms-ing today.

□ **pocket *one's* pride** (목적 달성을 위해) 자존심을 억누르다; To become humiliated.

□ **point *one's* finger at** 밀고하다; To inform on another person or group to authorities.

□ **pointy-head** 지식인; Intelligent person.

□ **poison** [익살] (강한) 술, 독주; One's favorite type of alcohol.

• What's your poison?

□ *poke in the brown eye* 항문 성교하다; To do anal sex.

□ **poke *one's* nose into** ~에(쓸데없이) 참견하다; To interfere or interlude.

254

- Did you poke her in the brown eye?

◻ *pole*　　　　　남성의 성기; Penis

- Man, that guy is such a pole.

◻ **pony up**　　　　돈을 내다[지불하다]; To pay for; To contribute an amount of money.

- Can you pony up some cash for the keg?

◻ **Ponzi scheme**　　　폰지형(型) 이자(利子) 사기 방식(피라미드식 이식(利殖) 사기 수법); An investment scam in which initial "investors" are paid off with money from subsequent "investors."

- The US and UK economies are officially sanctioned Ponzi schemes which are now unraveling.

◻ **poo**　　　　　응가, 똥; Feces. Also poo-poo. "Poo" is considered a childish term; "poo-poo" even more so. The term is mostly used by mothers, or female adults as a polite alternative to "shit".

- "Oh shit!" said the classy lady, "I just stepped in some doggie poo!"

◻ **poof**　　　　　방귀 뀌다; To fart.

◻ **pooh-bah**　　　높은 사람, 고관; 거만한 사람; 지도자, 대가; 중요한 인물; Haughty and important person with many titles.

◻ **pookie**　　　　가까운 사람들이 쓰는 용어; 여보, 자기; A term of endearment.

◻ *poon*　　　　　(여성의) 음부; Vagina. Also poon-tang.

- I gotta find me some poon.

◻ *poontang*　　　　(여성의) 음부; Female genitalia.

- I want some of that fine poontang!

□ **poop**　　　　　　　　똥; Feces

　• I got some poop on my shoe while walking through the park.

□ ***poop chute***　　　　항문; The anus; butthole

　• I'd stick it up her poop chute.

□ ***poop on you***　　　똥이나 처먹어라!; Piss on you!

□ **poop out**　　　　　(일 · 기능을 못하고) 나가떨어지다; To collapse; to
stop functioning.

　• My computer finally pooped out.

□ **pooped**　　　　　　녹초가 된, 기진맥진한; Tired; exhausted.

　• I'm too pooped to pop.

□ ***pooper***　　　　　엉덩이; Buttocks

　• She's got a nice pooper.

□ **poopy**　　　　　　기분 나쁜, 짜증 나는; Unpleasant, irritating

□ **pork**　　　　　　　속이다. 이용해 먹다; To take advantage of.

　• I had to cover Bob's work shift last night. He completely porked me!

□ **porn**　　　　　　　포르노 (영화 또는 잡지); Pornography

　• I was watching porn on my computer.

□ **posh**　　　　　　　멋진, 우아한; 호화로운; [경멸적] 상류의; Fashionable and elegant, wealthy, upper-class, opulent, expensive

　• That outfit is so posh!

□ **posh up**　　　　　향상시키다; To enhance.

256

□ **pot** 마리화나; Marijuana

- Man 1: Dude, what are you smoking? Man 2: Pot.
- "I smoke pot every now and then," Sarah said. "Is that a problem?" "If you bring it into the house with you, it might be," Shelly warned before Rachelle could speak.

□ **pot-head** 마리화나 상용자; A person who smokes a lot of marijuana.

□ **potty break** 화장실에 가기 위한 짧은 휴식

□ **potty mouth** 상스런 말씨(를 쓰는 사람); The mouth of a person who frequently swears.

- I'm going to wash that potty mouth of yours with soap!

□ ***pound sand*** 꺼져 버려; A dismissive retort; screw off.

- He probably told them to go pound sand.

□ **pour it on** (상대의 실패·약점 따위를 이용해) 전력을 기울이다; To exert effort.

□ **POV** 'Point of view'의 약어. 시점; 1인칭 관점 제작 포르노 영화; Acronym for "point of view."; a style of pornography in which the person holding the camera is one of the actors. The pornographic video is then from the "point of view" of someone engaging in sex acts.

- I've never done a real boy-girl scene. I've restricted myself to POV blowjobs but I've decided to move full into the industry.

□ **pow** 세게 때리다; To hit.

□ ***powder*** 코카인; Cocaine

□ ***powder one's nose*** 코카인을 (코로) 흡입하다; To snort cocaine.

- **powerhouse**　　유력 집단; A country or organization that has a lot of power or influence.

- **powers that be**　　(조직 · 국가 등의) 실세들; The person, people, organization, etc. that is in charge.

　• The decision is in the hands of the powers that be.

- **prairie dog**　　머리를 쳐들다. 대변이 급해 변이 나올 것만 같다; To stick one's head up out of a cubicle to look at something; to need to defecate so badly that the feces is coming out a bit, as a prairie dog looking out of its burrow.

　• I was trying to hold in my poop which caused me to prairie dog.

- **prank**　　(농담으로 하는) 장난; A childish trick.

- **pre-cum**　　정액 사출 전에 분비되는 무색 투명 액체; Clear lubricating fluid secreted from penis after arousal.

　• He saw his cock had left trails of pre-cum across her stomach.

- **prep**　　(비싼) 사립고 학생; young people, especially in America, who have often been to an expensive private school and who are conventional and conservative in their attitudes, behavior, and style of dress.

　• Only preps wear Abercrombie and Fitch.

- **preppy**　　(전형적으로) 비싼 사립학교 학생 같은 청소년; Clean cut; tucked in Abercrombie shirt with khaki pants and brown dress shoes. Usually people who are preppy are called "preps."

　• John looked very preppy today.

- **prick**　　남근(男根), 음경; Penis

　• The end of Adam's prick was wet with pre-cum.

- **prick**　　멍청한 놈; 지겨운[싫은] 녀석, 얼간이; Derisive term for a mean or unkind person; jerk. Usually used to refer to males.

258

- He is just a rich prick who thinks he can get away with everything.
- You prick!

▫ *prick tease*   몸만 달아오르게 하는 년(성관계를 원하는 듯 유혹하면서 끝내 허락하지 않는 여자를 가리키는 욕설); A person who gets a male excited by the high probability of later sex, but who has no intention of having sex with said male. Also see "cock tease."

- She's such a prick tease.

▫ primo   제1급의, 일류의, 최상의; The best of its kind; attractive, great, flawless; awesome. Also spelled "premo."

- Man, did you check out that chick? She was primo!

▫ private Idaho   자기 자신의 공상 속의 세계; One's daydreams and the internal landscape they inhabit.

- You're living in your own private Idaho.

▫ Problem exist between chair and computer   사용자의 잘못으로 인한 문제이다; The problem is caused by user error.

▫ Problem exist between chair and keyboard   사용자의 잘못으로 인한 문제이다; The problem is caused by user error.

▫ psycho   미친, 미친 사람; psychotic

- My ex-girlfriend is psycho.

▫ PTB   실세, 책임자, 담당자; Powers that be.

▫ *pube*   음모(陰毛), 거웃; A pubic hair.

- Carly found a pube in the lasagna.

▫ *pucker*   항문; Asshole

- Jenny rested her hands on Derrick's knees and presented her pucker to him.

□ **pucker up**　　　입을 오므리다. (입을 오므려 키스할 준비를 하다);
To prepare for a kiss.

• Pucker up baby!

□ *pucker-assed*　　　겁이 많은; Liable to fear.

□ *puckered brown eye*　　　항문; Anus

□ *puckered starfish*　　항문; Anus

□ **puff**　　　마리화나를 피우다; To smoke marijuana.

• You got some weed? Let's puff.

□ **puffed up**　　　자만심에 차서 우쭐한; Very proud of oneself and
thinking that he/she is important.

□ **puke**　　　게우다. 토하다; Vomit

• There's puke on the floor!

□ **pull an all-nighter**　밤을 새워서 하다; Work overnight.

□ **pull a fast one**　　~을 속여 넘기다, 속임수로 이기다; To try to deceive or fool someone in a quick yet daring or slick manner.

• That motherfucker tried to pull a fast one on me. There was no way the
car was worth that much.

□ **pull a gallstone**　　　괄목할 성과를 이루다; To accomplish something
remarkable.

• That guy without the leg just won the gold medal! He really pulled a
gallstone!

□ *pull a[or the] train*　　　(여자가) 차례차례 여러 남자와 성행위를
하다; When a group of men all have sex with one woman at the same
time, one right behind another.

- "That little slut," Allie remarked with a laugh. "Blowing high school guys? She's going to be pulling a train on the Padres if they're not careful."

□ **pull off**　　　　　(힘든 것을) 해내다[성사시키다]; To achieve.

- This is becoming an increasingly difficult task to pull off.

□ **pull *one's* leg**　　　놀리다. 농담하다; To kid.

- Are you pulling my leg?

□ pull *somebody's* chain　　　사람을 속여 화나게 하다; To deceive a person, usually in a kidding manner.

□ **pull strings**　　　(~에게 유리하도록) 영향력을 행사하다; To take advantage of one's influence to get something done.

- I had to pull a few strings, but I ended up getting us box seats.

□ pull the plug　　　~의 생명 유지 장치를 떼다; ~을 죽이다, 제거하다; To end something.

- Your group needs to reign in its spending, or we're going to have to pull the plug.

□ pull the plug on　　　~의 생명 유지 장치를 떼다; ~을 죽이다, 제거하다; To purposely bring about the end of something.

□ pull the rug out from under　　　배신하다; To betray a person.

□ *pull your finger out of your ass(butt)*　　　시간을 더 이상 지체하지 않고 행동을 시작하다; To stop sitting around or messing around and get ready for serious action.

□ pulverize　　　완전히 쳐부수다, 분쇄하다; To destroy completely.

□ pumped　　　열성적인, 흥분한; Excited; psyched

□ pumped up　　　열성적인, 흥분한; Excited; psyched

- punch *somebody's* lights out   때려서 정신을 잃게 만들다; To knock unconscious.

- punk   쓸모없는 사람; 조무래기, 똘마니, 풋내기; A disrespectful, rude, or otherwise unpleasant person.

- Your kid is a real punk.

- punk out   겁먹다; To become afraid.

- **push *one's* luck**   행운이 계속되기를 기대하다, 운을 너무 믿고 덤비다; To take a risk hoping to be lucky.

- push *somebody's* buttons   남의 성질을 돋우는 행동을 하다; To behave in such a way as to gain the desired reaction; to act in a way that one knows will upset, anger, or frustrate somebody; to aggravate.

- She knows how to push all his buttons.

- **push the panic button**   당황하여 쩔쩔매다; To do something quickly without thinking about it in order to deal with a difficult or worrying situation (often negative).

- push up daisies   죽다; To be dead.

- He's pushing up daisies.

- **pusher**   (마약) 밀매자; One who sells illegal drugs.

- I picked up two grams yesterday, from my pusher.

- pushover   호락호락한 사람; A person easy to persuade to do what you want.

- *puss*   여성의 음부; Female genitalia. From "pussy".

- This broad I meet last night had a huge puss.

- ***pussy***   여성의 음부; Vagina

262

- And every day from 3:00 to 5:40 p.m., Karlie would suck a dick, give a handjob or get her pussy licked.

□ ***pussy***   (성교 대상으로서의) 여성; 여성의 비하; A derogatory term for a woman or girl.

- Are you in the biz, or just an interested party? Shit man, all that pussy out there, who isn't an interested party? Me? I'm both. I am in the biz and very interested in pussy.

□ ***pussy***   겁쟁이. 꼬맹이; A coward or physically weak person; wimp

- I never said you were a pussy.

□ pussycat   (특히 예상 밖으로) 친근한 사람; A gentle person or animal.

- He's such a pussycat on TV.

□ put in the doghouse 찬밥 신세가 되게 하다; To lower someone's high self-opinion.

□ ***put on the crap/shit*** 찬밥 신세가 되게 하다; To lower someone's high self-opinion.

□ ***put one's ass on the line*** 위태로운[위험한] 상황에 있다, 목숨을 걸다; To take a huge risk.

□ put ***one***'s money on ~의 성공을 장담하다; To believe in.

□ put ***one's*** oar in 남의 일에 간섭하다; To interfere

□ put ***one's*** two cents in 자기 의견을 말하다; To state one's opinion.

□ put ***somebody*** in stitches 웃음보를 터트리다; To cause big laughter.

- put *somebody*'s nose out of joint　　화나게 하다; To offend and anger somebody; to upset and annoy somebody.

- **put *something* on hold**　　보류하다. 연기하다; To postpone.

- put *something* on ice　　보류하다. 연기하다; To postpone.

- **put *something* on the back burner**　뒷전으로 미루다; To put something on a low priority or you are procrastinating.

  • That must be another government policy put on the back burner.

- put the finger on　　[범인]을 경찰에 밀고하다; To inform on another person or group to authorities.

- put the heat on　　~에 강한 압박을 가하다, ~의 행동에 눈을 부라리다; ~을 엄하게 다루다[단속하다]; To coerce or intimidate.

  • The man put the heat on his colleagues' behavior.

- put the pedal to the metal　　차를 전속력으로 몰다; To speed in a vehicle.

- put the screws on　　(~를 상대로) 바짝 나사를 죄다[압박을 가하다]; To force a desired action using threats or intimidation.

- put the smack down　　~을 호되게 질책하다, ~을 실각시키다; To regulate, often by force.

  • The party started to get out of hand, so we had to put the smack down.

- put the smack down　　세게 치다; To hit hard.

- **put the squeeze on**　　(~을 하라고) ~에게 압박[압력]을 가하다; To put pressure on somebody to act in a particular way; make a situation difficult for somebody.

step. 17

□ **queer**   퀴어, (특히 남자) 동성애자; Homosexual, homosexual person.

• I've also been called poof, faggot, queer, little girl.

□ *quickie*   짧은 시간에 갖는 성관계; A very brief sexual en-
counter. May be performed in a non-traditional location such as a janitor's closet or bathroom.

• Pat and I had a quickie during his lunch break.

□ *quiff*   (여성의) 성기; Female genitalia.

• She's got a tight little quiff.

□ *quim*   (여성의) 성기; Female genitalia.

• Cassie's face was in Jenny's quim and Jenny was munching on Sahara's slick box.
• She's got a tight little quim.

266

step. 18

R

□ **R and R** 휴식; Rest and relaxation.

• I could use some serious R and R.

□ *rack* (여성의) 가슴; Breasts.

• Check out the rack on that woman!

□ *rag* 생리; 생리하다; Menstrual period; to menstruate.

• I've been ragging since Tuesday, and I feel horrible!
• My rag is really heavy this month.

□ **rage** 야단법석, 떠들썩한 파티, 댄스 파티; A fun activity or noisy dance party.

• That party was such a rage!

□ **raggedy-ass(ed)** 낡은, 오래된, 애처로운; Over-used, worn-out, pathetic

□ **railroad** (서둘러/강압적으로 무엇을 하도록) 몰아붙이다; To force or bully.

• The bill was railroaded through the House.

□ *raincoat* 콘돔; A condom.

• Did you wear a raincoat?

□ **rake it in** 한밑천 잡다[벌다]; To make a large profit.

□ **rake _somebody_ over the coals** 심하게 질책하다, 비난하다; To reprimand angrily.

□ *randy* (성적(性的)으로) 흥분한; Horny; to be sexually aroused or in a horny state of mind.

• I'm feeling so randy right now!

268

□ **rap**   징역형; 범죄 혐의; 체포, 구속; A criminal charge.

□ **rap sheet**   전과(前科) 기록; A list of one's past criminal charges.

> • Pontolillo has not been charged in the death of Donald D. Rice, 49, who had a long rap sheet of burglary arrests and was released from jail just two days before the altercation.

□ **rap** *somebody's* **knuckles**   심하게 질책하다, 비난하다; To reprimand angrily.

□ **rarin' to go**   ~하고 싶어서 좀이 쑤시다; ~하고 싶어서 근질근질하다; Excited to get started.

> • Mary is rarin' to go and can't wait for her university term to start.

□ **rat**   1. 쥐새끼 같은(비열한) 놈 2. 밀고자; 1. A criminal; a bad person. 2. Someone who reports misdeeds to an authority; narc, snitch

□ ***rat's ass***   무(無), 영; 조금의 관심[주의] (부정문에 사용); No; nothing; nothing to care.

> • "I don't give a rat's ass why you're here, move the fucking truck out of my parking space," Adam hissed.
> • I don't give a rat's ass what you think!

□ **rattlebrain**   머리가 텅 빈 사람; An empty-headed man.

□ **ratty**   1. 불쌍한, 처량한; 초라한. 2. 화를 잘 내는, 신경질 내는; In a poor condition; liable to anger.

> • He gets ratty if he doesn't get enough sleep.

□ **raunchy**   선정적인, 더러운, 지저분한; Nasty, gross, disgusting, revolting, etc. Also raunchy-licious.

> • Dude, that rotten trash is raunchy!

□ **raw deal**　　부당한 대우, 가혹한 처사; Unfair or unjust treatment; a bad deal.

□ **razzle dazzle**　　1. 소동, 야단법석; (대)혼란, 와글거림 2. (기법·효과 등의) 겉치레의 현란함; (극 등의) 화려한 연기 (장면); A noisy and showy display.

• It's entertainment now and the younger generation expect the razzle dazzle that comes before the fights.

□ **Read me?**　　내 말 알아들어?; Do you understand me?

□ **read my lips**　　내 말 잘 들어라; Pay close attention.

• What does he say now? In America, George Bush said, "Read my lips; no more taxes," but increased taxes and lost an election.

□ **read *somebody/something***　　이해하다; To understand.

□ **real deal**　　적법한 것, 진짜 물건; Something legitimate.

• This is the real deal, not a knock-off.

□ **real McCoy**　　(가짜가 아니라 진정한 가치를 지닌) 진짜[진품]; Something legitimate.

• This is the real McCoy, not a knock-off.

□ **red**　　공산주의자 (빨갱이); Communist

□ **red herring**　　(중요한 것에서) 관심을 딴 데로 돌리는 것; An argument used to distract someone from the real issue.

• Some people say that using ethanol as a fuel is just a red herring distracting people from the real issues of oil dependency and that what we really need is a complete replacement for fossil based fuels.

□ *red tide*　　생리 기간; Menstrual period.

□ **redneck** (모욕적으로 쓰여 교육 수준이 낮고 정치적으로 보수적인 미국의) 시골 사람; A person from a rural area. Origin: according to the stereotype (however accurate it may be,) people from rural areas spend a great deal of time working in the field. In doing so, the backs of their necks become sun burnt.

□ **reggie** 우회전; Right-hand turn. One either "does" or "makes" a reggie. See 'louie.'

• Do a reggie at the stop sign.

□ **recessionista** 리세셔니스타. 적은 예산으로 자신을 꾸미는 사람; A person whose clothes, whether cheap, second-hand, or suitably subdued, are considered appropriate to an economic downturn.

• It's no wonder some recessionista brides are turning to websites like TheDressList.com for second-hand wedding gowns.

□ **retard** 지능 지체아; 천치, 바보; An unintelligent person.

• You're such a retard.

□ **retch** ~을 토하다, 게우다; To vomit.

• That guy is retching everywhere and it almost hit that dog!

□ **rev up** 활성화되다, 힘이 붙다, 활기 띠다; To increase the speed at which something operates.

• Exercise is not likely to rev up your metabolism.

□ **rib** (친근하게) 놀리다; To make fun of.

• He ribbed me in the class all day.

□ **ride one's dick** 여성 상위의 체위로 성교하다; During intercourse, to be penetrated while on top.

• That girl was riding my dick last night.

- *ride the hershey highway*   항문 성교하다; To have anal sex.

> • Person A: Yo man, are you going to get a little tonight?
>   Person B: No dude, she is ragging.
> • Person A: Oh, so you're going to ride the Hershey Highway?

- **Right on!**   옳소[잘한다] (강한 찬성 · 격려를 나타냄); A phrase indicating approval, agreement, or just acknowledgement.

> • You're going dancing tonight? Right on.

- **right-winger**   우익, 보수주의자; A politically conservative person.

- **rip off**   ~에게 바가지를 씌우다; 바가지; To give someone a bad bargain; to steal from, or con someone.

> • Premier League tickets are a rip off.
> • This hamburger is a rip-off! I want my money back.

- *rip shit*   화가 많이 난; Enraged or otherwise highly emotional.

- *rip somebody a new asshole/one*   공격하다, 비난하다; To attack.

- **ripper**   훌륭한, 일류의; An excellent one of its type.

- **rise and shine**   (보통 잠자리에 있는 사람에게 하는 명령문으로 쓰여) 정신 차리고 일어나라[일어나서 움직여라]; Interjection used to wake someone up.

> • Rise and shine: time to start the day with all the latest tech news, rounded up in one place.

- **rock**   (가수 · 악단이) 감동[감명]을 주다; To be a talented musician or musical group.

> • This band rocks.

□ **rock** 코카인, 끽연용 결정(結晶) 헤로인; A piece of crack cocaine.

- Will you stop acting like I'm blowing bums for rock, for Christ's sake?

□ **rock and roll** 멋지다. 좋다; Statement of support, agree-ment, encouragement.

□ **rock 'n' roll** 멋지다. 좋다; Statement of support, agree-ment, en-couragement.

- Person A: We're going to a theme park tomorrow.
  Person B: Rock 'n' roll!

□ **rock star** 아주 매력이 있거나 재능이 있는 사람; The quality of being impressively fashionable or attractive; a talented person.

- You're such a rock star.

□ **rocket science** 고도의 지능이 요구되는 일; Something very dif-ficult. Used in the negative.

- Look, changing the oil may be messy, but it's not rocket science.

□ **rocket scientist** (일반적으로) 머리가 좋은 사람, 수재; A very clever or intelligent person.

- It doesn't need rocket scientist to solve the problem.

□ **rocking** 굉장한, 멋있는, 재미있는; Excellent; fun, exciting, lively, etc.

- Bar manager: Thank god, it's a slow night.
  Peck: Really? For a Sunday, this place is pretty rockin'.
- You guys had rocking gay sex in the bathroom?

□ *rod* 남성의 성기; Penis

□ *roll in the hay* (한 차례의) 성교; A session of sex.

- I'm kind of in the mood for a roll in the hay.

- **rolling in dough**   아주 돈이 많은; Very rich.

- **rolling in money**   아주 돈이 많은; Very rich.

- **Rolling on the floor laughing**   온라인 채팅을 할 때 이전의 포스팅이나 채팅, 상대방의 농담에 대한 열렬한 반응을 나타내는 말로 포복절도하는 모습을 나타냄; Text message used to indicate great amusement, usually exaggerated, at something.

- **rookie**   초심자, 초보자; A newcomer to a group or team.

- ***rosebud***   항문; Anus

  • We're going to get on the bed, spread our ass cheeks and give you a good look at our little rosebud.

- **ROTFLMAO**   온라인 채팅을 할 때 이전의 포스팅이나 채팅, 상대방의 농담에 대한 열렬한 반응을 나타내는 말로 포복절도하는 모습을 나타냄; Rolling on the floor, laughing my ass off.

- **ROTFLMFAO**   온라인 채팅을 할 때 이전의 포스팅이나 채팅, 상대방의 농담에 대한 열렬한 반응을 나타내는 말로 포복절도하는 모습을 나타냄; Rolling on the floor, laughing my fucking ass off.

- **rough up**   ~를 두들겨 패다; To hurt.

- **roughhouse**   난투를 벌이다; 시끄럽게 놀다, 야단법석을 떨다; To play roughly.

- **roughneck**   거친 남자; Crude male.

- **rub elbows**   명사들과 사귀다; ~와 교제하다; ~와 친밀하게 일하다; To socialize.

  • He rubs elbows with the rich and famous.

- **rub in**   (기억하고 싶지 않은 일을) 자꾸 들먹이다[상기시키다]; To repeatedly or pointedly bring up a sore subject.

- Louise: What? I only know two restaurants. And they have cloth napkins.
- Bob: Don't rub it in.

□ *rub one off*　　　자위하다; To masturbate.

- Go take a shower and rub one off, you'll feel better.

□ *rub one out*　　　자위하다; To masturbate.

- "Look at him," she said, tapping Shelly on the shoulder. "He is just sitting there ogling us like we're in a butcher shop window. I'm surprised he's not rubbing one out."
- I was so horny I had to rub one out.

□ rub out　　　~를 죽이다[살해하다]; To kill.

□ rub *somebody's* nose in it　　　남의 언동[실패]을 야단치다, 벌주다; 남에게 잔소리를 퍼붓다; To reprimand other's failure; to punish.

□ **rubber**　　　콘돔; A condom.

- Always wear a rubber during sex.

□ **rubber stamp**　　　(법률/계획 등을) 잘 살펴보지도 않고 인가하다; To approve without debate or significant thought.

- I can't believe the board just rubber stamped that measure.

□ **rubberneck**　　　(차를 타고 지나가면서) 고개를 돌려 보다; Someone who slows down on the highway to stare at an accident.

- The traffic jam was caused by rubber-neckers slowing down for a gawk at the accident.

□ **ruckus**　　　야단법석, 대소동; A great deal of noise, argument, or confusion.

□ **rule the roost**　　　(무리 사이에서) 가장 강한 영향력을 행사하다[지배권을 쥐다]; To be the person who controls a group, family, community, etc.

□ **rumble**　　　갱들의 싸움(gang fight); A brawl; a fight.

275

• There is a rumble tomorrow in the park.

□ **run for the hills**   도망가다; To run away.

• The rest of us would have taken the offer and ran for the hills.

□ **run off at the mouth**   (분별없이) 말을 줄줄 늘어놓다; To speak unwisely.

• I hate you running off at the mouth!

□ **run on empty**   자력(資力)[방책]이 다하다; 힘을 잃다, 역부족이다; To be reaching the end of one's reserves of strength, patience, energy, money, or some other necessary item.

• I think his energy and mental reserves are almost running on empty.

□ **run out of gas/steam**   (일이)진척이 안되다, 멈추다; To stop functioning.

□ **run-in**   언쟁, 싸움; A fight.

S

□ *sack*　　　　　　　고환; 남자다움; 용기; Testicles, courage

　• Get a sack and go ask her out.

□ **sack**　　　　　　해고하다, 파면하다; To dismiss from a job; fire

　• Four hundred workers face the sack.

□ sack out　　　　　자러 가다, 잠자리에 들다; To sleep.

□ *sad-ass*　　　　　불쌍해 보이는; Looking very unhappy.

□ *safety meeting*　　직원들이 근무 중에 몰래 모여 마약을 하는 시간; A break in the workday when employees gather to ingest drugs.

　• There is going to be a safety meeting in 5 minutes.

□ *salad tossing*　　항문 구강성교; Anilingus

　• She's into salad tossing.

□ *salami*　　　　　　남성의 성기; A penis.

□ salty　　　　　　　(때로 약간 저속하지만) 재미있는, 저속한; Corny or childish.

　• That was the saltiest joke I've heard in a long time.

□ saphead　　　　　바보, 얼간이; Fool; idiot

□ **sassy**　　　　　　멋지게 옷을 입는; Stylish

　• Those clothes are sassy!

□ *sausage party*　　남자들만의 파티; A gathering with many more males than females. Connotes displeasure.

　• Let's take off, this is just a sausage party.

□ Savvy?　　　　　　알겠느냐?; Do you understand me?

278

□ Savvy!	알았다!; To understand!
□ say uncle cry uncle.	항복하다, 패배를 인정하다; To accept defeat; to
□ Say what?	뭐라고?; Could you repeat that?
□ scab	항상 빌리기만 하고 갚지는 않은 사람; Someone who borrows things and doesn't expect to pay them back.

• He is always scabbing cigarettes.

□ **scalp**	암표를 팔다; To sell tickets to an event for more than their list price.

• He was trying to pick up some cash scalping tickets.

□ **scam**	사기; A fraudulent business scheme; swindle

• My parents lost their retirement in some internet scam.

□ scare *somebody* stiff	굉장히 겁을 주다; To scare badly.
□ *scare the bejesus out of*	굉장히 겁을 주다; To scare badly.
□ *scare the crap out of*	굉장히 겁을 주다; To scare badly.

• I am kind of embarrassed at how I acted. I sort of smacked Eric and Shelly's dad around a little and scared the crap out of her little brothers. It wasn't one of my better days.
• No, but honestly, you two scared the crap out of me.

□ **scare the hell out of**	굉장히 겁을 주다; To scare very much.

• Sock: You don't think she's gonna come after us, do you?
  Sam: God, I hope not. She scares the hell out of me.
• Sock: Well, all women scare the hell out of you.

□ scare the living daylights out of much.	굉장히 겁을 주다; To scare very

- scare the pants off *somebody*   굉장히 겁을 주다; To scare very much.

- scare the pants out of *somebody*   굉장히 겁을 주다; To scare badly.

- **scare the shit out of**   굉장히 겁을 주다; To scare someone tremendously.

  • Dude, you scared the shit out of me.

- *scared shitless*   겁을 많이 먹은; Really scared.

  • OMG, that movie was freaky! I was Scared Shitless!

- schiz out   미치다; To go insane.

- schizo   정신분열증 환자; A person with schizophrenia.

- schlep   싫은 녀석, 무능한 사람, 귀찮은 사람; A lowly person.

  • He's such a schlep.

- *schlong*   남근(男根), 음경; Penis

- schlong   싫은 녀석. 지겨운 녀석; Displeasing person; dick

  • You are such a schlong!

- *schlong juice*   정액; Semen

- schloomp   바보, 얼간이; Fool, idiot

- *schlort*   단소 음경; A short penis. (A play on the word schlong.)

  • A schlong is better than a schlort.

- schlub   바보, 얼간이; A clumsy, oafish person.

- schmaltz   몹시 감상적인 곡, 감상주의; Too sentimental.

  • A schmaltzy wedding.

- schmaltzy 몹시 감상적인. (또는 schmalzy, shmaltzy, shmal-zy); Too sentimental.

  • A bathroom stop took almost 30 minutes because they had to peruse every item in the schmaltzy gift shop.

- *schmeck* 헤로인; Heroin; schmecker – heroin user. A Yiddish variation on "smack".

  • Let's shoot some schmeck!

- *schmeckel* 남성의 성기; Pejorative. derivative of schmuck. Yiddish derivative for penis.

  • That guy is such a schmeckel.

- schmo 멍청이, 얼간이; An unintelligent person.

- **schmooze** 향후 사업 성공을 위해 사교를 하다(한담을 나누다. 수다 떨다); To interact socially with people, usually for future business gains. To use flattery and ingratiation as a modus operandi.

- schmuck 멍청이, 얼간이; A general insult; jerk; asshole. From the Yiddish term, an obscene term for penis.

  • You read in the tabloids every day, some schmuck hits it big and falls to pieces because he wasn't ready for success.

- schmutz 오물; 더러움, 얼룩; An unpleasant, unidentified substance.

- schnockered 술 취한; Very much drunken.

  • He was so schnockered he fell off the bar stool.

- schnook 별 볼 일 없는 인간, 멍청이; A stupid or gullible person.

- schnozz 코; Nose

  • Check out the schnozz on that guy!

□ *schwartz*   남성의 성기; Penis

• I see your schwartz is as big as mine.

□ **scoop**   최신 정보; The latest information.

• What's the scoop on the upcoming hiring freeze?

□ scoot   서둘러 가다; To go or leave quickly.

• Wow, is that the time? I've got to scoot!

□ **scope out**   ~을 자세히 살피다, 이성을 훑어보다; To examine or investigate; To stare, usually at a member of the opposite gender.

• I was scoping out that hot soccer player after practice.

□ scorch   심하게 질책하다, 비난하다; To reprimand angrily.

□ **score**   성공하다, 득점하다; To succeed.

□ *score*   [여자를] 손에 넣다; [마약을] 입수하다; To have sex.

• Guess who scored last night?

□ score a touchdown   성공하다, 득점하다; To success.

□ **scout's honor**   (보이) 스카우트의 영예를 걸고 말하는 것. 정말이다; To make a strong promise.

• Lee: Scout's honor?   Don: On my mother's grave.

□ scram   도주; 도주하다; To leave; to run away.

• Let's scram!

□ scratch   (행사/경기 참가 등을[에서]) 취소[제외]하다; To get rid of, to give up on.

□ **screaming**   매력 있는; Attractive

• That man is screamin'.

282

□ ***screw***   섹스하다; To have sex.

- She's pretty. Look, if she was there in '92, and if she looked anything like that, I promise you I totally screwed her.

□ **screw**   (사람에게서 특히 많은 돈을) 우려[뜯어]내다; To deceive; to cheat.

□ **screw**   사라지게 하다. 꺼져 버리게 하다; An expression of anger. Roughly, "let (one) be screwed".

- Person A: He just called and said he's not coming.
  Person B: Well, screw him!

□ **screw**   ~을 엉망으로 하다[망치다]; To err; mess up.

- He screwed that interview.

□ **screw around**   시간을 낭비하다; To waste time.

□ **screw around with *something*** 망치다, 엉망으로 만들다; To not take a task seriously.

□ ***Screw off!***   꺼져; A dismissive retort; buzz off; go away.

□ ***screw the pooch***   완전히 망치다, 완전히 실패하다; To make an irreparable (possibly tragic) mistake. To fail completely.

- GB has screwed the pooch on the economy, and everyone knows it.
- Q: How did you do on the exam?
  A: I totally screwed the pooch.

□ **screw up**   ~을 엉망으로 하다[망치다]; To err; mess up.

- They screwed up that paint job.

□ ***Screw you!***   엿 먹어라!; A contemptuous dismissal; An expression of anger.

- Person A: You suck at fishing.
  Person B: Screw you!
- Screw you! I'll do what I want.

- **screwed up** 혼란한, 당혹한, 난장판이 된; To be in serious trouble, broken, ruined, defective

- **screw-up** 실수투성이의 사람; A person who makes many mistakes.

  • He's such a screw-up.

- **screw-up** 실패, 실수, 실책; A mistake.

  • It was a huge screw-up.

- **screwy** 나사가 풀린 듯한, 이상한; Strange

  • My car has been acting screwy lately.

- **scrog** 망치다. 고장 내다; To damage or ruin. Also spelled skrog.

  • The data tapes got scrogged in transit.

- **scrounge** (공짜로) 얻어 내다; To get by asking or begging.

- *scud* 멀리서 보면 매력적인 여성이지만 가까이서 보면 아님; Pertaining to the attractiveness of a girl you see. Good from far, but far from good.

  • When I was across the room she looked good, but as I got closer I realized she was a scud.

- **scum** 인간쓰레기, 쓰레기 같은 인간; A bad person or group.

  • Stay away from that scum.

- *scum* 정액; Semen

- **scumbag** 쓰레기 같은 인간, 더러운 놈; An undesirable person - usually one who is without morals or decency. See also scum.

  • Tevon's the dealer they clock for. He runs the projects - real scumbag.

284

- scupper   실패하게 하다, 좌절시키다; To put an end to.

- scuzzbag   인간쓰레기, 쓰레기 같은 인간; A bad person or group.

- **Search me!**   난들 아나[난 모른다]; I have no idea.

- **see where _somebody_ is coming from**   ~의 처지를 이해하다, ~의 입장을 이해하다; To understand another's viewpoint.

    • I can see where you are coming from, Calleva, however I most disagree.

- **See you later, alligator!**   Robert Charles Guidry의 원곡인 'See You Later, Alligator'를 1955년 Bill Haley and His Comets'가 rock-and-roll 로 편곡하여 불러 유명하게 된 인사말; A casual farewell, often responded to with the rejoinder, "After a while, crocodile!"

- _seed_   정액; Semen

- **sell**   (아이디어/서비스/후보자 등을 받아들이도록) 납득시키다; To convince.

    • I sold my boss on letting me work from home once a week.

- **sell down the river**   남을 속이다, 배신하다; To betray a person.

- **sell like hotcakes**   불티나게 팔리다; To be sold very quickly in large quantities.

    • Every scene Derrick Driller has released has sold like hotcakes.

- **sell out**   (~을 위해) 신념[원칙]을 버리다; 배신하다; To betray a person; To exit a previous arrangement, change one's mind, change one's usual behavior, etc.

    • They will sell out on you in a minute.

- **sell _somebody_ a lemon**   고장 난 물건(특히 자동차)를 팔다; To sell defective or damaged goods.

- **sell _somebody_ bill of goods**   야바위를 치다; To play a trick upon a person.

□ send *somebody* packing   해고하다, 퇴짜 놓다; To dismiss from a job; fire.

□ send *somebody* to the cleaners   빈털터리를 만들다; To cheat; to deceive.

□ send *somebody* to the showers   해고하다, 퇴짜 놓다; To dismiss from a job; fire.

□ set about   ~를 공격하다; To start a fight.

□ **settle a/the score**   복수하다; To seek revenge.

□ settle accounts   복수하다; To seek revenge.

□ **sew up**   성사시키다, 매듭짓다; Accomplish

   • They think they have the election sewn up.

□ *sex up*   성욕을 불러일으키다; 성적 매력을 더하게 하다; To engage sexually with a person.

   • I want to sex you up, girl.

□ sexy mama   아주 섹시한 여자; An extremely attractive woman with striking sex appeal.

   • Man, what a sexy mama!

□ shabby   다 낡은, 허름한; Things or places looking old and in bad condition.

□ shack up   동서(同棲)하다; 불의의 관계를 가지다; To hook up in a sexual manner and spend the night with someone. A person who shacks-up may be referred to as a "shacker."; Have a sex.

   • I don't think his father was too thrilled when he shacked up with his girlfriend.
   • Who did you shack-up with last night?

286

□ *shaft* 남성의 성기; Penis

• Wow, he's got a big shaft.

□ *shag* 섹스, 성교; A session of sex.

• Fancy a shag?

□ shake a leg (남에게 하는 말로) 빨리빨리 시작해라[움직여라]; To hurry.

• Alright, ladies, shake a leg. Keep truckin'.

□ shake the money tree (큰) 이익을 낳다, 크게 벌다; To make a large profit.

□ shakes 떨림; Body shaking from a fit of fear.

□ shanghai (어떤 일을) 속여서 하게 하다; To trick someone into taking a job; to trick someone into joining the crew of a ship.

□ shape up 태도를 개선하다; 더 열심히 일하다; To improve your work or your behavior.

□ sharpie 교활한 사람; 빈틈없는 사람; A person of sharp intelligence.

□ *shawty* 자기보다 나이가 어린 사람의 호칭; A person younger than one's self. Origin: hip-hop slang. "shorty"

• What's up, shawty?

□ shedload 엄청난 양(특히 돈); A large amount.

• I've got shedloads of work to do.

□ sheisty 욕심 많은, 구두쇠인; Deceitful; untrustworthy; greedy. (Also "shiesty")

• I wouldn't hang out with him, he's shiesty.

- **shekels** 셰켈(이스라엘의 통화 단위); 돈; The standard monetary unit of modern Israel, divided into 100 Agorot; money.

- **shell out** (~에 거금을) 들이다[쏟아붓다]; To pay a lot of money.

  - I had to shell out quite a bit for that ring.

- **shellack** 얻어맞다. 큰 점수 차로 지다; To take a beating, or lose a game badly by a large score.

  - The team took a real shellacking from everywhere.

- **shenanigans** 1. 허튼소리(nonsense), 장난 2. 속임, 사기, 기만 (deceit); Trickery; misbehavior.

  - Our entrepreneurs are the best, despite the shenanigans of a venal government.

- **shiesty** 욕심 많은, 구두쇠인; Deceitful; untrustworthy; greedy (Also "sheisty")

  - I wouldn't hang out with him, he's shiesty.

- **shindig** 떠들썩한 파티; A noisy party.

  - Look, just get us into the shindig tonight.

- *shit* 똥, 대변; Feces

  - There is shit on the floor.
  - I don't want anyone pissing or shitting on me. I don't mind drinking your cum and I wouldn't care if Sarah or Allie squirted in my mouth while cumming. But I don't want to be pissed on.

- *shit* 제기랄, 빌어먹을(bullshit); Exclamation expressing displeasure; exclamation of disbelief or Skepticism; used to emphasize a point or request; Also sheesh; used to convey surprise or alarm.

  - You're telling me that you hooked up with her and her mom? Shit.
  - Shit, I missed the bus!
  - Shit, calm down.

288

□ **shit** [부정문에서] 무(無), 아주 조금; Anything, Used in the negative to mean "nothing".

• There ain't shit going on.

□ **shit** 쓸모없는 것; 조악한 물건; Something not worth mentioning.

• I'm tired of his shit.

□ **shit** 겉치레; 겉치레만의 이야기; 거짓말; To attempt to deceive; lie to.

• That watch is yours? You're shitting me!

□ **shit** 품질이 형편없는 것. 기분이 나쁜 것; Of poor quality; bad

• "You're blocking my parking space," Adam said as he pulled beside them. "Move that piece of shit to visitor parking or I'll have it towed away."
• Why do you listen to that shit music?

□ **shit a brick** 몹시 조바심내다; 화내다; [감탄사적으로] 우라질!, 빌어먹을!, 쳇!; To freak out; go crazy; get extremely upset.

• It's not that bad, don't shit a brick!

□ **shit fucker** 병신. 바보; A person who is being an idiot or a stupid ass.

• You such a shit fucker.

□ **shit in _one's_ shoes** 아주 놀라다; To feel fear.

□ **shit list** 블랙리스트; A list of people one is angry with.

• Congratulations! You just made my shit list.

□ **shit on** 속이다, 형편없이 대하다; To cheat; to treat poorly.

• Are you shitting on me?

□ *shit oneself*   겁을 먹다; To feel fear.

□ *shit out of luck*   아주 재수 없는; Without hope, in an irreparable bad situation.

> • You have no money for cab fare? Well then I guess you're shit out of luck!

□ *shit storm*   형편없는 상황; A terrible mess.

> • "So you elected to deflect the shit storm your way, huh?" he asked with a grin. "Bet you won't do that again soon."
> • We're in the middle of a shit storm now.

□ **Shit!**   체!, 빌어먹을!, 우라질!; Vulgar exclamation of displeasure.

□ *shit-bag*   바보, 멍청이; Dumb ass; jack ass.

> • You fucking shit-bag.

□ *shitface*   얼빠진[멍청한] 얼굴을 한 놈; General insult.

> • Hey, shitface.

□ *shithead*   똥 쌀 놈, 싫은 놈; A despicable person.

> • You're a real shithead!

□ *shithole*   거지 소굴 같은 곳; A filthy, disgusting or dilapidated place or establishment.

> • I would be willing to bet she has washed her hands of that whole fucked up shithole you call a town and everyone in it.

□ *shitkicker*   촌놈; Cowboys or cowgirls and by extension rednecks in general.

> • What do you mean you've got no money you, you fucking shit kicker?

□ *shitless*   겁을 먹다; I'm scared shitless.

□ *shitlist*   블랙리스트; A list of people one is angry with.

- You just put yourself on my shitlist.

□ **shitload**   대량, 다수, 잔뜩; A large amount.

- Carl just showed up with a shitload of beer.
- I've made a shitload of money in the last week. Tate said he would cut me a check for the download fees at the end of the week.

□ *shits*   놀람; A fit of fear.

□ *Shitsure!*   그렇고 말고, 물론이지, 옳소; Certainly; Definitely

□ *shitter*   변소; Toilet

□ **shitty**   1. 엉망진창인, 형편없는 2. 개 같은, 더러운; Inferior; worthless; despicable; Displeasing or of poor quality.

- I got a job offer from someplace called Dropping Point. He got shitty when I told him no.
- That movie was shitty.

□ *shlong (schlong)*   남성의 성기; Penis

- "Get the fuck out of here with that shit," Matt scoffed. "I've watched you lick a bitch's asshole out while another bitch sucked your schlong from behind. I've had a contest with you about how many bitches we could bang in one night. And now that you're scoring some regular pussy you don't want to give up the details?"
- You got a big shlong!

□ shnockered   술에 (많이) 취한; Extremely inebriated.

- I'm going to get so shnockered at the party!

□ shoestring   소액의 돈; A small amount of money.

□ **shoo-in**   쉽게 우승할 사람; A certainty; in a competition, the probable winner.

□ *shoot (one's) load* 사정하다; To ejaculate.

• She looked so good I thought I was going to shoot my load in my pants!

□ *shoot (one's) wad* 사정하다; To ejaculate.

□ shoot *oneself* in the foot   자신에게 문제를 일으키다; To cause problems for oneself.

□ **shoot the breeze** 잡담하다, 쓸데없이 지껄이다; To chat; to talk idly.

• Some of my former students spotted me and came over to say hi and shoot the breeze.

□ *shoot the shit*   말 같지 않은 소리를 지껄이다; To talk meaningless things.

□ shoot up   총격(전); To fire guns repeatedly in or into.

• The gangsters shot up the speak-easy.

□ *shoot up*   (정맥에) 마약을 주사하다; To inject a drug.

□ **short fuse**   성격이 급함; A short temper.

• Her short fuse is always getting her into trouble.

□ *shorty*   여자; A young female. Origin: hip-hop slang; a person.

• "Uh-oh! Uh-oh! "K" to the "N" to the "O-P-E" she's the dopest little shorty in all Pawnee, Indiana. Leslie Knope, seriously, you get sexier every day. And that is not a line. That is for reals."
• What's up, shorty?

□ **shot**   시도; An attempt.

□ shot to hell   아주 망한, 엉망이 된; Completely damaged.

□ **shotgun**   (승용차 · 트럭의) 조수석(에 먼저 타기); The passenger seat in a vehicle.

292

- I get shotgun!
- I get to sit shotgun.

□ **shotgun wedding**　(신부의 임신 등으로 인해) 급히 치르는 하는 결혼식.
속도위반 결혼; A wedding where the woman is pregnant.

- Wasn't that a shotgun wedding?

□ *Shove it!*　집어치워[말도 안 되는 소리 하지 마]; Angry retort.

- Shove it, jerk.

□ *Shove it up your ass!*　집어치워[말도 안 되는 소리 하지 마]; A
contemptuous dismissal.

□ *shove off*　꺼져라; Leave

- Why don't you just shove off, man?

□ **shove** *one's* **oar in**　쓸데없는 참견을 하다, 공연히 덥적거리다; To interfere; to interlude.

□ **show** *somebody* **the door/gate**　쫓아내다, 해고하다; To dismiss
from a job; fire

□ **showboat**　과시하다; To perform or behave in a showy and
flamboyant way.

□ **showstopper**　하드웨어나 소프트웨어를 사용할 수 없게 만드는 오
류; A bug that makes hardware or software unusable.

- I do not think that climate and environment of itself is a show stopper to
our being able to deploy.

□ **shrink**　정신과 의사; A psychologist or psychiatrist.

- It's like he's on posh drugs, you know, the sort that shrinks for rich-and-
famous people give their customers to keep them around, you know?

□ *shucks*　이런, 어머, 아뿔싸(당혹감/실망감을 나타내는 소리);
An exclamation of disappointment, annoyance, etc.

□ shut *one's* barn door	바지 지퍼를 올리다; To zip one's fly.	
□ shut out	영패시키다, 완봉승을 거두다; To defeat impressively.	
□ **Shut the fuck up!** infix intensifier.	아가리 닥쳐!; Shut up with "the fuck"	
□ *Shut your trap!*	아가리 닥쳐!; Shut up your mouth!	
□ *sicko* or gross person.	이상 심리 소유자, 정신병자 같은 사람; A disturbing	

• I don't need to feel like some sicko just because I wear someone's clothes.

□ sidekick	조수; A person who accompanies one helps him/her.	
□ sideline seem unimportant and not included in what people are doing.	열외로 취급하다; To make something/someone to	
□ siff	지불을 거부하다; To refuse to pay.	
□ sign up for	~에 서명하다, ~을 믿다; To believe.	
□ **simmer down** To grow calmer or quieter, as after intense rage or excitement.	(화·흥분 후에 차츰) 진정하다 [화를 가라앉히다];	
□ **sing a different tune** change one's opinion/attitude.	견해[의견, 태도 따위]를 바꾸다; To	
□ singing the blues	울상을 짓고 있는, 침울한; Depressed	
□ sink *one's* teeth into	~에 기세 좋게 달려들다; To start a task.	
□ sissified	패기 없는, 유약한; Effeminate; of weak male.	
□ sissy	계집애 같은 사내(애); Effeminate, weak male.	

• To my dad, people who taught at colleges and people who wore ties were 'sissies' – all of them.

□ ***Sit on it and rotate!***　　　엿 먹어라!; A contemptuous dismissal.

□ **sit tight**　　　움직이지 않고 가만히 있다; To stay in one place
and wait patiently.

- Annie: Sit tight. I'll be back. I said sit tight!
- Carlo Reni: That's not something I'm good at - sit tight.

□ **six feet under**　　　(죽어서) 매장된, 묘에 (들어가); Dead and buried.

- Her grandfather has been six feet under for some time now.

□ ***sixty nine***　　　남녀 동시 구강성교; Simultaneous oral sexual
stimulation: from the physical position of head to tail.

- 69 is a popular sexual position.

□ ***skank***　　　훔치다; To steal.

- He skanked my pencil.

□ ***skank***　　　매춘부; Whore; prostitute

- They worried he might hook up with a skank and start bringing them
around.

□ ***skank***　　　불쾌한 것[사람], 기분 나쁜 녀석[것]; Messy, run
down, dilapidated

- My flat is real skank, just look at the fridge.

□ **skeevy**　　　초라한, 더러운; Gross, creepy; ICKY, etc.

- He's so skeevy.

□ **sketchy**　　　의심스러운, 이상한; Of questionable character;
strange

- I'd stay away from that guy, he looks sketchy.

□ **skid row**　　　사회의 밑바닥; A poor area of a town; GHETTO.

- He became a skid row type of drunkard.

□ *skin*   콘돔; A condom.

□ skin *somebody* alive   ~을 몹시 꾸짖다[벌주다]; ~을 완전히 해
치우다; To reprimand severely.

□ skin-flint   구두쇠, 수전노; A mean person who hates spending money.

□ **skinny-dip**   알몸으로 헤엄치다(치기); To swim naked.

- At least once a month I would catch girls skinny dipping in the pool.

□ **skip town**   갑자기 떠나다, 몰래 도망치다; To leave without a trace.

□ **skipper**   선장, 주장; Captain

□ **skosh**   적은, 적은 양의 (일본어에서 유래); A tiny amount; a
little bit; tad; smidgen; jot (from Japanese)

□ **slack**   기회(여유), 여지; Tolerance

- Give him some slack - he's just a kid.

□ *slackass*   게으름뱅이; A lazy person.

- Shaw: You haven't been in here in a while.
  Bar owner: Nope, just wanted to know if you slackasses have cleaned up
  my place yet or not. I've got a business to run, you know?
- Shaw: Yeah, I know. We're on it. We're on it. We're on it.

□ slacker   태만한 사람, 게으름뱅이; A lazy person.

- Those people are real slackers.

□ slack-jaw   태만한 사람, 게으름뱅이; A moron or lazy person,
typically residing in a rural area; BUMPKIN

□ *slag*   갈보; A promiscuous female (UK slang).

• She's been slagging around like the girl in that Police song, 'Roxanne.'

□ **slam dunk**　　　성공이 확실한 것; A sure thing.

• This will be a slam dunk.

□ *slammer*　　　교도소, 유치장; Prison; jail

• "I should have called out 'Spousal Abuse!'" Shelly joked. "But then I'd have to bail you out of the slammer."

□ Slap me five!　　　하이파이브하자!; A request for a "high-five."; a greeting or celebratory gesture of slapping hands (the five refers to the number of fingers) "high" in the air–often above the head.

□ **slap on the wrist**　　가벼운 꾸지람(에 불과한 것); A light punishment.

• The judge gave the defendant a slap on the wrist.

□ slathers　　　대량, 다수, 듬뿍; A large amount.

□ slaughter　　　(시합 등에서) 완승[압승]을 거두다; To defeat impressively.

□ slave away　　　힘들게 일하다. 노예처럼 일하다; To work extremely hard.

• I've slaved away fixing my own broken cars in 30 degree weather.

□ slay　　　(전쟁/싸움에서) 죽이다; To defeat; to kill.

□ **sleaze**　　　부정직한 사람, 부도덕한 사람; A vulgar, contemptible, untrustworthy people.

• He is a real sleaze. I used to dance and he was there every night. He would drop $10,000 on a girl and then she'd leave with him.
• That girl was a sleaze.

□ sleazebag　　　부정직한 사람, 부도덕한 사람; Sleaze; a bad person.

□ **sleep around**　　여러 남자[여자]와 자다[성관계를 갖다]; To have sex with many people.

• He's never at home because he sleeps around so much.

□ **sleep on** *something*　　　~에 대해 하룻밤 동안 생각해 보다; To sleep through the night before making a big decision.

□ *sleeve*　　　팔을 다 덮은 문신; A tattoo that covers all or much of a person's arm.

□ **sleuth**　　　탐정, 사복형사; A detective.

□ **slime**　　　(더럽고) 끈적끈적한 물질, 점액; A thick, wet, unpleasant substance.

□ **slimeball**　　　더러운 인간; A bad person.

□ *sling the crap*　　　거짓말하다; To lie.

□ *sling the shit*　　　거짓말하다; To lie.

□ *slip through the backdoor*　　　항문 성교를 하다; To perform anal sex.

• Last night, I slipped through her backdoor.

□ **slip up**　　　실수를 하다; To make a mistake (Usually written either slip-up or slipup).

• Magnifying oversights and seeing slipups as proof of catastrophe, they unleash hostility, anger, despondency, or jealousy.

□ *slit*　　　여성 성기; Female genitals.

• Every female has a slit.

□ **slob**　　　(지저분한) 게으름뱅이; A dirty or messy person.

• What do you expect of Moyles? He's a disgraceful slob.

□ **slog**　　　(시간이 오래 걸리는 힘든/지루한 일을) 열심히 하다; 힘겹게 걷다; Tedious and time-consuming work.

298

• It's a hard slog, but somebody has to do it.

□ **sloppy**   엉성한, 대충하는, 단정치 못한, 너저분한; Messy, imprecise

• Yeah, he was pretty sloppy last night.

□ sloshed   술 취한; Quite drunk.

□ slouch   (게으르게) 구부정하게 서다; Shoulders and head bent to look lazy and unattractive.

□ **slug**   (주먹으로) ~을 강타하다; (공을) 세게 치다; 싸우다; To hit; to punch.

• I slugged him in the face.

□ slug it out   (싸움 · 시합에서) 결판이 날 때까지 싸우다; To fight very hard until one person or group finally wins.

□ slug-fest   심한 타격전, 난타전; A severe fight.

□ *slut*   1. 난잡하게 놀아먹는 계집, 잡년 2. 지저분하고 게으른 계집; A promiscuous woman.

• Stay back, slut!

□ *slutty*   난잡한; Having loose sexual morals or sexually promiscuous.

• I can't believe she wore such a slutty dress to the wedding!

□ smack   탁 소리가 나게 치다; To hit; to slap.

• He got smacked right in the jaw.

□ smack   공격적인 언행, 비난; Offensive speech about another person.

• I hear you've been talking smack about me.

□ **smack down**   엎어 메치다; To beat with physical violence.

• Frank got smacked down by that 350-pound bouncer.

□ **small beer**   보잘것없는 사람 (것); A trifling matter.

□ **small fry**   별 볼 일 없는 사람; Something or someone unimportant.

□ **small potatoes**   하찮은 것[사람]; 소액; Something insignificant; small amount.

• You've been spending too much on that account. It's small potatoes.

□ **small talk**   한담(특히 사교적인 자리에서 예의상 나누는 것); Discussion about non-sensitive topics in a social setting. Usually performed while meeting someone for the first time, or simply out of politeness.

• Well, you're in paradise with a handsome Italian. Adapt, overcome, make small talk.

□ **smart-ass**   수재, 수완가; 건방진 녀석, 우쭐하는 놈; Someone who replies to questions or situations satirically or in a condescending manner.

• She's a smart-ass teacher.
• I can't stand smart-asses, but when I pictured one, it wasn't hard to be one.

□ **smash**   (노래/영화/연극의) 엄청난 히트[대성공]; A greatly successful thing, especially a movie or a song.

• That movie was a huge smash!

□ **smash and grab**   (가게의) 진열장을 깨고 물건을 탈취하는; A robbery performed by smashing a window, grabbing things from inside, and leaving quickly.

□ **smash-mouth**   격렬한, 공격적인, 난폭한; Raw, real, hardcore, manly

• Kentucky is a smash-mouth, half court defensive team that can really guard people.

300

| smidgen | 아주 조금; 아주 작은 조각; A small amount. |

| smoke | 물리치다; To defeat. |

- She said she wasn't planning to go full out but she smoked us in speed and endurance.

| *smoke* | 마리화나를 피우다; To smoke marijuana. |

- Do you want to smoke?

| **smoke and mirrors** | 교묘한 속임(수); Something deceptive. |

- It turns out the presentation was rigged. The whole thing was smoke and mirrors.
- It was also Graeber, a lifelong hater of corporate smoke and mirrors, who coined the movement's ingenious slogan, "We are the 99%."

| *smoke crack* | 마약을 하다; To do drugs. |

| *smoke dope* | 마약을 하다; To do drugs. |

| *smoke pole* | 펠라티오를 하다; To perform fellatio. |

| **smoking** | 아주 매력적인; Extremely attractive. |

| smooch | 키스(하다); 애무(하다), 페팅(하다)(pet); A kiss; To Kiss. |

- You're the cutest boy in school. We're gonna have an awesome summer. Smooches, Brenda

| *smut* | 난잡한 여자; Promiscuous female. |

- She's a smut.

| snack | 매력적인 사람; Attractive female or male. |

- The boy I like is a total snack!

| SNAFU | 대혼란; Acronym for situation normal: all fucked up; Messed up as usual. |

• Well, that's typical, they're just snafu!

□ **snag** 훔치다; To acquire; to steal.

• He snagged the money from his mom's wallet.

□ **snag** 암초[뜻하지 않은 장애]; A problem, especially one causing a delay.

• There is just one small snag - where is the money coming from.

□ snap *somebody*'s head off 심하게 꾸짖다; To reprimand angrily.

□ **snapperhead** 바보, 멍청이; An idiot.

• Shut up, you snapperhead!

□ **snatch** 와락 붙잡다, 잡아채다, 잡아 뺏다; To obtain quickly.

□ ***snatch*** 질(膣), 여자의 성기; Female genitalia.

• Her snatch smells.

□ ***snatch*** 여자(의 비속어); Derogatory term for a disliked female; BITCH

• She is such a snatch!

□ **snazzy** 아주 맵시 있는, 세련된; Fashionable; of fashion; good; to be stylish.

• My goodness, that bikini really looks snazzy on you!

□ **sneak** 좀도둑질하다; To acquire discretely.

• I sneaked a cake when they were out of the room.

□ sniff *something* out 냄새[후각]로 ~을 알아[찾아]내다; To uncover; to observe a person to judge their abilities.

□ **snitch** 일러바치다; To betray a person.

□ **snitch**　　　　　밀고자; A person who informs on (i.e. reports the misdeeds) of someone else.

- I don't want to be a lousy snitch⋯ Ryan has been using the color printer for his business a lot.

□ **snitch**　　　　　훔치다; To steal.

□ **snooker**　　　　　속이다, 기만하다; To deceive; to take advantage of; cheat; swindle

- We got snookered. I saw you doing it and you saw me doing it and the next thing we know, it's our freaking job.

□ **snooty**　　　　　오만한; With an attitude of superiority; pretentious

- I hate how snooty she is.

□ **snore**　　　　　지루한 것, 잠이 올 정도로 지루한 일; Something boring, not interesting, makes you fall asleep.

- That TV show was a snore.

□ **snot**　　　　　오만하고 버릇없는 자식; An impudent or arrogant person.

- The new supervisor is such a snot that nobody likes her at all.

□ **snot(nose)**　　　　　오만하고 버릇없는 자식; An arrogant and annoying person.

□ **snot-rag**　　　　　콧수건; 더러운; Repulsive, displeasing

□ *snow*　　　　　코카인; Cocaine

- Do you have any snow?

□ *snowball*　　　　　여성이 구강 사정 후의 남성의 정액을 키스로 교환하는 행위; A sexual practice where a person performs fellatio on a male until the male ejaculates, then spits the semen into the male's mouth.

• She gave him a snowball.

□ **snowball's chance**　　가망성이 전혀 없는 일; Hopeless things; abbreviation of "Snowball's chance in hell."

□ **snuff _somebody_ out**　　죽이다; To kill.

□ **So what!**　　그래서? (어쩌라고); I don't' care.

□ **soak**　　많은 돈을 우려내다; To cheat.

□ **_SOB_**　　개새끼, 개자식; Acronym for "son of a bitch."

• He swore that he would be a s.o.b. if he was lying.

□ **soccer mom**　　사커 맘(자녀를 스포츠, 음악 교습 등의 활동에 데리고 다니느라 여념이 없는 전형적인 중산층 엄마를 가리킴); The stereotypical suburban mother.

• Soccer moms indeed! Psychographic segmentation for marketing and advertising extended to politics.
• She will be a big appeal to all the soccer moms in middle America.

□ **sock it to _somebody_**　　세게 치다, 강타하다; To hit.

□ **soft on**　　~에 빠져 있다; Attracted to.

□ **soft touch**　　쉬운[만만한] 사람, 돈을 내기 쉬운 사람; A person easily persuaded or imposed on, esp. to lend money.

□ **SOL**　　더 이상 방법이 없음; Acronym of "shit out of luck", meaning that there is nothing one can do to remedy some situation.

• I guess that means you're SOL.

□ **something else**　　(비슷한 유형의 다른 것들보다) 훨씬 더 대단한 것[사람/일]; Wonderful, impressive.

• Those girls are something else.

□ ***son of a bitch***   나쁜 자식; A bad person.

□ ***son of a bitch***   제기랄!; Exclamation of negative emotion. For example: anger, disappointment, etc.

  • Oh, son of a bitch! Mom lied again.

□ ***son of a bitch***   아주 어려운 문제; An extremely difficult or unpleasant problem.

□ ***son of a gun***   나쁜 자식; A bad person.

□ ***son of a gun***   제기랄!; Exclamation of negative emotion. For example: anger, disappointment, etc.

  • He's an arrogant son of a gun, but that confidence will pass on to the players.

□ *son of a whore*   나쁜 자식; A bad person.

□ SOP   표준운용절차; Acronym for "standard operating procedure".

  • What's the SOP in this situation?

□ **sophomore slump** 2년 차 증후군; A lack of success during a second attempt of something.

  • Our first album was awesome, but we faced a bit of a sophomore slump.

□ **sound bite**   (특히 정치인의 연설에서 따온) 효과적인 어구. 뉴스 스토리의 전개과정과 직접 관련 있는 사람의 간단한 논평을 녹음해 둔 것; Particularly interesting, short portion of an audio recording.

  • He comes here with only sound bite politics rather than any constructive help.

□ **Sounds like a plan!** 좋은 생각이야!; That sounds great!

- **soup up** (자동차 · 컴퓨터 등의) 성능을 높이다; To increase the capability of. Usually applied to motor vehicles.

- *space cadet* (마약 중독자처럼) 멍한 사람; A spacey person; one who has difficulty grasping reality; someone who frequently doesn't pay attention.

- *space out* (특히 마약에 취해) 멍해 있다; To lose one's concentration; to forget to do something.

  - I was supposed to pick him up at the airport but I spaced out.
  - Stop spacing out and work on your homework.

- *spank it* 자위하다; To masturbate. Most commonly applied to males.

  - You weren't out on a date last night – you were home spankin' it.

- **spare tire** 허리둘레의 군살; A large amount of fat around a person's midsection, resembling a car tire.

  - It is so frustrating to keep losing weight but not see the "spare tire" go away.

- **spark plug** (동료 등을) 분발시키는 사람; An energetic person who facilitates change by setting events in motion.

- **spat** 싸움; A fight

- **spaz** 가끔씩 미친 것 같이 행동하는 사람; A person who often acts in an irrational or spontaneous fashion.

- **spaz out** 경련하다, 몸이 굳어지다, 몹시 흥분하다; To react with extreme or irrational distress or composure.

  - When he learned I was cheating on him, he totally spazzed out.

- *speedball* 코카인과 헤로인 섞은 것; A mixture of cocaine and heroin, usually injected.

  - He woke up in hospital after speedballing.

306

□ *spend* 정액, 사정하다; Semen; To ejaculate.

• She hadn't said anything but Karlie could tell from the look on Sarah's face that the driver had known exactly what she was doing - fingering her twat and eating the remnants of Adam's spend.

□ spieler 능숙하게 말을 떠벌리는 사람; A person who speaks very well.

□ **spiff up** 몸치장을 하다, 모양을 내다, 멋을 부리다; To dress up.

□ spiffy 멋진, 세련된; Smart, stylish; very good, excellent; COOL

• That's spiffy!

□ **spike** (남의 음료/음식에 몰래 술/독약 등을) 타다[섞다]; To secretly put alcohol in a non-alcoholic beverage.

• We spiked the punch at the high-school dance.

□ spike up 뭔가 하기 전에 약물을 하다; To get ready by consuming a drug.

• Let's spike up before we go to the concert.

□ **spill** *one's* **beans** 발설하다; To give something away; to tell secret information.

□ **spill** *one's* **guts out** 비밀을 불다; To give something away; to tell secret information.

□ **spill the beans** (비밀을) 무심코 말해 버리다; To give something away; to tell secret information.

• I spilled the beans and told Jackie I loved her.

□ spin doctor (정치인/기관 등의) 공보 비서관, 홍보전문가; A person (usually involved in Public Relations) who attempt to put a positive "spin" on bad news that surfaces about a client.

• Yet again, the Government are putting spin doctors ahead of real doctors.

□ **spineless**　　　　　줏대가 없는; Not having the courage to say something; not standing up for oneself; not having the courage to say no.

• She should've said something and not be so spineless.

□ *spinner*　　　　　왜소한 여성; A petite female. Origin: a woman small
enough that she can be spun around while on top of a man during sex.

• The girl I hooked up with last night was a spinner.

□ **spit**　　　　　(욕설·폭언 등을) 내뱉다, 내뱉듯이 말하다 (out); To
speak or utter with contempt, hate, violence, etc.

• Don't leave[keep] me in suspense. Spit it out.

□ **splendiferous**　　　대단히 훌륭한; Excellent, outstanding. A combination of the words splendid, fantastic, wonderful, and fabulous, generally
used to indicate that things are extremely awesome in every degree.

• That's splendiferous, man!

□ split a gut　　　　크게 웃다; To laugh uncontrollably.

□ split a gut　　　　지독하게 노력하다; To exert effort.

□ split *one's* gut　　배꼽이 빠지도록 웃다; To burst into loud laughter.

□ split *one's* side　　배꼽이 빠지도록 웃다; To burst into loud laughter.

□ *splurge*　　　　　사정하다; To ejaculate.

• He splurged on his bed sheets.

□ **sponge**　　　　　(돈/먹을 것 등을 얻기 위해) 빌붙다, 뜯어먹다; To
get money from other people.

□ *spooge*　　　　　정액; Semen

□ **spoon**　　　　　남자가 여자를 뒤에서 껴안고 잠자다; To sleep with another person at your back, faced the same direction as you are, usually a male behind a female. Also may include fondling, kissing, or arms around each other. Meaning doesn't always have to be serious: can be used to joke on another person usually in a friendly way.

• Kenneth and Will spoon together every night.

□ **spread it on thick**　　　과장하다, 허풍 치다; In speech or writing, to be overly effusive.

□ **spunk**　　　　　정액; Semen

• He jacked off and shot spunk all over his hand.

□ **spunky**　　　　　용감한, 투지[열의]에 찬; Courageous, feisty

□ **square off**　　　　(~와) 싸우다[싸울 준비를 하다]; To start a fight.

□ **squeak by/through**　　　간신히 성공하다, 겨우 곤경에서 벗어나다[헤어나다]; To achieve a successful result with great difficulty.

□ **squillion**　　　　(수가) 엄청나게 많음; An extremely large but unspecified number, quantity, or amount.

□ **squirt**　　　　　(여성이) 사정하다; To ejaculate (used for woman).

• "Oh yes," she said as he dropped to his knees on the floor and pushed her knees apart. "Fuck yes! Eat my snatch! Make me squirt in your fuckin' face!"

□ **squish**　　　　　우유부단한; Indecisive and/or weak.

□ **stab in the back**　　　(자기를 믿는) ~의 뒤통수를 치다[~를 배신하다]; To betray a person.

• I can't believe I trusted you with my secrets, then you stabbed me in the back.

□ **stacked**　　　　　[여성이] (특히) 가슴이 풍만한, 포동포동한; Large breasted.

• Pamela Anderson is stacked!

□ **stage father**　　어린 연기자의 아버지; The father of a child actor.

• So the new gossip is that Marcus is becoming a real stage father, after his daughter has been in only 1 play. She didn't even have a speaking role!

□ **stage mother**　　어린 연기자의 어머니; The mother of a child actor.

• So the new gossip is that Linda is becoming a real stage father, after her daughter has been in only 1 play. She didn't even have a speaking role!

□ **stage parent**　　어린이 연기자의 부모; An over-bearing parent of a child actor.

□ **stallion**　　잘생기고, 체격이 좋은 남성; An extremely hand-some, well-built man - usually a stripper - whose body is in great shape.

• Damn, he's got the body of a stallion!

□ **stand up**　　(특히 연인 사이에서) ~를 바람 맞히다; To skip a pre-arranged meeting, especially a date.

• She stood me up!

□ *stank*　　추한; 오싹한; With poor personal hygiene/promis-cuous/generally gross.

• She's a stank hoe.

□ **stark-naked**　　홀딱 벗은, 실오라기 하나 안 걸친; Completely naked.

□ **steal**　　(값이 너무 싸서) 거저나 마찬가지; Very cheap.

• This suit is a steal at $80.

□ **steamroll**　　힘으로 강제하다. 힘으로 밀어붙이다; To coerce and intimidate.

□ **steep**　　비싼; Expensive

310

◻ **step on it**　　(특히 빨리 차를 몰라는 뜻의 명령문으로) 세게[빨리] 밟아라; To drive quickly.

◻ step on *one's* cock　　위험을 자초하다; To cause problems for oneself.

◻ **step on the gas**　　(특히 빨리 차를 몰라는 뜻의 명령문으로) 세게[빨리] 밟아라; To drive quickly.

◻ step-dude　　계부; Stepdad

• I've got to go to my step-dude's family's Thanksgiving this year.

◻ *STFU*　　입 닥쳐!; Shut the fuck up!

◻ stick　　벽촌. 촌놈; A person who lives in a rural area.

• That guy is such a stick!

◻ stick figure　　봉선화(棒線畵) (머리 부분은 원, 사지와 체구는 직선으로 나타낸 인체[동물] 그림). 바짝 말라 해골만 남은 사람; A very simple type of drawing made of lines and dots, often of the human form or other animals. In a stick figure, the head is represented by a circle.

• She is so thin that she is like a stick figure.

◻ ***Stick it up your ass!***　　엿이나 먹어라[알게 뭐야]; A contemptuous dismissal.

◻ stick *one's* neck out　　무모한 짓을 하다, 위험을 자초하다[자초하는 짓을 하다]; To take a risk.

◻ **stick *one's* nose into**　　~에 참견하다, 간섭하다; To interfere; to interlude; poke one's nose into.

◻ stick up for　　~을 변호하다, 옹호하다(defend); [권리 따위]를 지키다; To support of defend.

◻ sticks　　벽촌; A remote area; backwoods; a city or town regarded as dull or unsophisticated.

□ stiff	값비싼; Very expensive.
□ **sting**	(사기꾼의) 교묘한 사기; Fraud; cheating

• It was a sting operation and the target was knocked out.

□ stinker	아주 기분 나쁜 인간, 골칫거리; A misbehaving person. A fairly childish term.
□ **stinking**	지독한, 역겨운, 엄청난; Very. Used especially in "stinking rich".
□ stinking of money	돈이 엄청 많은; Very rich.
□ stinking with	~가 역겨울 정도로 많은; With extremely large amount of.
□ stinkpot	악취를 풍기는 것, 역겨운 놈; Repulsive thing(person); displeasing thing(person).
□ stoked	1. 열중하여, 열광하여. 2. 몹시 취한; (마약으로) 기분이 좋아진. 3. 흥분하여, 행복하여; Excited or energized.

• Break starts at noon Friday. Classes resume 10 days later. I am stoked. Walt and I are going to Frisco.

□ stomp	짓밟다; To defeat.
□ stomp on	짓밟다; To defeat.
□ **stone-broke/stony-broke**	빈털터리; Completely without money.
□ *stoned*	(마리화나/술에) 취한; Under the influence of marijuana.

• Well sure, now the tortoise makes sense. It's the only pet that you can catch when you're stoned.

□ *stoner*	마리화나 상용자; A person who frequently smokes marijuana.

◻ **stool**　　　　　　　대변(大便); Feces; POOP

◻ **straight**　　　　　　동성애자가 아닌, 이성애의; Heterosexual

◻ **straight**　　　　　　좋다, 괜찮다; Fine; okay

◻ **straight scoop**　　　특종; Scoop

◻ ***strap-on***　　　　　부착용 모조 성기; A fake penis (dildo) attached to a harness that a female can "strap on" to penetrate another.

◻ **strapped (for cash/money)**　빈털터리의; Without money. Shortened form of "strapped for cash."

◻ **strapped out**　　　　돈이 떨어진; Pressed for money.

◻ **streak**　　　　　　　나체로 사람들 앞을 달리다; To run naked.

◻ **streak**　　　　　　　전속력으로[쏜살같이] 가다; To run very quickly.

◻ **strike it lucky**　　　행운을 만나다; To be lucky.

◻ **strike oil**　　　　　큰 벼락부자가 되다; To become very rich quickly.

◻ **string puller**　　　　배후 조종자; A person influential through manipulation.

◻ **strong-arm**　　　　　강압적인, 강권을 쓰는; Coercing or intimidating.

□ **strung out**
Tired
(육체적 · 정서적으로) 소모(고갈)된; Exhausted;

□ **stuck on**
~에 빠져[미쳐, 반해]; To be obsessed with.

• He's still stuck on his ex-girlfriend.

□ **stuck-up**
거드름 피우는, 거만한; Pretentious

• She's stuck up.

□ *stud*
성적으로 매력 있는 남자; An attractive male; a
sexually talented male.

• Police officer: (Referring to a fellow police officer pretending to be a gay
male prostitute.) Look at that stud – that's all man.

□ *Stuff it!*
~따위는 엿이나 먹어라, 멋대로 해라 (강한 거절이나
반감); Angry retort.

□ *stunner*
굉장한 미인; 굉장히 매력적인 것; An attractive person.

□ **stupidhead**
바보, 멍청이; A fool; a person who is clueless.

□ *suck*
구강성교를 하다. 성기를 빨다; Often a reference to
fellatio.

• You can suck it right into your hot little mouth. You can lick it right up
and keep him so he can do this to you, Love.

□ *suck*
혐오감을 주다, 아주 불쾌하게 하다. 형편없다; To be
inadequate, displeasing, or of poor quality.

• Ah, hell. I'm too young to gamble. That sucks!
• Their new CD sucks.

□ *suck ass*
아첨하다, 알랑거리다; Someone that sucks up to
another person.

• This girl at work is a suck-ass to the boss.

314

□ **suck it**　　　그만둬라; An expression of anger; bite me; fuck off. Literally, "Suck my genitals."

- If you don't like my project, you can suck it.
- Suck it.

□ suck it up　　　닥치고 참다; To deal with something displeasing without complaining.

□ suck it up and take it　　　닥치고 참아라; To deal with something displeasing without complaining.

- "So you're saying we have to suck it up and take it?" Rachelle asked.

□ **suck off**　　　성기를 빨다. 구강성교를 하다. 구강성교; To perform fellatio; for a male to receive oral sex.

- Yo, I got a suck off, from that bitch last night.

□ *suck on that*　　　엿 먹어라!; A retort; take that. Also suck that.

□ *suck one's dick*　　　엿 먹어라!; A retort; "take that". Also suck that.

□ *suck that*　　　엿 먹어라!; A retort; "take that". Also suck on that.

□ *suck up*　　　알랑대다, 아부하다; 아부하는 사람; A person who behaves overly fawning so as to win favor. To flatter and otherwise make an attempt to ingratiate oneself; to be obsequious.

□ **sucker**　　　잘 속는 사람. 바보; Imbecile; a person that got screwed.

- Can you dig it, sucker?
- You sucker.

□ *sucker for*　　　~에 홀딱 반하다; To attracted for.

□ sucker punch　　　불시의 타격; To attack sneakily.

- *sugar daddy*   (보통 성관계 대가로 자기보다 훨씬 젊은 여자에게 많은 선물과 돈을 안겨 주는) 돈 많은 중년 남자; A rich older man who gives money and presents to a young girl in return for her company, affection, and usually sexual intercourse.

- *sugar mom*   (보통 성관계 대가로 자기보다 훨씬 젊은 남자에게 많은 선물과 돈을 안겨 주는) 돈 많은 중년 여자; A rich older woman who gives money and presents to a young man in return for his company, affection, and usually sexual intercourse.

- Sunday dad   일요일에만 아이들을 보게 되는 아빠; A father who only sees his children on Sunday, by choice.

- Sup?   무슨 일이야?; What's up?

- superfly   멋진, 마음에 드는, 매력적인; Excellent, superior, way cool or off the chain.

  • Kyle and Chris are superfly.

- **Sure as hell!**   틀림없다!; Certainly, Definitely

- *Sure as shit!*   틀림없다!; Certainly, Definitely

- Sure as the devil!   틀림없다!; Certainly, Definitely

- **sure bet**   틀림없음. 확실함; A certainty

- sure shot   틀림없음. 확실함; A certainty

- **sure thing**   틀림없음. 확실함; A certainty

- swag   스타일이 좋음; Style. From swagger.

  • That boy got some swag.

- swagger   "쿨"한 스타일이나 태도; Style, attitude, or general demeanor that is "cool".

316

□ **swallow** (의심 없이) ~을 받아들이다, 곧이곧대로 듣다; To believe a lie.

□ *swallow* 구강성교 중 남성의 정액을 삼키다; To swallow a man's ejaculate during oral sex.

□ **swallow hook, line, and sinker** 모든 경고 신호도 무시하고, 덜컥 믿어 버리다 (미끼를 물다); To accept in every respect, ignoring every warning sign.

□ **swamped** 눈코 뜰 새 없이 바쁜; To be overloaded with work.

□ **swank** 오만하고 건방진; Arrogant and conceited.

□ **swank** 매력적인, 스타일 있는; Attractive or stylish. Also swanky.

□ **swankalishious** 매력적인, 스타일 있는; Elegant, sophisticated, classy

□ **sweat it out** 열심히 (땀 흘려) 일을 해내다; To exert effort.

□ **sweep** (스포츠 경기에서) 완승을 거두다[휩쓸다]; To defeat.

□ **sweep *one* off *one*'s feet** ~를 정신없이 (사랑에) 빠져들게 하다; To make someone fall in love with ~.

□ **sweet on** ~를 아주 좋아하다[~에게 반하다]; To feel attracted to.

- Between the two of us, I know he's sweet on her.

□ **sweetheart deal**   담합; An abnormally favorable contractual arrangement.

- Also, how you treat each customer doesn't have to be the same. If Allie, Sarah, Shelly and Karlie cut a sweetheart deal by sleeping with the boss, who am I to complain.

□ **swell**   아주 좋은[즐거운/멋진]; Cool, sweet, bitchin', great, good. (Generally, in response to a question.)

- A: "How are you?" or, "How 's it going?"
  B: "Swell, just swell."

□ *swing both ways*   양성애자이다; To be bisexual.

□ *swinger*   부부 교환 행위를 하는 사람; A member of a couple that trades partners with other couples, for the purpose of sexual intercourse.

- On our first date Tom and I went to a swinger club.

step. 20

T

□ ta da	최고. 멋진 것; The best; the bomb.

• That chick's ass is ta da!

□ *Ta ta, MOFO!*	아기들의 옛날식 작별 인사말인 ta-ta와 mother fucker의 축약형인 MOFO가 결합된 것; Goodbye, mother fucker.

□ tad	적은 양; A small amount.

□ take a beating	대패[참패]하다; To be defeated.

□ take a chill pill	마음을 가라앉히다. 진정하다; To relax.

• He needs to take a chill pill.

□ *take a crap*	대변보다; To defecate.

• I've got to go take a crap.

□ take a dive	일부러 져주다; To purposely lose a fight, to fail.

□ *take a dump*	대변보다; To defecate.

• I've got to go take a dump.

□ take a fall	유죄 판결을 받다; To receive a guilty verdict.

• So she took the fall for everyone.

□ *Take a flying fuck!*	뒈져 버려; A contemptuous dismissal.

□ *take a hike*	가다, 사라지다; [명령형으로] 썩 꺼져, 저리 가; Angry retort. Literally: "Leave!"

□ *take a leak*	소변보다; To urinate.

• I need to take a leak.

□ **take a licking** 패배하다, 얻어터지다; To suffer a defeat or a beating.

□ ***take a piss*** 소변보다; To urinate.

• He goes to the toilet and starts taking a piss.

□ ***take a powder*** 갑자기 떠나다; 달아나다; To run away, to leave.

□ **take a shine to** ~에 (홀딱) 반하다; To become attracted.

• I think you'll get the job. They seemed to take quite a shine to you.

□ **take a squint at** 곁눈으로 살짝 보다; To take a quick look; to examine quickly.

□ **take a swipe at** ~을 겨누어 배트를 휘두르다, ~을 공격하다; To attack unexpectedly.

□ ***take a whiz*** 소변, 쉬하다; To urinate.

• I've got to go take a whiz.

□ **take down** 공격하다, 체포하다; To defeat.

□ **take for a spin** 시운전하다; To take a ride in or on a motor vehicle, for fun; to "test drive" a motor vehicle.

• There it is, Meg. What do you say we take it for a spin?
• Let's take this baby for a spin!

□ **take it easy** 일을 쉬엄쉬엄하다; 긴장을 풀다; To relax.

• I'm just taking it easy… watching some TV.

□ **take it easy** (명령형으로 쓰여) 진정해라[걱정 마라]; To relax.

□ **take it easy** 알아서 해!, 잘 가라, 또 만나자; Goodbye!

□ ***take it in the ass***   속다. 이용당하다; To be taken advantage of; GET SCREWED. Also take it up the ass.

• We really took it in the ass on that deal.

□ take it on the lam   걸음아 날 살려라 하고 도망치다; To escape; to run away.

□ ***take it up the ass***   항문 성교의 상대가 되어주다; To be on the receiving end of anal sex.

□ take on   ~와 시합을 하다[겨루다/싸우다]; To challenge.

□ take *oneself* off   떠나다, 달아나다; To go away; to run away.

□ ***take shit***   트집을 잡히다. 모욕을 당하다; To accept insults from a person without fighting back. Also "take it".

• Man, are you going to take shit from him like that?

□ take *somebody* down on a peg   콧대를 꺾다, 기세를 꺾다; To lower someone's high self-opinion.

□ take *somebody* to the cleaners   (속여서) 빈털터리로 만들다; To cheat; to deceive.

□ take *someone* down a peg   콧대를 꺾다, 기세를 꺾다; To lower someone's high self-opinion.

□ ***take the piss out of***   놀리다; To tease in an aggressive way.

□ ***Take your finger out of your ass(butt)***   가만히 앉아 있지만 말고 뭔가 행동을 시작하라; Stop sitting around or messing around and get ready for serious action.

□ ***Take your thumb out of your ass(butt)***   가만히 앉아 있지만 말고 뭔가 행동을 시작하라; Stop sitting around or messing around and get ready for serious action.

322

- **taking it easy**   편안한, 진정된; Relaxed

- **talk turkey**   진지[심각]하게 말하다, 탁 터놓고 말하다; To speak openly and without reserve.

- *tallwacker*   남성의 성기; Penis

- **tangle**   분규, 싸움; A fight.

- **tank**   완전히 망하다; To decline and fail suddenly; come to an end.

  • His regime will tank soon.

- **tard**   저능아; A shortened form of retard; Mentally retarded or just a stupid person.

  • You are a real tard.

- *tart*   바람난 여자, 매춘부; A person, usually female, that is a show-off or just a stupid bimbo.

  • That chick with the short skirt is such a tart.

- *tasty*   섹시한, 육감적인; Someone really good, attractive, or just cool.

  • Check out that tasty chick!

- **Ta-ta**   안녕, 잘 가; Goodbye!

  • Person A: See you tomorrow!   Person B: Ta-ta.

- **tattle tale**   수다쟁이, 고자쟁이(talebearer); A person who frequently reports misbehavior.

  • My little brother is such a tattle tale.

- **TBTB**   (조직 · 국가 등의) 실세들; The powers that be.

- **team up**　　　　(~와) 한 팀이 되다[협력하다]; To work together with another person or group in order to do something.

- tear *somebody/something* down　　심하게 꾸짖다; To reprimand angrily.

- tear *somebody* new asshole/one　　공격하다; To attack.

- tech weenie　　컴퓨터와 관련된 것에만 빠져 있는 바보; A person, a bit of a nerd, who is fascinated by all things technical, particularly computer-related.

- **tee off**　　　　시작하다; To begin.

- teeny　　　　작은; Small

- teenybopper　　팝 음악, 패션 등에 관심이 아주 많은 어린 십대 (10~13세 사이의) 소녀; A (usually female) teenager who follows popular trends.

  • Sure, we fans may not be teeny boppers anymore, but we are mature and successful women who adore this group.

- teeny-weeny　　작은; Small

- **tell it like it is**　　있는 그대로 말하다, 솔직히 말하다; To speak openly and honestly.

- Tell it/that to the marines　　네가 하는 말은 못 믿는다; I don't believe it(you).

- Tell me another (one)!　　너의 말은 못 믿는다; I don't believe it(you).

- tell *somebody* where to get off　　화를 내며 꾸짖다; To reprimand angrily.

- Ten-four!　　(특히 무선 통신에서) 알았다, 오케이, 오버; "Message understood." Used in radio transmissions, e.g. CB radio, police radio.

□ *tent pole*	발기; An erection.	

□ **terminally stupid**	아주 멍청한; Stupid; Retarded

□ **terminate**	죽이다; To kill.

□ **testy**	짜증을 잘 내는; Liable to anger.

□ **thanks for nothing** 아무것도 안 해 줘서 고마워!; Retort used to indicate displeasure with someone's lack of help.

□ That tears it! 그걸로 이젠 끝이다. 더 이상은 대응을 못한다; I am losing my ability to cope!; Cry of frustration.

□ that time of the month 생리 기간; A menstrual period.

> • It's that time of the month again.

□ *the fuck* damn 등 대신에 쓰는 강의어(强意語); An infix intensifier used with some verbs that use prepositions or prepositional phrases.

> • After the police came, he shut the fuck up.
> • What the fuck is the matter with you?

□ *the heck* the hell 대신에 쓰는 강의어(强意語); Intensifier, usually expressing confusion or displeasure. Also "in heck", "in the heck."

□ *the shit hit the fan* 난장판이 되다, 난리 나다; Something bad happened.

> • When my parents got home, the shit hit the fan.

□ *the shit out of* 아주 심하게; Used with a verb (and a direct object) to indicate the action was performed in some impressive way (e.g. aggressively, quickly, well, etc.)

> • They beat the shit out of that guy.

□ thickhead	우둔한 사람; Stupid	
□ thickie	우둔한 사람; Stupid	
□ third degree	엄한 심문; Interrogation	

• She really gave me the third degree.

□ ***This sucks!*** 정말로 후졌다. 이것 정말 싫어!; To identify something as worthless, contemptible, or maddening.

□ **thong** 끈 팬티; A long thin strip panty made of leather, plastic, or rubber.

□ **thrash** 때려눕히다; To defeat.

□ ***threesome*** 스리섬(세 명이 함께 하는 성행위); A session of sex involving 3 people.

• Austin: Hold on a tick. "Things to do before I die" "Have threesome with Japanese twins". – Austin Powers in Goldmember (2002 film)

□ **throw a fit** 발작을 일으키다; 엄청 화내다; To feel extreme anger.

□ **throw down** 싸우다; To fight.

• Look, they're about to throw down!

□ **throw in the sponge** 패배를 인정하다; To quit, to surrender.

□ **throw in the towel** 패배를 인정하다; To quit, to surrender.

• Most people throw in the towel when they break down and eat a candy bar, go a few days without exercising, or buy a pack of cigarettes.

□ **throw it down** 파티를 열다; To host a party.

• Is Mike going to throw it down tonight?

- *throw __somebody__ out on his/her ass* 내쫓다, 해고하다; To dismiss; to fire.

- throw __somebody__ out on his/her ear 내쫓다, 해고하다; To dismiss; to fire.

- throw the book (of rules) at [범죄자 등을] 종신형[중형]에 처하다, ~을 엄하게 벌하다; To prosecute to the full extent of the law.

  - Personally, I think the police wanted blackmail information more than they wanted to prosecute. But when she wouldn't come off with names, they threw the book at her. From what I heard, the only thing she said the police was 'I have no idea what you're talking about.'

- **throw up** 토하다, 게우다; To vomit.

  - I threw up my breakfast.

- thud 쿵 하고 내리치다; To hit.

- thug 폭력배; A gang member or "ruffian".

  - I got mugged by a thug.

- thump 내리치다; To hit.

- thunk 내리치다; To hit.

- thwack 내리치다; To hit.

- tidy sum 많은 양; 많은 금액; A large amount.

- tie one on 고주망태가 되다; To get drunk.

  - I really tied one on last night.

- **tiger mom** 자녀 교육에 열성적인 동양계 엄마. 2011년 Amy Chua의 "Battle Hymn of the Tiger Mother"에서 유래. 타이거 마더. 엄격함과 동시에 사랑과 믿음을 바탕으로 아이를 양육하는 엄마로서, 예의범절 및 상대에 대한 존중을 교육하고 좋은 성적을 얻도록 함; An Asian mother giving strict upbringing to her children. The term comes from "Battle Hymn of the Tiger Mother" by Amy Chua published in 2011.

  • She also has a tiger-mother in tow, which doesn't help.

- **tight** 인색한; A person reluctant to spend money or personal items.

  • My mom's tight. She won't give me $10.

- **tight ass** 구두쇠; 인색함; A stingy person.

  • Chris is such a total tight ass!

- **tight spot** 난처한 입장, 궁지; A difficult situation, a troublesome situation.

  • If dad had another stroke, then he's in a tight spot.

- *tight-ass* 고지식한 사람, 딱딱한 사람; 구두쇠; A stingy person; an uptight person.

  • You might have noticed that Sean is a bit of a tight-ass. He has firm convictions about right and wrong and he clings to them pretty fiercely.

- **tightwad** 구두쇠, 수전노; A stingy person.

  • My mom's such a tightwad, she wouldn't spend $30 on a DVD player.

- **time of the month** 생리 기간; A menstrual period.

  • We don't want to go to your baby shower. We don't have a time of the month. We don't love pink.

- **tip *somebody* off** 밀고하다, 비밀을 알려주다; To give something away; to tell secret information.

- **tipsy**   술이 약간 취한; Drunken

  • After drinking all that vodka, I'm feeling kinda tipsy.

- *tit*   젖꼭지, 유두(teat); (~s) 유방; Breast. Likely from the word "teat".

  • To see you today, in your loose T-shirt and shorts, a person might think you were soft, maybe even a little overweight. I mean, you have the tits and ass of a woman who weighs a lot more than you do.

- *titty*   젖꼭지, 유두; 유방; Breast. Usually but not always used in the plural.

  • You like how my titties bounce.
  • Excuse me. Your titty is exposed.

- *titty fuck*   젖가슴 사이 마찰 성교; A session of "sex" with breasts that are pushed together.

  • That was a nice titty fuck.

- **toad**   보기 싫은 놈[것], 주는 것 없이 미운 사람[것]; A very unpleasant man.

  • I've never met that toad you used to date.

- **toady**   1. 아첨꾼, 알랑쇠 2. 아첨하다, 알랑거리다; Flattering or being pleasant towards a person in the hope of getting some advantage.

- **toast**   완전히 망가지다; Permanently broken.

  • Cam drinks a glass of wine and he's toast.
  • I think the motherboard in my computer is toast.

- **toe the mark/line**   규칙에 따르다; To behave in a respectable and respectful manner. to obey the rules or orders.

- **tons**   아주 많은 양; Many or much.

□ **Toodle-oo!** 안녕히; Goodbye!

□ **tool about[or around]** 빈둥거리다; To waste time, mess around.

• I'm going to get a car like this!" Allie declared. The car was small, like Allie (and like Leslie), and it was cute, like Allie (and like Leslie). Adam could see Allie tooling around L.A. in one.

□ **top banana** (뮤지컬 등의) 주역 배우; (단체의) 제1인자, 중심 인물; The leading comedian in vaudeville, burlesque, etc.; leader of a group.

□ **top brass** 고급 간부들; People in the highest positions.

□ **top dog** 톱의, 최고의, 가장 중요한; The leader.

□ *top heavy* 유방이 큰; Large breasted.

□ **top-notch** 최고의, 아주 뛰어난; Excellent, highest-rated.

• That girl is top notch.

□ *toss salad* 항문 구강성교를 하다; To perform anilingus; RIM.

• She just tossed his salad.

□ **toss *somebody* out** 쫓아내다, 해고하다; To dismiss; to fire

□ **toss-up** 반반(의 가능성); A situation that could end in multiple outcomes, each of which is equally likely.

• So far the election is still a toss-up.

□ *totty* 섹시한 여자(특히 남성들이 쓰는 말로 보통 여성들에 겐 모욕적으로 여겨짐); An attractive person.

• Your new girlfriend is quite the totty.

- **touchdown** 성공, 득점; A success.

- touched in the head 머리가 약간 이상한; Crazy

- touchy 걸핏하면 화내는; Liable to anger.

- **tough it out** 어려움을 참고 견디어 내다; To exert effort.

- tough nut 다루기 힘든 사람; A very difficult person to deal with.

- *Tough shit!* 그것참 안됐네. (하지만 나는 상관없어); Too bad (for you), but I don't care.

  • Oh, your new job is hard? Tough shit.

- tough spot 곤란한 위치; Problematic situation.

- *tough titty* 그것참 안됐네. (하지만 나는 상관없어); Too bad (for you), but I don't care.

  • You don't like it? Tough titty.

- TP 화장실 휴지; Acronym for "toilet paper".

  • We're out of TP.

- trailer park trash 트레일러 파크에서 거주하는 부랑인; Dirty, uneducated, poor people with no job who waste what money they have on unnecessary things like liquor or stereos and televisions instead of buying clothes and food for their dirty kids that they don't take care of because they're too busy getting drunk and acting like assholes.

  • I don't want to go to the flea market, it's going to be full of trailer park trash.

- **train wreck** (열차사고가 난 것처럼) 엉망진창; A person whose life is in total disarray.

  • Why are you dating that train wreck? She hasn't had a job in five years.

□ *tramp* 잡년, 화냥년; A disreputable female.

• Wait wait wait wait wait. Is your "friend" that top heavy tramp in reception?

□ *tramp stamp* 여성이 등 아래에 한 문신 (짧은 상의와 밑 위가 짧은 바지를 입으면 보임); Tattoo on a woman's lower back at the belt line.

• She got a tram stamp? That's all you need to know!

□ trash 쓸모없는 인간, 인간쓰레기, 건달; A low-class person.

• Why are you dating that guy? He's trash.

□ trash 망가트리다, 못 쓰게 만들다; To ruin; destroy; mess up.

□ trash 거짓말, 난센스; Nonsense; full of lies.

□ tree-hugger 급진적인 환경 보호 운동가; A term used to describe an individual who is fanatical about nature.

• She's such a tree-hugger that now she's out protesting against blowing your nose on Kleenex.

□ *tribbing* 여성 둘이 성기를 비비는 동작; the lesbian act of rubbing or grinding vulva-to-vulva for sexual stimulation.

□ *trim* (늘씬한) 여자; Slender woman.

• I saw some nice trim today.

□ tripe 허튼소리, 거짓말; Nonsense; full of lies.

□ troll 트롤(인터넷 토론방에서 남들의 화를 부추기기 위해 보낸 메시지. 이런 메시지를 보내는 사람); In an online community or discussion, to attempt to lure others into combative argument for purposes of personal entertainment and/or gratuitous disruption.

332

- Watching faceless online passerby troll bloggers or mock fellow scribblers can be a drag.

□ **trophy wife**　　　트로피 와이프(나이 많은 남자의 젊고 매력적인 아내) 성공한 중 · 장년 남성들이 수차례의 결혼 끝에 얻은 젊고 아름다운 전업주부; An attractive (usually younger) wife of a wealthy, famous, or important man.

- New research reveals that Alpha Males don't want trophy wives any more.

□ **truck**　　　움직이다, 출발하다; To move or to go.

- Alright, ladies, shake a leg. Keep truckin'.

□ truck it　　　급하게 출발하다; To leave in a hurry.

- When I saw the teacher coming, I started truckin' it!

□ *trunk*　　　엉덩이; Buttocks

- She had a nice trunk.

□ TT4N　　　안녕(주로 인터넷 채팅에서 사용); "Ta-ta for now", i.e. "goodbye for now." Used mainly in computer-based conversation.

□ tuck in *one*'s tail　　　꼬리를 감추다, 굴욕을 당하다; To become humili- ated.

□ tude　　　태도; Attitude

- I got the same 'tude, dude.

□ **tune out**　　　상관[주의]하지 않다; ~에 귀를 기울이지 않다; To ignore

- They tune us out when we tell them to wait. They see the other side of the coin as being interesting.

□ *tunnel of love*　　　질. 여자의 성기; Vagina

- I wanna be in your tunnel of love.

□ *turd* 똥; 똥 같은 놈; Feces; a piece of fecal matter; loaf

• There's a big turd in the toilet.

□ *turd cutter* 항문; Buttocks

• That girl has a fine turd cutter.

□ turkey 멍청한[쓸모없는] 인간; Insignificant or stupid person.

□ **turn a blind eye** ~을 못 본 체하다; To ignore a misdeed.

□ **turn chicken** 겁이 나다; To become afraid.

□ **turn in** 잠자리에 들다; To go to bed.

• I think I'm going to turn in. See you in the morning.

□ **turn off** (성적인) 흥미를 잃게 하는[싫증이 나게 하는] 것; Something one finds unattractive.

• Bad breath is a total turn-off.

□ **turn on** (성적으로) 흥분[자극]하다[시키다]; To excite someone sexually.

• She had been turned on as hell watching him with Jenny Cinnamon earlier, but fucking in front of Karlie was 10 times the thrill.

□ turn *one*'s stomach 구역질 나게 하다; To make a person vomit.

□ turn *somebody* in 밀고하다; To give something away; to tell secret information.

□ turn *somebody* out 내쫓다, 해고하다; To dismiss; to fire.

□ **turn the trick** 목적을 이루다, 일이 잘되다; Accomplish a goal; succeed

□ turn up *one*'s toes   죽다; To die.

□ **turn up the heat**   압력을 높이다; 강압적으로 하다; Apply great or increased pressure.

□ turn yellow   무서워서 얼굴빛이 변하다; To become afraid.

□ *tush*   엉덩이; The buttocks.

□ *tushie*   엉덩이; The buttocks.

□ twacked   망가진, 고장난; Messed up, wrong, not working
correctly.

• That computer program is twacked. I'll have to reinstall it.

□ *twat*   (여성의) 성기; 여자의 음부를 가리키는 비어; Vulva

• Last time, Rachelle popped her nipple out and flashed her barely covered
twat at Adam half a dozen times.
• Right before she started getting bitchy, she was sitting across from Adam
and Karlie. She pulled her shorts aside, stroked her little twat and licked
her finger.
• I licked Katie's twat last night.

□ *twat*   등신, 멍청이; A displeasing person; idiot

• "Oh, you sneaky little twat," she hissed.

□ **twenty-four seven** ('하루 24시간, 일주일에 7일간'의 뜻으로) 언제나,
항상; Constantly. Etymology: abbreviation of "twenty-four hours a day,
seven days a week".

• That restaurant is open twenty-four seven.

□ *twerk*   엉덩이를 흔들며 섹시하게 춤추다; To dance in a
sexual manner, usually involving shaking on the buttocks.

• She was twerkin' like you know what last night.

□ **twerp**　　　　　천한 놈, 바보; A fool; a twit.

- By all accounts, even your spineless twerp of a husband's, it belongs to her.
- Now you've broken it, you twerp!

□ *twinkie*　　　　매력적인 젊은 여성; An attractive girl.

- That's a hot little twinkie.

□ **twist** *one's* **arm**　강압적으로 시키다; To coerce; intimidate

□ **twisted**　　　　제정신이 아닌; Mentally disturbed or unsound.

□ **twit**　　　　　얼간이, 멍청이, 바보; A foolish or annoying person.

- I would assume the two twits trying their best to look like tough guys are your brothers.
- Adam stared down at the pompous little twit with the anger he had been feeling since hearing what the two women inside had been called.

□ **twitchy**　　　　불안해하는; Susceptible to twitching a lot.

□ **two-bit**　　　　별 볼 일 없는, 하찮은; An inferior item or trivial sum.

- He goes around acting like a two-bit hood.

U

□ **uber**　　　　최고의; 최대의; Ideal, prefix meaning "super-".

• He's an uber-carpenter.

□ **Ucky!**　　　　우웩!; Disgusting

□ **umpteen**　　　아주 많은, 무수한; Many; countless.

• I've told you umpteen times, but you keep mistaking the same mistake.

□ **unflappable**　　(곤경에서도) 흔들림 없는, 동요하지 않는; Remaining composed and level-headed at all times.

□ *Unfuckingbelievable!*　　절대로 믿을 수가 없어!; I'm shocked.
I can't not believe.

□ **unwind**　　　긴장을 풀다; To relax.

• I'm tired of work. I'm going home to unwind.

□ **up _one's_ alley**　　능력·취미에 맞는, 장기인; One's area of expertise.

• Does that sound like it might be up your alley?

□ *up shit creek*　　궁지에 몰려; In serious trouble, possibly a shortened version of "up shit creek without a paddle".

□ *up the ass*　　완전히, 철저히, 엄청 많은; In an excessive amount, usually too much. Also "up the butt."

• I've got e-mails up the ass!

□ *up the gazoo*　　대량으로, 엄청 많은; An excessive amount of something.

□ *up the wazoo*　　대량으로, 엄청 많은; An excessive amount of something.

• He's got money up the wazoo!

338

- **up to scratch**　　표준에 달하여[기대에 부응하여]; Of acceptable quality, in good condition.

- **up to snuff**　　표준에 달하여[기대에 부응하여]; Of acceptable quality, in good condition, meeting standards or expectations.

  • I don't think this batch of macaroni and cheese is quite up to snuff.

- *up to the ass with*　　~이 엄청 많은; With a large amount of.

- **up to the eyeballs with**　　~이 엄청 많은; With a large amount of.

- *Up your ass!*　　엿 먹어라, 알게 뭐야; A dismissive retort.

  • Stick it up your ass.

- *up yours*　　빌어먹을!, 뒈져라!; A dismissive retort.

  • Lightman: You almost blew his bloody head off.
  Turley: Up yours, man!

- **upbeat**　　긍정적인, 낙관적인; Optimistic; cheery

  • The film ends on a surprisingly upbeat note.

- **upchuck**　　토하다, 게우다; To vomit.

  • He upchucked his lunch.

- *upper decker*　　화장실 세면대에 대변보고 도망치는 행위; The act of defecating in the top basin of a toilet bowl causing it to clog. Usually done as a mean spirited prank.

  • I hid an upper decker in that jerk's toilet before we left.

- **uptight**　　너무 격식을 차리는; Overly formal, conservative, repressed, rigid

step. 22

V

□ **vamoose**　　　　급히 떠나다; To leave.

- Hastert approved calling the bluff of anti-victory Democrats last week by demanding a floor vote on the idea of vamoosing Iraq immediately.

□ **vamp**　　　　요부(妖婦); An attractive female, who is constantly flirting with men.

- She is so vamp!

□ **vamp it up**　　　　섹시함을 강조하다; To increase the sexiness.

□ **Variety is the spice of life**　　　변화가 인생을 즐겁게 한다; Variety is what makes life enjoyable.

□ **varmint**　　　　말썽꾸러기(특히 아이); A misbehaving child.

□ **veggie**　　　　채소. 채식주의자; Vegetable

- Serve with baked potato and your favorite veggie.

□ **vexed**　　　　화가 난; Very angry.

- He was getting all vexed.

□ **vibe**　　　　~에 공감하다, ~와 뜻이 통하다. ~와 죽이 맞다; To get along well in a relationship.

- I like him. I think we could vibe.

□ **vibe**　　　　분위기, 낌새, 느낌; Feelings; premonitions; atmosphere

- I'm picking up some pretty negative vibes.
- The coffee shop has a nice vibe.

□ **viral**　　　　입소문이 나서 인기를 끄는; Popular due to being forwarded between people who know each other.

- Concerns about the Internet's harmful effects on our brains and lives have gone - well, viral.

□ **voyeur**   (성적으로) 엿보기 좋아하는 사람, 관음자(觀淫者);
Someone who gets sexual pleasure from secretly watching other people having sex or taking their clothes off.

> • Her fingers were underneath her dress, her panties at her feet. She felt like a voyeur but she wasn't embarrassed. She would have loved to go join them.

W

□ **w/**	~와 함께, 같이; With	

□ **w/o**	~없이; Without	

• Are you coming w/ or w/o your spouse?

□ *wack off*	자위하다; To masturbate. Typically used for male masturbation.	

• I was really horny so I wacked off.

□ **wacko**	미친, 제정신이 아닌; 분별없는; Crazy	

• He's wacko.

□ *wad*	사정하다; To ejaculate.	

• Have you not wadded in months?

□ *wad*	정액; Semen	

□ **wake up and smell the coffee**	정신 차리고 상황을 직시하라; A command/invitation to accept reality.	

• Wake up and smell the coffee, man! Your ex-wife is not coming back.

□ **walk out on** *somebody*	~를 버리다; To abandon.	

• The husband walked out on his family one day and never returned.

□ **wallop**	세게 치다; To beat somebody up.	

□ **wall-to-wall with**	~로 가득히 깔린; Covered with something from wall to wall; a large amount.	

□ **waltz**	어려움 없이 해내다[완료하다]; To do something in a relaxed and confident way.	

• The recruits have waltzed through their training.

- **waltz**   힘들이지 않고 신속히 움직이다; To move quickly and effortlessly.

- *wanger*   음경; Penis

  • Just as he was about to plunge his wanger into Jonny, Jones arrived.

- **wank**   잘난 체하는 남자; A smug, self-involved person, usually male.

  • What a wank.

- *wank off*   자위하다. 수음하다; To masturbate.

  • Oh yeah, he's in the other room wanking off.

- *wanker*   음경; Penis

  • Crikey, he's got a huge wanker!

- **wanker**   재수 없는 새끼(특히 남자를 가리키는 욕); An unpleasant person; jerk A general insult.

  • You are such a wanker!

- *wankie*   음경; Penis

  • He got a small wankie.

- **wannabe**   유명인을 동경하는 사람(유명인을 동경하여 행동/복장 등을 그들처럼 하는 사람); One who aspires to be like another person or group of people.

  • I'm just a wannabe Emacs user, so could you explain why that's a bad idea?

- **washed out**   돈이 다 떨어진, 기운 없는, 지친; With no money left.

- **waste**   망가트리다; To destroy.

  • She wasted her car when she got in that wreck.

□ **waste of space**   아무짝에도 쓸모없는 사람; An utterly worthless person, one unworthy of the space which he occupies.

□ **wasted**   너무 피곤한; Too tired to proceed.

• I'm wasted, man.

□ *watersport*   배뇨(排尿)를 수반하는 성행위; Sexual play with urine.

• Though Matt and Coop had been known to engage in water sports on occasion Jake thought the whole concept was disgusting.

□ **way**   훨씬, 멀리; Very

• This is way cool!

□ **way good**   아주 좋은; Extremely good.

□ **way-in**   유행의, 세련된; Extremely fashionable.

□ **weak sister**   도움이 필요한 사람, 거추장스러운 사람; A person in a group who is regarded as weak or unreliable.

□ **wear the pants**   (아내가) 남편을 깔고 뭉개다, 내주장하다; To be in charge.

□ **weasel**   처벌을 교묘히 면하다; To escape punishment.

• They can manipulate words to weasel their way out of anything.

□ *wee wee*   남성의 성기, (아동어로) 고추; A penis.

□ **weed**   마리화나; Marijuana

• Narrator: In fact, it was a box of Oscar's legally obtained medical marijuana··· Primo bud. Real sticky weed. - "Prison Break-In", Arrested Development (TV, 2005), Season 3 Episode 7.

□ *weenie*   남성의 성기, (아동어로) 고추; Penis

□ weeny	나약한 사람; A wimp.	
□ **weirdo**	괴짜, 별난 사람; A weird person.	
□ *well hung*	(남성이) 성기가 큰; Having a large penis.	

• I just want for once a small, professional, decisive, well-hung man in his 40s.

□ **wet blanket**	흥을 깨는 사람; A person that kills fun or humor.

• I hate to be a wet blanket, but I thought the show was terrible.

□ **wet** *one's* **pants** 아주 놀라다(바지에 오줌을 쌀 정도로 놀라다); To feel fear.

□ **wet** *oneself* 아주 놀라다(바지에 오줌을 쌀 정도로 놀라다); To feel fear.

□ **wet** *oneself* 아주 크게 웃다(바지에 오줌을 쌀 정도로 웃다); To have a big laugh.

□ whack	세게 치다; To punch.
□ whack	미치다; Crazy

• She is whack.

□ *whack off* 자위하다, 수음하다; To masturbate. Usually used in reference to male masturbation.

• Leave me alone! Go whack off or something.

□ **whacked out** 미친, 제정신이 아닌; Crazy; alternative spelling of "wacked out".

□ **whale into** *somebody* 맹렬히 공격하다; To attack.

□ wham 치다, 때리다; To punch.

□ ***wham bam, thank you ma'am*** 짧고, 형식적이며, 일회적 섹스; A brief sexual encounter.

349

> • The guys just want 'wham, bam, thank-you ma'am.' They don't care about building a relationship.

□ *whang*　　　음경; Penis

> • Suck my whang.

□ whap　　　치다, 때리다; To punch.

□ **What (in) the hell is going on?**　　여기서 도대체 무슨 일이 일어나고 있는 거야?; Vulgar expression of "What is going on?"

□ **What gives?**　　웬일이냐?; A casual greeting, similar to What's happening? What's happening/happenin'?

□ *What in the fuck is this shit?*　　이건 도대체 뭐야?; What is this?

□ What the devil?　　뭐[뭐라고]? (놀람 · 분노를 나타낼 때); Vulgar expression of "What~?"

□ *What the fuck?* 뭐[뭐라고]? (놀람 · 분노를 나타낼 때); Vulgar expression of "What~?"

□ *What the fuck?*　　"도대체 ~뭐야?"의 속어 표현; An interjection signaling incomprehension or befuddlement.

□ *What the fucking hell?*　　"What~"의 속어 표현; Vulgar expression of "What~?"

□ **What the hell?**　　도대체 무엇[왜]~?; Vulgar expression of "What~?"

□ **Whatever!**　　아무래도 좋아. 난 상관없어; I don't' care.

□ What's clicking?　　잘 지내?; A greeting similar in form to "What's up?" or "What's crackin'?", but more related to new trends on the Internet.; What's going on?

□ What's cooking?　　무슨 일이야? What's going on?

□ What's the haps?　무슨 일이야? What's going on?

□ **what's what**　뭐가 뭔지(무엇이 유용한지, 중요한지 등등); What things are useful, important, etc"

- I get dumped from the fucking cover. I was promised that cover. Vi was counting on that fucking cover, dude. So I called to tell them what's what.

□ **wheel is turning but hamsters' dead** 약간 멍청한; Stupid; Retarded

□ **wheeler-dealer**　(사업/정치에서) 권모술수에 능한 사람, 수완가; A person who is good at getting what he/she wants, often by dishonest or unfair methods.

□ **when the chips are down**　막상 일이 닥치면; When the things become really difficult and messy.

□ **when the going gets tough** 상황이 힘들어지면; when the things become really difficult and messy.

- Amateurs fall by the wayside when the going gets tough.

□ *when the shit hits the fan*　일이 정말로 어렵게 되거나 걷잡을 수 없을 때; When the things become really difficult and messy.

- It seems like you are always around when the stuff hits the fan.

□ **where the rubber meets the road** 실력[진가]이 시험되는 장(場); At the most important point.

- Talking about prognosis is where the rubber meets the road.

□ whip　패배시키다; To defeat.

- We whipped them in semifinals.

□ *whip somebody's ass*　때려 눕히다; To defeat.

□ **whipper-snapper** 건방진 애송이; Arrogant young person.

□ *white*　　　코카인; Cocaine

□ **whiz**　　　잽싸게 하다; To move quickly and effortlessly.

□ ***whiz***　　　소변을 보다; To urinate.

• I've got to go whiz.

□ **whiz**　　　수완가, 전문가, 명인, 명수; A person with skill in a particular subject or trade.

• She's a real whiz when it comes to math!

□ **whiz-bang**　　　소형의 초고속 포탄, 주목을 받는 신기술, 훌륭한; Impressive or flashy. Typically used to refer to new technology.

• Another long-range change involves a shift in focus from relying heavily on expensive, whiz-bang hardware such as spy satellites.
• This software update has a lot of new whiz-bang features!

□ **whiz-kid**　　　신동; 젊은 수재; A person who is very good and successful at something, especially at a young age.

□ ***Who gives a (flying) fuck?***　　　나는 상관없어. 누가 상관한다고 그래?; I don't' care.

□ **Who gives a damn?** 나는 상관없어. 누가 상관한다고 그래?; I don't' care.

□ ***Who gives a fart?*** 나는 상관없어. 누가 상관한다고 그래?; I don't' care.

□ ***Who gives a frig?*** 나는 상관없어. 누가 상관한다고 그래?; I don't' care.

□ ***Who gives a shit?*** 나는 상관없어. 누가 상관한다고 그래?; I don't' care.

□ **who-done-it (whodunit)**　　　추리 소설, 스릴러 영화; A work of fiction in the crime mystery genre.

352

• This riveting mystery is a "whodunit" at its best.

- **whole bag of tricks** 전부, 모조리 다; Everything

- **whole bag of wax** 전부, 모조리 다; Everything

- **whole enchilada** 전부, 모조리 다; Everything

- **whole hog** 전부, 모조리 다; Everything

- **whole kit and caboodle** 전부, 모조리 다; Everything

- **whole lot** 아주 많이; A large amount of.

- **whole nine yards** 모든 것[(필요한 것이 다 들어간) 완전한 것]; Everything

- **whole shebang** 전부, 모조리 다; Everything

- **whomp** 결정적으로 패배시키다; To beat severely.

• The Seahawks are gonna whomp the Lancers!

- *whoop somebody's ass* 패배시키다; To defeat.

- **Whoops!** 아이코, 어머나; An interjection expressing discovery of an error or mistake and, often, an implicit apology.

- *whooty* 엉덩이가 크고 매력적인 백인 여성; A white female with attractive, large buttocks. Possibly from "white"+"booty".

- **whopper** 엄청 큰 것; Something big.

• Weatherman: With these unstable pressure systems, I predict a whopper of a storm is coming our way.

- **whopping** 엄청 큰; Very large.

- **whore** 창녀; Prostitute; promiscuous person. Usually (but not always) used to apply to promiscuous females.

□ **whump**	때리다, 치다; To punch.
□ **wiggle out of**	(교묘히) 빠져나오다; To escape from.

• He used his cleverness to wiggle out of doing work.

□ **wild about**	~에 몰두하다; To be attracted with.
□ **willies**	소름 끼침; Nervousness, jitters, or fright (esp in the phrase "give (or get) the willies")
□ *willy*	(특히 아동어로) 고추; Penis

• Stop clutching your willy. It's disgusting.

□ **wimp**	겁쟁이, 약골; Lacking physical prowess or stamina.
□ **wimp out**	(하려고 하던 일을) 겁을 먹고 안 하다; To lose courage.
□ **win out/through**	(어려움에도 불구하고) 성공하다[해내다]; To succeed through perseverance.
□ **windbag**	수다쟁이, 떠버리; A talkative person who says nothing of substance.
□ *wingman*	섹스 상대방을 고르는데 옆에서 도움을 주는 남자; A male who helps a person find a sexual partner for the night, e.g. by speaking positively about the person.

• I got this girl's number last night. My wingman kept her friends out of the way.

□ **wipe out**	~을 완전히 파괴하다[없애 버리다]; To destroy.

• The entire town was wiped out.

□ **wiped out**	녹초가 된, 기진맥진한; Exhausted; tired

• I'm pretty wiped out. I think I'll go to bed.

□ wire puller   배후 조종자; A person who uses private or secret influence for his own ends.

□ **wired**   흥분한, 에너지가 넘치는; Full of energy.

• How can you be so wired when you got only 3 hours of sleep last night?

□ **with a vengeance**   호되게, 심하게, 맹렬히; To an extreme degree.

• It began to rain again with a vengeance.

□ with it   유행을 아는[유행에 맞는/최신식의]; Knowing the latest trend; hip

□ without a bean   땡전 한 푼 없는; With no money left.

□ *without a pot to piss in*   찢어지게 가난한; Extremely poor.

□ without a red cent   찢어지게 가난한; Extremely poor.

□ **wizard**   귀재; A person with deep, expert knowledge of that subject matter.

• We're looking to hire a Unix wizard.

□ wonk   특정한 분야만 아는 전문가; 일만 아는 사람, 일[공부]벌레; An expert; a person who is obsessively interested in a specified subject.

□ *wood*   발기한 남성의 성기; 발기; An erection.

• Girl, you're so hot. You're giving me wood.

□ *woody*   남성의 발기; A male's erection.

• Ashley gives me a woody.

□ *work (one's) ass off*   매우 열심히 일하다; To work hard.

A
B
C
D
E
F
G
H
I
J
K
L
M
N
O
P
Q
R
S
T
U
V
W
X
Y
Z

- Louise: You've been working your you-know-what off? I've been working my ass off! Night and day training!
  Bob: Louise, take it easy.

□ **work like a charm**　　기적같이 이뤄지다[성공하다]; Quickly have the effect you want; work like magic.

□ **workaholic**　　일 중독자, 일벌레; A person who works excessively. From "alcoholic" – a person addicted to alcohol.

- He's well known as a workaholic.

□ **worked up**　　(몹시) 흥분한; Agitated or angry.

□ **worm out of**　　교묘히 면하다; To escape punishment.

- I'd like to see him worm out of this charge.

□ **worth a bundle**　　가치가 높은; Having a high value.

□ **wrap (*one's*) mind around**　　이해하다; To understand.

- We have things that need to get done that don't necessarily include following souls around town with you. OK? Can you wrap your little head around that?

□ **wrap *something* up**　　(합의 · 회의 등을) 마무리 짓다; To finish.

- That just about wraps it up for today.

□ **wreck**　　완전히 패배시키다; To defeat badly.

- Dude, I just got wrecked at video games.

□ **wriggle out of**　　교묘히 면하다; To escape from.

□ **wuss**　　쪼다, 병신; Wimp, sissy, coward. Also wussy.

- Michael: Oh, that's a pretty tough race.
- Steve Holt: Only for a wimp, a wuss….

□ X   엑스터시; Ecstasy, a particular street drug.

• I've stayed away from crack and heroin but I've taken X and other pharmaceuticals.

□ **XOXO**   포옹과 키스 (채팅 약어); An abbreviation for hugs and kisses, usually placed at the end of a letter.

And who am I?
That's one secret I'll never tell···
You know you love me. XOXO, Gossip Girl.

step. 25

Y

- **yadda yadda yadda** 시시한 소리, 그렇고 그런 소리 (이미 알고 있거나 지루한 내용이라서 그만 줄이는 말); Etc; And on and on and on in a similar vein. Popularized by the Jerry Seinfeld TV show.

  • He said he was having problems and yadda-yadda-yadda.

- **Yahoo!** 야호(신나서 외치는 소리); How exciting!; exclamation of delight; hooray

- **yank *somebody*'s chain** 남을 속이다, 곤란하게 하다; To tease or goad someone by lying.

  • The man nodded and finally seemed to accept that Adam wasn't just yanking his chain.

- **yapper** 입; Mouth

  • Shut yer bloody yapper, ya motor-mouth.

- **Yeep!** 이크!; An exclamation of surprise.

- **yellow** 겁이 많은, 겁쟁이 같은; Liable to fear.

- **yes-man** (윗사람에게 잘 보이려고) 무조건 예라고 하는 사람, 예스맨; A person who always agrees with superiors.

- **Yikes!** 이키(갑자기 놀라거나 겁을 먹었을 때 내는 소리); An exclamation of surprise.

- **Yipes!** 아야!, 이크!, 어렵쇼! (아픔 · 놀람 등을 나타내는 소리); An exclamation of surprise.

- **Yippee!** 야호!; How exciting!

- **YO!** 야, 어이(젊은이들의 인사말); 흑인 영어와 Italian Americans들의 대화에서 많이 사용됨; Yo는 1976년도에 발표된 영화 '록키(Rocky)'의 주인공 록키 발보아(Rocky-Balboa)역의 실베스터 스탈론(Sylvester Stallone)이 영화에서 "Yo, Adrian!"라고 말하면서 유명해짐; A greeting or exclamation to attract attention.

- yokel   (무식한) 촌놈, 무지렁이; A person from a rural area; hick

- york   토하다, 게우다; To vomit.

  • I drank so much last night, I yorked all over myself.

- ***You bet your (sweet) ass!***   당연하지; Certainly; Definitely

- **You bet your life!**   당연하지; Certainly, Definitely

- **You bet!**   물론이지[바로 그거야]!; Certainly; Definitely

- **You betcha!**   물론이지[바로 그거야]!; Certainly; Definitely

- **You can say that again!**   정말 그렇다[(당신 말에) 전적으로 동의한다]; I agree completely; I know that already.

- **you know what**   그것 말이야, 있지 그거; A general replacement for vulgar nouns.

- ***You know where you can stick it?*** 알아서 꺼져라!; A contemptuous dismissal.

- **You said a mouthful!**   맞았어, 바로 그거야; That's right!

- **You'd better believe it!**   믿어도 돼, 틀림없다니까; It's sure!

- You're damn tootin'! 맞는 말이다!; You are right!

- ***You're FOS!***   너의 말은 다 거짓말이다!; You are full of shit. I don't believe you.

- ***You're full of shit!***   너의 말은 다 거짓말이다!; I don't believe it(you).

- **You're telling me!** 내 말이 바로 그 말이에요/전적으로 동의해요!; I agree completely; I know that already.

□ yuck	역겨운 것; A gross substance.
□ Yuck!	욱(역겨울 때 내는 소리); Disgusting
□ Yucky!	욱(역겨울 때 내는 소리); Disgusting
□ yummy	아주 맛있는; Delicious; desirable

- Q: Let's take the rest of the week off and go to Cancun for a stint⋯ sounds yummy?
  A: Absolutely⋯ yummy yummy!

□ *yummy mummy*   (애가 있는) 매력적인 여성; Exclamation used when food tastes good or looks good. Has come to also be used when one sees someone attractive.

- She is yummy mummy.

step. 26

Z

□ **zap**　　　　　　　　망가트리다, 고장내다; To damage (fry) an electronic component with electricity.

• When I stuck a pen in my power supply, it zapped the hard disk.

□ **zap**　　　　　　　　재빠르게 하다; To go/move very fast.

□ **zero**　　　　　　　인기 없는 사람; An unpopular person.

• I can't believe you hang out with that zero.

□ **zilch**　　　　　　　무(無), 영(零); Nothing

□ **zillion**　　　　　　엄청난 수; A very large number.

• Do I have to say "sorry" zillion times?

□ **zing along**　　　　빠르게 움직이다; To move/go very fast.

□ **zingy**　　　　　　흥분시키는, 매력적인; Excited

□ **zip**　　　　　　　영(零), 무(無); Nothing

• The score was three-zip.

□ **zip**　　　　　　　(차·총알 등이) 핑 하고 소리 내며 나아가다; To move/
go very fast.

□ **zippy**　　　　　　아주 빠른; Very fast.

□ **zonk**　　　　　　한 방 때리다, 기절시키다, 때려눕히다; To punch.

□ **zonk off**　　　　　푹 잠들다; To sleep.

□ **zonk out**　　　　　푹 잠들다; To sleep.

□ *zonked*　　　　　　(피로·술·마약에 취해) 완전히 맛이 간; Extremely
intoxicated. Usually refers to alcohol intoxication but can also apply to
marijuana or other drugs. extremely tired.

• Did you see that guy at the party? He was zonked!

□ *zonked*　　　　　지쳐 빠진, 녹초가 된; Exhausted.

• We were so zonked after The Late Show.

□ Zowie　　　　　야!, 와! (놀람 · 감탄을 나타냄) ('자우이'라고 발음함); How exciting!; exclamation of delight; hooray